# FOSS Next Generation

# Science Resources

Full Option Science System
Developed at
The Lawrence Hall of Science,
University of California, Berkeley
Published and distributed by
Delta Education,
a member of the School Specialty Family

© 2016 by The Regents of the University of California. All rights reserved. No part of this book may be reproduced or transmitted in any form or by any means, electronic or mechanical, including photocopying or recording, or by any information storage and retrieval system, without permission in writing from the publisher.

1511920
978-1-62571-447-3
Printing 1 — 10/2015
Webcrafters, Madison, WI

**Table of Contents**

# FOSS Science Resources

Energy .................................................. **1**
Soils, Rocks, and Landforms ...................... **125**
Environments ...................................... **201**
References ......................................... **309**

**Physical Science**
# FOSS Science Resources
# Energy

# Table of Contents

**Investigation 1: Energy and Circuits**
Edison Sees the Light . . . . . . . . . . . . . . . . . . . . . . . . . . . . 5
Energy Sources . . . . . . . . . . . . . . . . . . . . . . . . . . . . . . . . 10
Series and Parallel Circuits . . . . . . . . . . . . . . . . . . . . . . . 15
Science Practices . . . . . . . . . . . . . . . . . . . . . . . . . . . . . . . 21
Engineering Practices . . . . . . . . . . . . . . . . . . . . . . . . . . . 22
Thinking Like an Engineer . . . . . . . . . . . . . . . . . . . . . . . 23
Engineering a Solar Lighting System . . . . . . . . . . . . . . . 27

**Investigation 2: The Force of Magnetism**
When Magnet Meets Magnet . . . . . . . . . . . . . . . . . . . . . 32
Magnificent Magnetic Models . . . . . . . . . . . . . . . . . . . . 39
Make a Magnetic Compass . . . . . . . . . . . . . . . . . . . . . . 42

**Investigation 3: Electromagnets**
Electricity Creates Magnetism . . . . . . . . . . . . . . . . . . . . 46
Using Magnetic Fields . . . . . . . . . . . . . . . . . . . . . . . . . . 49
Electromagnets Everywhere . . . . . . . . . . . . . . . . . . . . . . 51
Morse Gets Clicking . . . . . . . . . . . . . . . . . . . . . . . . . . . . 60

**Investigation 4: Energy Transfer**
Energy . . . . . . . . . . . . . . . . . . . . . . . . . . . . . . . . . . . . . . 67
What Causes Change of Motion? . . . . . . . . . . . . . . . . . 76
Bowling . . . . . . . . . . . . . . . . . . . . . . . . . . . . . . . . . . . . . 80
Force and Energy . . . . . . . . . . . . . . . . . . . . . . . . . . . . . . 81
Potential and Kinetic Energy at Work . . . . . . . . . . . . . . 85

**Investigation 5: Waves**
Waves . . . . . . . . . . . . . . . . . . . . . . . . . . . . . . . . . . . . . . 88
More about Sound . . . . . . . . . . . . . . . . . . . . . . . . . . . . . 93
Light Interactions . . . . . . . . . . . . . . . . . . . . . . . . . . . . . 102
Throw a Little Light on Sight . . . . . . . . . . . . . . . . . . . . 108
More Light on the Subject . . . . . . . . . . . . . . . . . . . . . . 113
Alternative Sources of Electricity . . . . . . . . . . . . . . . . . 116
Ms. Osgood's Class Report . . . . . . . . . . . . . . . . . . . . . 122

# Edison Sees the Light

"The **filament** burns out too quickly," Mr. Edison said. "We have to find a better material to make a longer-lasting filament."

Thomas Edison (1847–1931) was the most famous inventor of his time. He invented the phonograph, the motion-picture camera, the first copy machine, and hundreds of other things. He is most famous, however, for improving a product he *didn't* invent, the electric **lightbulb**.

The problem with lightbulbs before 1879 was that they burned out too quickly. The filament is the part of the lightbulb that actually makes the **light**. When an **electric current** flows through the filament, the filament gets so hot that it glows and gives off light. The hotter the filament gets, the brighter the light. But the hotter the filament gets, the faster it burns out.

**Edison with his lightbulb**

Edison's short-lived lightbulb was a simple device. It was much like a modern incandescent lightbulb. In an incandescent lightbulb, two stiff support **wires** hold the filament. A clear glass globe surrounds the filament for protection. The glass globe is attached to a metal casing. The tricky part is how the support wires, which are part of the **circuit**, connect to the metal casing.

One support wire attaches to the side of the metal case. The other support wire attaches to a small metal disc at the bottom of the base. The base **contact point** must not touch the main part of the metal case. This is important. When **electricity** travels to the lightbulb in a circuit, the electricity must flow *through* the filament.

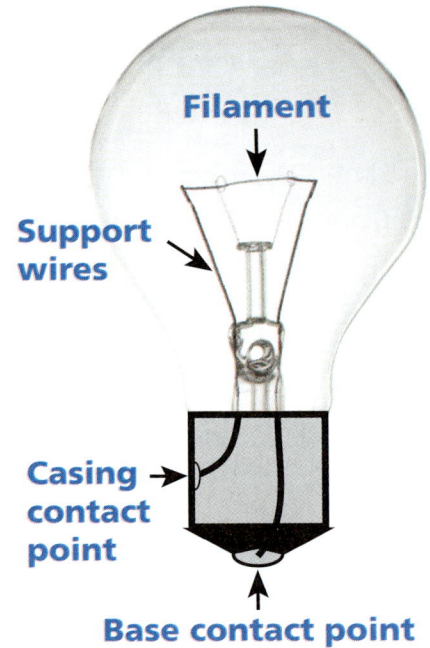

When you put a lightbulb in a circuit, electricity can be delivered to the lightbulb. When the circuit is complete, the electric current will flow. The electric current has **energy**. The energy produces **heat** and light as the lightbulb does its job. Energy leaves the lightbulb system as light.

Edison tackled the filament problem with hard work. He is credited with saying, "Invention is 1 percent inspiration and 99 percent perspiration." Edison directed his team to try every imaginable material to find the best filament. It is said that they tried and rejected 2,000 materials. Edison needed help.

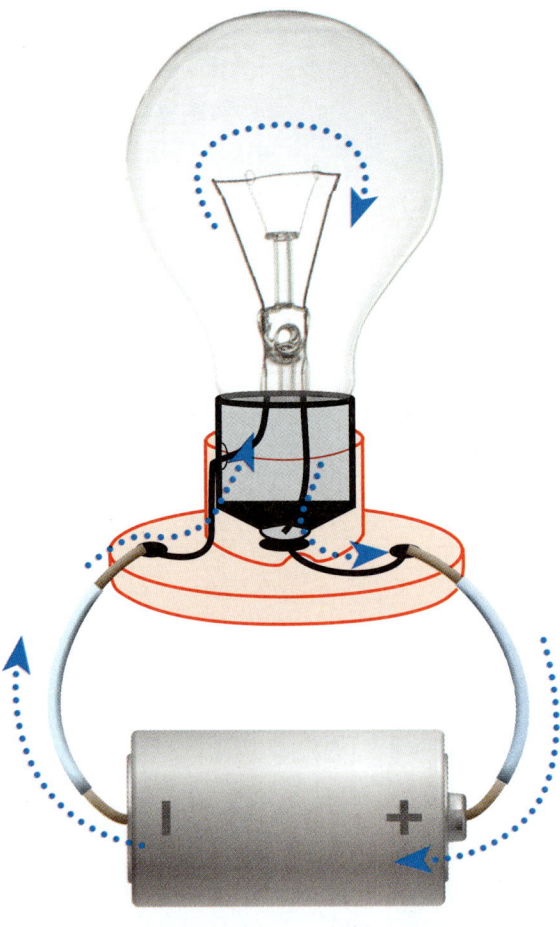

A lightbulb in a circuit

Help came in the form of Lewis Latimer (1848–1928). Latimer was an experienced draftsman and inventor. He had been working on the filament problem, too. Latimer discovered that a carbon-coated cotton thread made a good filament. He got a patent for the carbon filament. Inventors get patents from the government when they invent something new. When Edison tried the carbon filament in his lab, he agreed that it was the best material. Edison bought the patent from Latimer. Now Edison could use the carbon filament in his lightbulb.

**Lewis Latimer**

Edison had to solve one more problem to make a useful lightbulb. He knew that things need oxygen to burn. He predicted that if he could remove the air from the glass globe, there would be no oxygen, and the filament would not burn up. He was right. This new lightbulb lasted months instead of days.

Thomas Edison had seen the light. Now it was time to show this new **light source** to the world. It was New Year's Eve in 1879. Edison's team strung lights from their lab to the train station. A crowd of more than 3,000 people came to see what would happen.

It was a very dark night, and all the gaslights had been turned off. Edison stepped up to the platform and threw the switch. All the lights came on. The crowd cheered.

Edison understood the importance of electric lighting. It could change the American way of life. That's why he asked Latimer to join his team in 1884. Latimer stayed with Edison for years. He wrote patents for new inventions and books on electrical engineering.

**Edison's lab**

7

Many years later, in 1918, the team of scientists and **engineers** gathered to celebrate Edison's birthday. They called themselves the Edison Pioneers. Lewis Latimer was the only African American among the engineers. He also was one of the 28 founding Pioneers.

## Lightbulbs Today

In Edison's time, the only way known to make electric light was to make a filament so hot that it glowed. The glowing filament gave off a lot of heat and a good amount of light. It takes a lot of energy to make light by heating a filament. Today we have alternative ways to make light that don't need nearly as much energy.

The long white tubes that produce light are called fluorescent lamps. A fluorescent lamp does not have a filament. Instead the tube is filled with gas. When an electric current travels to the lightbulb, the gas begins to glow and give off light. The light is not quite as bright as an incandescent lamp. But the amount of energy needed to produce the light is far less than the energy needed to heat a filament.

The Edison Pioneers in 1920

We also have compact fluorescent lightbulbs. The tube is much thinner, and it is wound into a **coil** to save space. Compact fluorescent lightbulbs screw into standard sockets designed for incandescent lightbulbs. Replacing all of your incandescent lightbulbs with compact fluorescent lightbulbs can save a household several hundred dollars every year.

In 1962, a new light-producing **technology** was developed. It was a tiny device called a light-emitting diode (LED). LEDs produce light by using a small amount of energy to emit a ray of light. The LED doesn't waste energy by producing heat. The first LEDs were dim and produced only red light. But they were extremely efficient.

As electrical engineers continued to develop new LEDs, they developed amber- and green-colored LEDs. The colored lights made it possible to convert traffic lights to LEDs. This saved cities a lot of money. Eventually, an LED was developed that produced pure, bright white light. The newest technology for lighting homes and businesses is LED lighting because modern LEDs can produce bright white light using much less electricity, resulting in huge cost savings. You might have seen flashlights that use clusters of small bright lights instead of a single lightbulb. Those small bright lights are modern LEDs.

# Thinking about Lightbulbs

1. How do you know when energy is moving in a lightbulb circuit?
2. Describe the path taken by electricity through an incandescent lightbulb.
3. What are some of the reasons why lamp technology has changed?

**Modern LEDs**

# Energy Sources

Energy makes things happen. Every action is caused by energy. For example, energy makes things warm. Energy makes things move. Energy makes sound and light. Energy is everywhere, and it makes things happen.

There are many ways we can observe energy at **work**. Some of those ways are heat, **motion**, **sound**, and light. Most of the energy we use comes from the Sun. Energy comes from the Sun as light and heat. Light and heat can make things happen. Think about standing in the sunshine. You can see the light and feel the heat.

**The Sun constantly radiates energy that reaches Earth.**

**A toaster plugged into a wall socket**

**Listening to a portable music player powered by a battery**

Electricity is used to make hundreds of different things happen. Electricity can make light. Electricity can make sound. Electricity can make things move. Electricity can make things hot or cold.

Many electric appliances, such as toasters and lamps, have a cord with a plug on the end. They are plugged into a wall socket. The socket is connected to a wire. The wire is connected to a **generator** at a power plant many miles away. You are using the electricity as it is being generated. A lamp uses electric current to produce light. A toaster uses electric current to produce heat. As long as your lamp or toaster is connected to the **energy source**, it will do its work.

But what if you want to take your music player with you to the beach? There is no place to plug in a music player at the beach. But you can still listen to music. You just need a **battery**. A battery is a portable source of **stored energy**.

## Stored Energy

A battery is a source of stored energy. Batteries are full of chemicals. The chemicals in a battery can produce electricity. Electricity from batteries is the same as electricity from a wall socket, but portable. Electricity makes many things happen. Batteries can make sound in a music player and light in a flashlight. The stored energy in batteries can also start a car, power a cell phone, or drive a toy boat across a pond.

Batteries come in all sizes. Hearing aids that fit inside a person's ear have tiny batteries. Batteries that provide the energy to start and drive cars and buses are large. Hybrid vehicles that run on both an electric engine and a gasoline engine have lots of batteries to serve different functions.

**Hearing aids are powered by stored energy in tiny batteries.**

**A car battery**

**Huge batteries power this electric school bus.**

Some communities have electric buses, even electric school buses. The batteries take up most of the space under the seats. The energy in these large batteries flows through wires as electric current. The current powers electric **motors**. The motors turn the bus wheels to move the bus. This bus never has to go to the gas station.

Electric cars are starting to show up on city streets and highways around the United States. They never stop for gas because they need a different source of energy for refueling. Electric cars need to have their batteries recharged. Recharging a battery requires connecting the battery to a source of electricity. Batteries produce electricity when the chemicals in them react. The reaction forms new chemicals and produces electricity. When the chemicals have all reacted, they stop producing electricity. By connecting the battery to an energy source, the chemicals are changed back into their starting conditions. The recharged battery is again ready to produce electricity as a product of the chemical reaction in the battery.

**An electric car is recharged by connecting it to an energy source.**

So how is an electric car recharged? The driver parks the car near an energy source. The driver plugs an extension cord from an energy source into the car. While the car sits there, the batteries recharge. Recharging can happen at home or at a recharging station. Recharging can also happen at work or at a shopping center.

Electricity is the most popular way to transfer or move energy to get a job done. Producing electricity involves changing an energy source into electric current. Scientists are looking for alternative sources of energy to produce electricity. Some alternative sources of energy are light and heat directly from the Sun, moving air or wind, heat generated inside Earth, and moving water.

## Questions to Explore

1. What is energy?
2. What can electricity do?
3. What is a battery?

# Series and Parallel Circuits

**E**lectric current comes from an energy source. The source might be a D-cell battery, a **solar cell**, or a wall socket. When a **component**, like a lightbulb, is connected to a source of electricity, the lightbulb will make light. When a different component, like a motor, is connected to an electricity source, the motor shaft will turn. How do you connect a lightbulb or a motor to an electricity source?

You can use a D-cell to light a lightbulb. Metal wires carry the electricity. If you try to get the lightbulb to light using one wire like this, the lightbulb will not shine.

**An incomplete circuit**

The trick is to use two wires. One wire connects the base of the lightbulb to one end of the D-cell. The second wire connects the metal casing of the lightbulb to the other end of the D-cell. This setup results in a bright, shining lightbulb. It is called a **complete circuit**, or a **closed circuit**. The places on a D-cell and lightbulb where wires touch the component are called contact points.

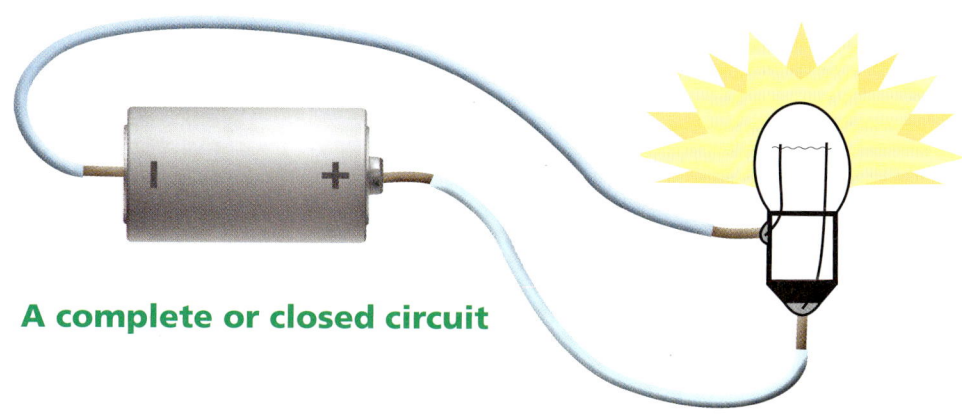

**A complete or closed circuit**

15

If you disconnect one of the wires from the lightbulb or from the D-cell, the lightbulb will stop shining. This is because the pathway through which the electric current flows to the lightbulb is broken. A circuit with a break is called an **incomplete circuit**, or an **open circuit**.

It is important where the wires connect to the D-cell and the lightbulb. One wire must connect to the positive (+) end of the cell. The other wire must connect to the negative (–) end of the cell. The other end of one of the wires must connect to the metal casing of the lightbulb. The other end of the second wire must connect to the base of the lightbulb. These connections make a closed circuit. The electric current will flow, and the lightbulb will shine.

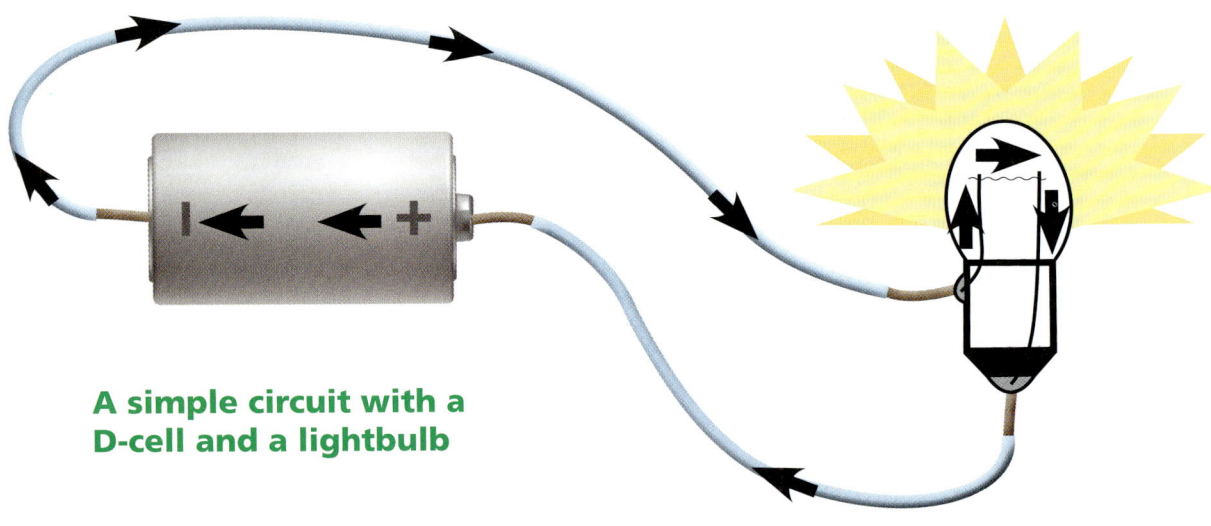

**A simple circuit with a D-cell and a lightbulb**

You might want to connect two lightbulbs to a D-cell. How can you do this? There are two ways. You can open the one-lightbulb circuit and put a second lightbulb into the circuit. Now the electric current flows through two lightbulbs in one circuit. This is a **series circuit**. There are two lightbulbs and one D-cell connected in series. In a series circuit, current has only one pathway to flow from the source (D-cell) to the components (lightbulbs).

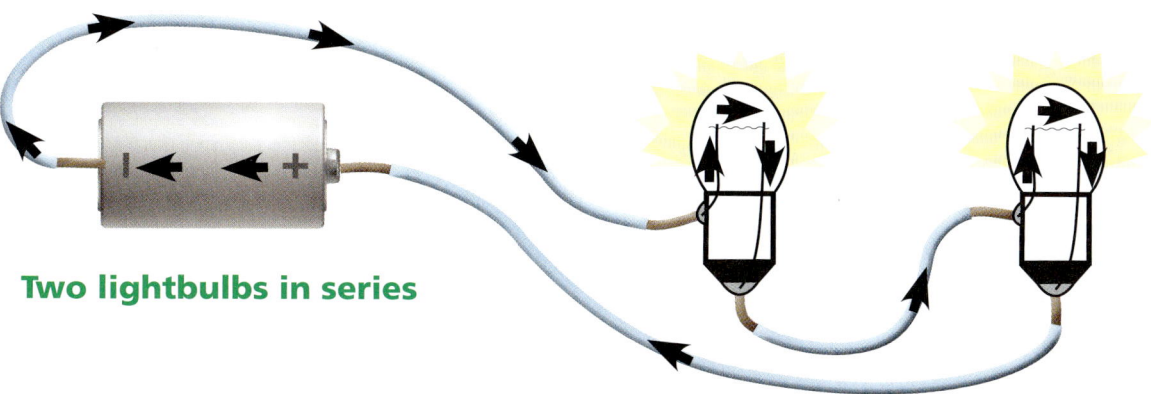

**Two lightbulbs in series**

There is another way to add a second lightbulb to the one-lightbulb circuit. You can use two wires to connect the second lightbulb to the first lightbulb. This is called a **parallel circuit**. There are two lightbulbs in parallel connected to a D-cell. In this parallel circuit, each component (lightbulb) has its own pathway to the energy source (D-cell). Lightbulb 1 is in the blue-arrow pathway; lightbulb 2 is in the red-arrow pathway.

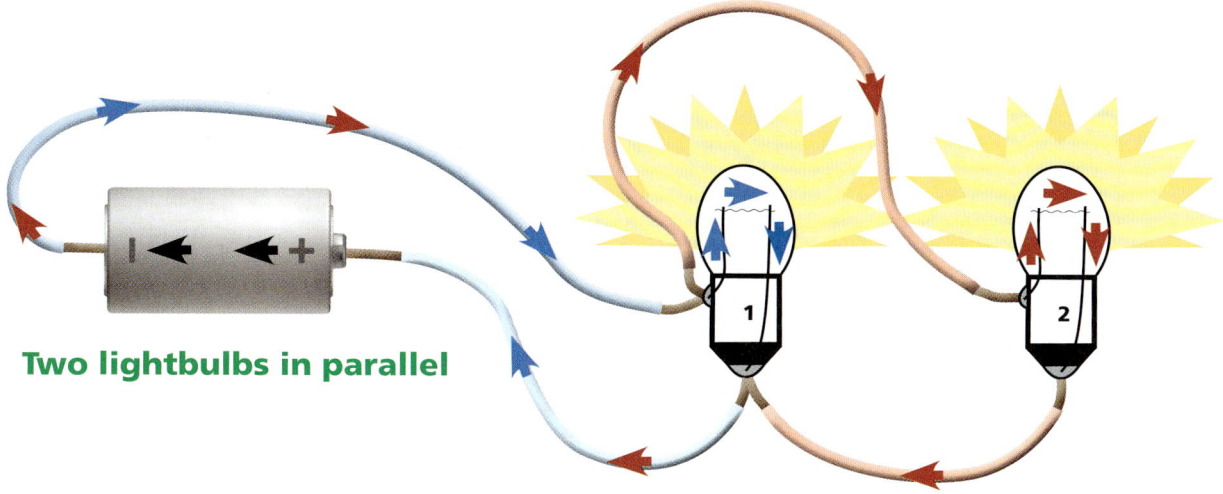

**Two lightbulbs in parallel**

# Which Circuit Should You Use?

Suppose you want to light two lightbulbs. Is there any reason to put them in parallel rather than in series? Yes. The reason becomes clear when you compare the two kinds of circuits. Two lightbulbs in series both shine with a dim light. Both lightbulbs in parallel shine brightly. If you want bright lights, put the lightbulbs in parallel.

Why is there a difference? Two lightbulbs in series have to share the energy of the D-cell. There is only one pathway for the electric current. The current flows from the negative end of the cell through the first lightbulb. It then goes through the second lightbulb and back to the positive end of the cell.

Two lightbulbs in parallel do not have to share energy of the D-cell. Each lightbulb has its own pathway to the source of electricity. Even though some wires are shared for part of the pathway, more than one pathway lets each lightbulb get its own electricity. That's why lightbulbs in parallel shine more brightly.

So, is it better to connect your lightbulbs in series or in parallel? It seems like parallel would be better because you get two bright lights. But there is a cost. The energy of the D-cell will drain much faster when it is supplying electricity to two lightbulbs in parallel. When lightbulbs are connected in series, the D-cell lasts longer, but the lights are dimmer.

**Two or more lights connected in parallel shine brightly.**

## Adding More D-Cells to a Circuit

If you want to put two or more D-cells in a circuit, they can be connected in series or in parallel. Which of these circuits shows two cells in series? Which shows two cells in parallel?

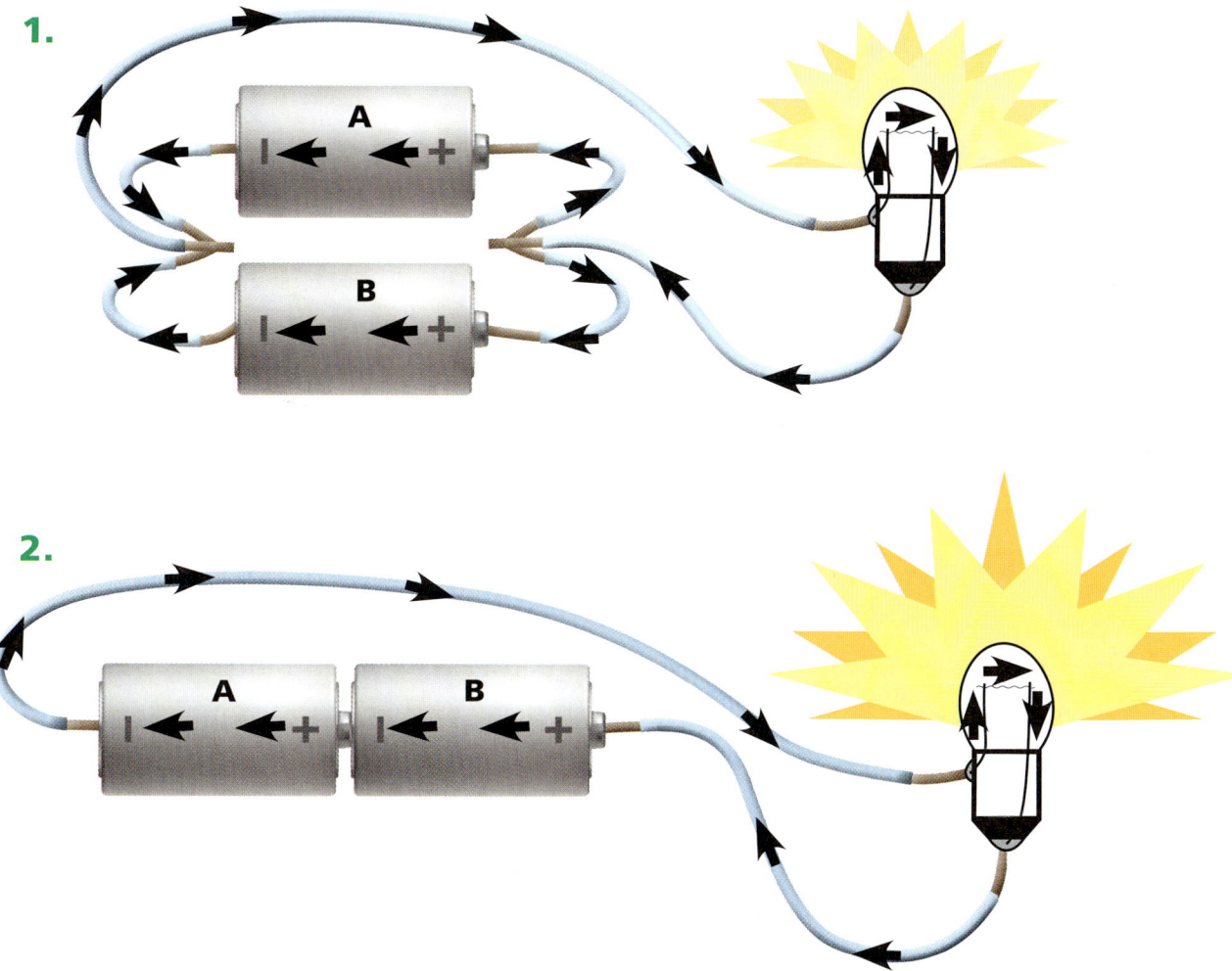

In circuit 1, cells A and B are in parallel. Each cell delivers electricity to the lightbulb in its own pathway. In circuit 2, electricity is delivered to the lightbulb by two cells working together in the same pathway. As a result, the lightbulb in circuit 2 will be twice as bright as the lightbulb in circuit 1.

Here is an interesting circuit made with lightbulbs and D-cells. How would you describe this circuit?

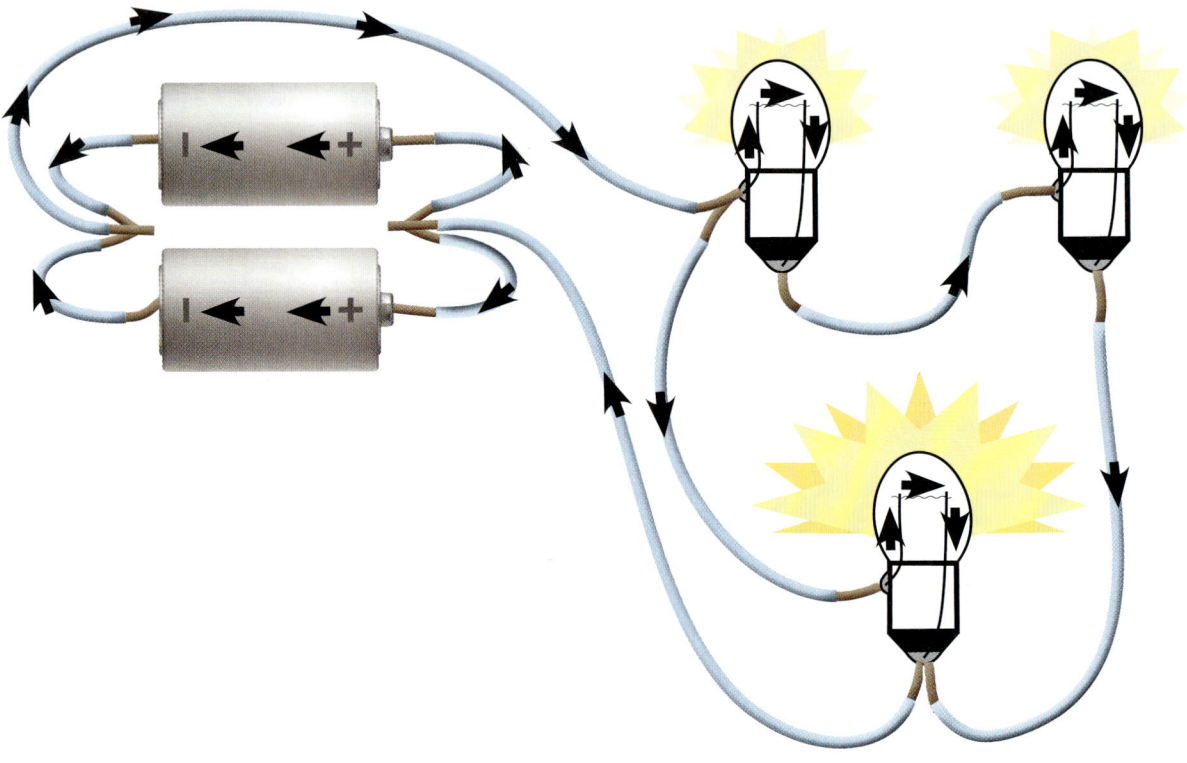

This circuit is one lightbulb in parallel with two lightbulbs in series, powered by two D-cells in parallel. If you said that, you got it right.

# Thinking about Circuits

1. What is the advantage of wiring two lightbulbs in parallel?
2. Why are two lightbulbs in series with a D-cell dim?
3. Do you think the lights in your home are wired in series or in parallel? Why do you think so?

# Science Practices

1. **Asking questions.** Scientists ask questions to guide their investigations. This helps them learn more about how the world works.

2. **Developing and using models.** Scientists develop models to represent how things work and to test their explanations.

3. **Planning and carrying out investigations.** Scientists plan and conduct investigations in the field and in laboratories. Their goal is to collect data that test their explanations.

4. **Analyzing and interpreting data.** Patterns and trends in data are not always obvious. Scientists make tables and graphs. They use statistical analysis to look for patterns.

5. **Using mathematics and computational thinking.** Scientists measure physical properties. They use computation and math to analyze data. They use mathematics to construct simulations, solve equations, and represent different variables.

6. **Constructing explanations.** Scientists construct explanations based on observations and data. An explanation becomes an accepted theory when there are many pieces of evidence to support it.

7. **Engaging in argument from evidence.** Scientists use argumentation to listen to, compare, and evaluate all possible explanations. Then they decide which best explains natural phenomena.

8. **Obtaining, evaluating, and communicating information.** Scientists must be able to communicate clearly. They must evaluate others' ideas. They must convince others to agree with their theories.

Scientists ask questions and communicate information. Are you a scientist?

# Engineering Practices

1. **Defining problems.** Engineers ask questions to make sure they understand problems they are trying to solve. They need to understand the constraints that are placed on their designs.

2. **Developing and using models.** Engineers develop and use models to represent systems they are designing. Then they test their models before building the actual object or structure.

3. **Planning and carrying out investigations.** Engineers plan and conduct investigations. They need to make sure that their designed systems are durable, effective, and efficient.

4. **Analyzing and interpreting data.** Engineers collect and analyze data when they test their designs. They compare different solutions. They use the data to make sure that they match the given criteria and constraints.

5. **Using mathematics and computational thinking.** Engineers measure physical properties. They use computation and math to analyze data. They use mathematics to construct simulations, solve equations, and represent different variables.

6. **Designing solutions.** Engineers find solutions. They propose solutions based on desired function, cost, safety, how good it looks, and meeting legal requirements.

7. **Engaging in argument from evidence.** Engineers use argumentation to listen to, compare, and evaluate all possible ideas and methods to solve a problem.

8. **Obtaining, evaluating, and communicating information.** Engineers must be able to communicate clearly. They must evaluate other's ideas. They must convince others of the merits of their designs.

**Engineers use models.**

# Thinking Like an Engineer

How did you decide what circuit is best for a string of lights? You learned about the problem. You looked for ideas about solving it. You were thinking like an engineer.

**Engineers solve problems.**

## What Do Engineers Do?

Engineers solve problems, such as how to make or fix something. First, engineers define the problem carefully. They decide on the **criteria** for a good design. This means finding out what the **solution** must deliver.

Here are the criteria for the string of lights.
- All the bulbs are brightly lit.
- When one bulb burns out, the other bulbs stay brightly lit.

Engineers must also consider **constraints**. The constraints are the design limits. Here are some constraints on the design for the string of lights.
- The materials are easy to get.
- The string is inexpensive to make.
- It is safe for people, pets, and the environment.

**You need to think about the criteria and constraints when deciding what circuit to use for a string of lights.**

Next, engineers design solutions to the problem. They gather materials and **tools**. Then, they build and test a **prototype**. Does it meet the criteria of a good design? Often the solution does not meet all the criteria. So the team revises the design. They always consider the constraints. Is the solution inexpensive? Are the materials easy to get? Is it safe and easy to use?

### Elements of the Engineering Design Process

Let's review the process of engineering design.
1. Understand the problem thoroughly.
2. Define the criteria for and constraints on a solution.
3. Plan a solution.
4. Build the solution.
5. Test the solution and evaluate its performance.
6. Revise the plan, based on data from the test.
7. Repeat steps 4–6 until the solution satisfies the criteria and constraints.
8. Obtain a patent and go into production.

## A Better Lightbulb

Think about Thomas Edison (1847–1931) working on the lightbulb. The filament burnt out too quickly. His team developed a plan to solve this problem. They made hundreds of different prototypes and tested them.

Think about the criteria for a solution to this problem: How do you make an inexpensive lightbulb that lasts a long time and uses little energy? Edison and his team found a good solution. Ever since, engineers have been designing light sources that meet new criteria.

What would the criteria be for a portable lighting system used in places without electricity? What would the constraints be?

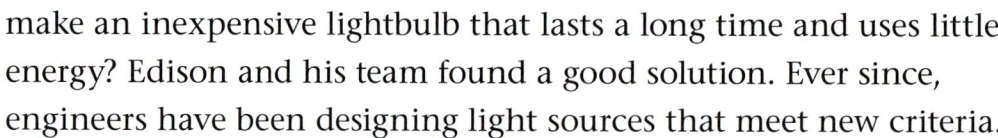

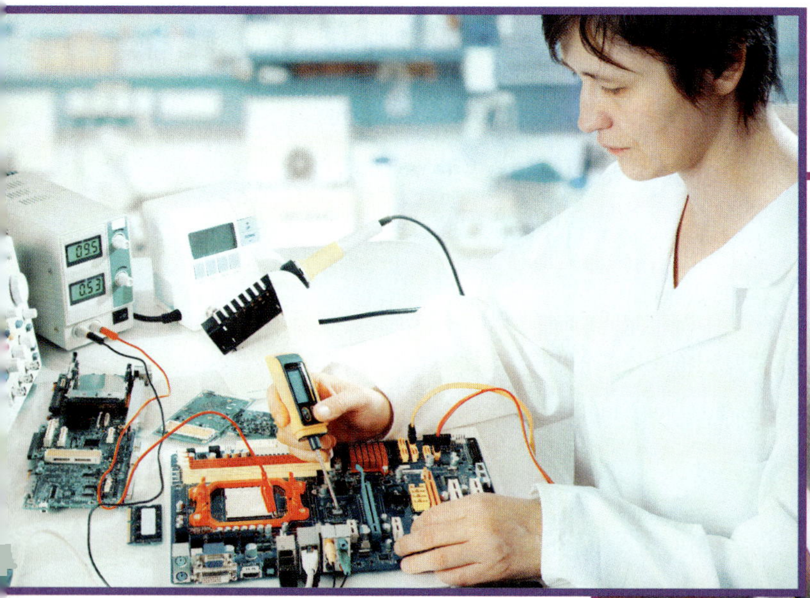

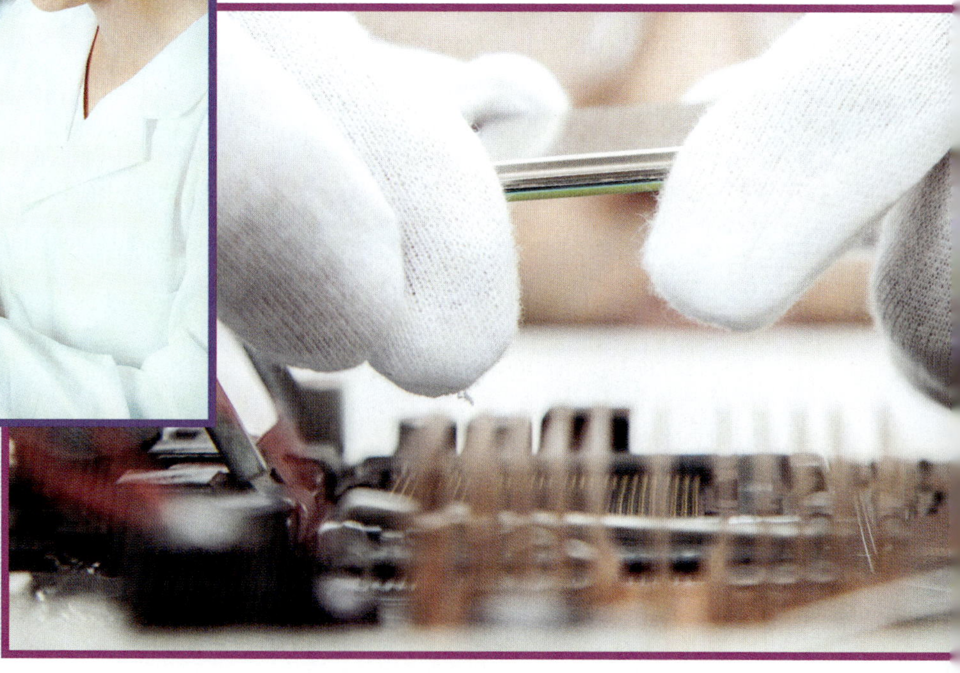

**Computer engineers work on designing new computer systems.**

# Engineering a Solar Lighting System

In 2008, Dr. Laura Stachel was in northern Nigeria. There she observed emergency care at a state hospital. She realized that lack of reliable electricity was a huge problem. Because of frequent blackouts, midwives and doctors struggled to diagnose and treat women with pregnancy problems. Emergency surgeries were interrupted. Dr. Stachel worked with her husband, Hal Aronson, a solar energy educator in Berkeley, California, to solve the problem. They created a solar system to provide electricity for important parts of the hospital. Other health workers in the area began to ask for solar lighting for their clinics, too. Mr. Aronson and Dr. Stachel formed a nonprofit company, We Care Solar. Mr. Aronson designed the We Care Solar Suitcase. This solar system is easy to move, easy to install, durable, and inexpensive to maintain. Mr. Aronson sat down with FOSS to talk about how he engineered this device.

**Q: Can you describe the problem that you set out to solve?**

**A:** The primary problem is the lack of good-quality light, or any light at all. Good-quality light is needed to properly treat sick people. For example, doctors need to see where a mother is bleeding to be able to stop the bleeding.

**Mr. Aronson and Dr. Stachel**

**Q: We know you made Solar Suitcases to help solve the problem. Can you tell us a little about them?**

**A:** The Solar Suitcase is designed to provide medical-quality light all night long. It is designed to do this every night of the week. In order to accomplish this, we start with the energy requirements of the two medical lights and build in a sealed rechargeable battery. We size the solar panels so that they can fully recharge the battery every day.

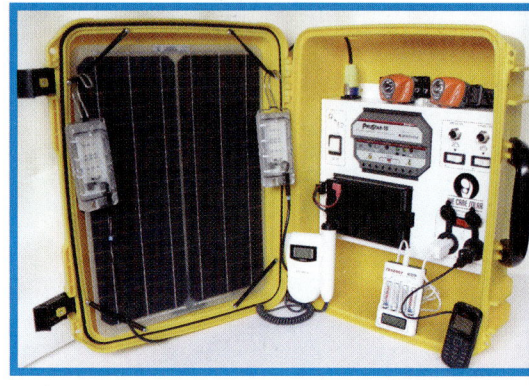

**A Solar Suitcase**

Solar Suitcases have been used in a range of settings. The case is waterproof because doctors often bring them to disaster sites and set them up in tent cities. We use special connectors for the lights, so that the connection is robust and others cannot pull power from them.

**Q: Why didn't you use typical connectors such as light sockets or regular outlets?**

**A:** The Solar Suitcase has a relatively small battery. The key to a well–functioning Solar Suitcase system is to use high-quality, energy-efficient loads. If people tried to plug in other lights, they would have neither the performance nor the efficiency. The lights would not be able to stay on all night long.

We also want to avoid other appliances being plugged into the system, in order to make sure that the battery is full when night comes.

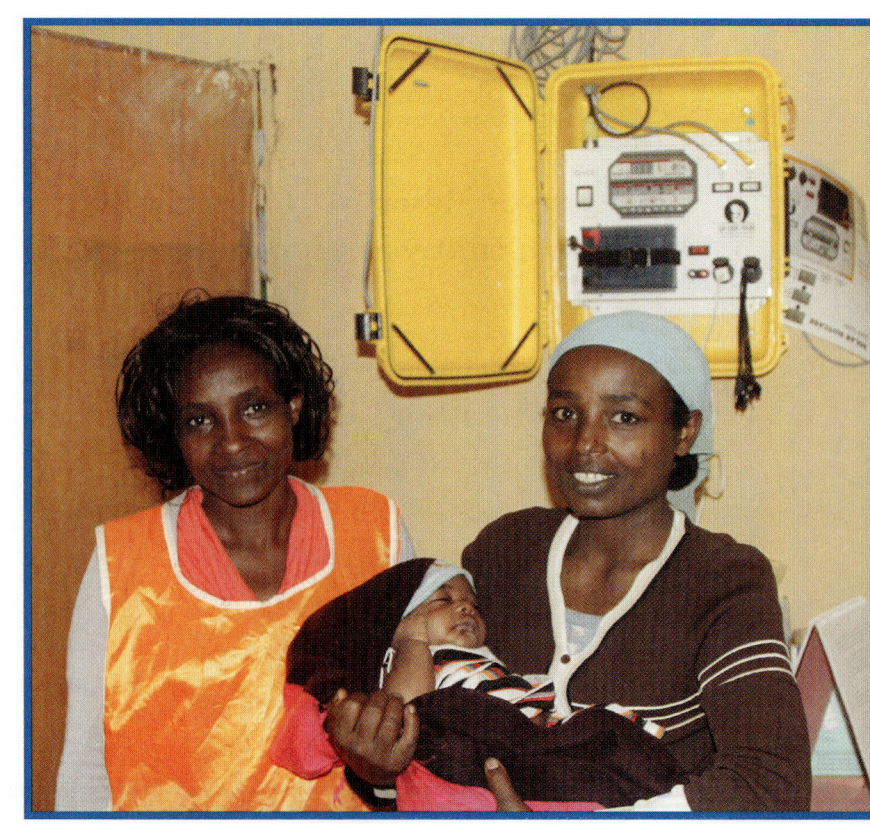

**Q: How do you use models or prototypes in your work?**

**A:** Once we understood the needs of health workers, we built prototypes of systems that we thought would solve their needs: provide adequate light, be easy to use, be easy to maintain, be durable. We then sent the prototypes out into the field and followed up to learn what worked well and what needed improvement. We have been through this process six to ten times.

Tinkerers will never get it perfect the first time. The point is to do your best, get it out there, hope that it will be useful, and learn from where it fails. Instead of being saddened or frustrated by failures, which I typically am, I learned to see them as useful information for making improvements.

**Q: How do you determine if your design solves the problem?**

**A:** At one level, we have learned that it has solved a problem. The clinics report back that more women are coming to use the clinic now that it has good light. Also, we hear that health-center staff, nurses, and midwives, can do their work and are no longer scared at night. Doctors at hospitals, such as Dr. Chirangi from Shirati Hospital, send us photos. The Solar Suitcase kept the light on in the operating room after the grid power failed, and so his surgery was successful.

**Q: What are the major constraints in your work?**

**A:** Where our systems are installed is far away from where we live. So it is a major effort for us to do the maintenance. The answer is to work with skilled in-country partners who have the resources to maintain the systems.

**Engineers and technicians need to consider where to install solar panels on the metal roof. What might be some of their considerations?**

**Q: Who takes care of the system once it's installed?**

**A:** We train the district health workers and local technicians to maintain the system. We provide tools, we teach them how to use the tools and conduct installations, and we teach them troubleshooting. When we leave, one person is in charge of the system, so they have real ownership.

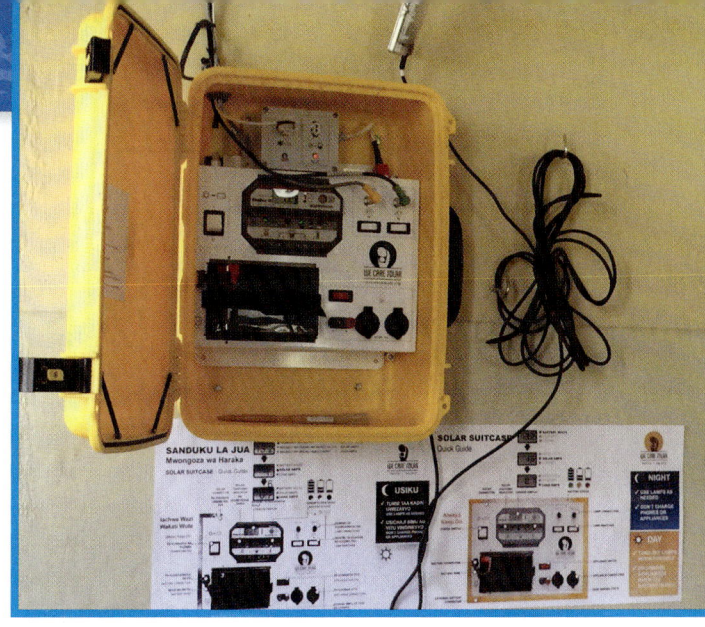

A Solar Suitcase installed in a clinic. Note the diagrams beneath it. These diagrams help people know how to use the system.

## Summary

Over 1,000 Solar Suitcases have been assembled and shipped around the world! And that's not all. In addition to providing power for healthcare, We Care Solar started another program, called We Share Solar. We Share Solar gives students around the United States the opportunity to build Solar Suitcases for orphanages and schools in other countries.

### Thinking about Engineering a Solar Lighting System

1. Why didn't Mr. Aronson want people to plug their TVs and other appliances into the Solar Suitcase?

2. Why is it important for engineers to test their prototypes?

3. Think of three questions you might have for Mr. Aronson. Share your questions with your group and come up with one group question to share with the class.

4. How else might a Solar Suitcase be used to solve problems in rural areas?

# When Magnet Meets Magnet

You know what a refrigerator **magnet** is. It's an object that might look like a flower, a piece of fruit, or a seashell. And, most importantly, it sticks to the refrigerator.

Refrigerator magnets come in thousands of sizes, colors, and shapes. But they all have one thing in common. When you look on the back, you see a piece of black flexible material or a hard, black object. The flexible piece or black object that sticks to the refrigerator is a **permanent magnet**.

The magnet might look different from the doughnut-shaped one you used in class. But it works just the same. The shape on the front is a decoration. It's the magnet that sticks to the refrigerator.

The most interesting thing about magnets is that they stick to refrigerators and to a lot of other things. But they don't stick to everything. If you test all the different objects around your kitchen, you will soon discover that magnets only stick to some metal objects.

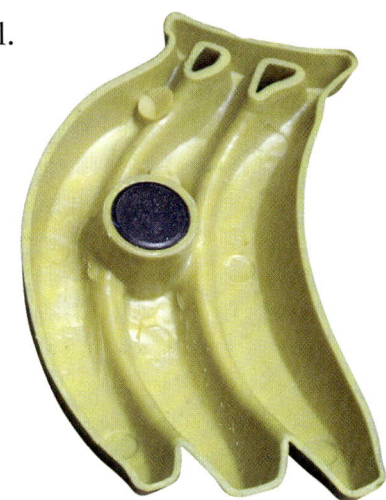

**A permanent magnet on the back of a refrigerator magnet**

**Refrigerator magnets**

Visit FOSSweb to explore more about magnets!

After more testing, you will find that magnets stick to one kind of metal. That metal is **iron**. Iron can be mixed with other metals to make steel. Magnets stick to steel because steel is mostly iron. Magnets do not stick to objects made of most other metals. For example, magnets do not stick to aluminum pots, copper coins, silver spoons, gold rings, or brass hinges. The general rule is *if a magnet sticks to an object, the object is iron or steel.*

When you bring two magnets together, two things can happen. Sometimes magnets pull on each other and stick together. When they pull and stick, we say they **attract**.

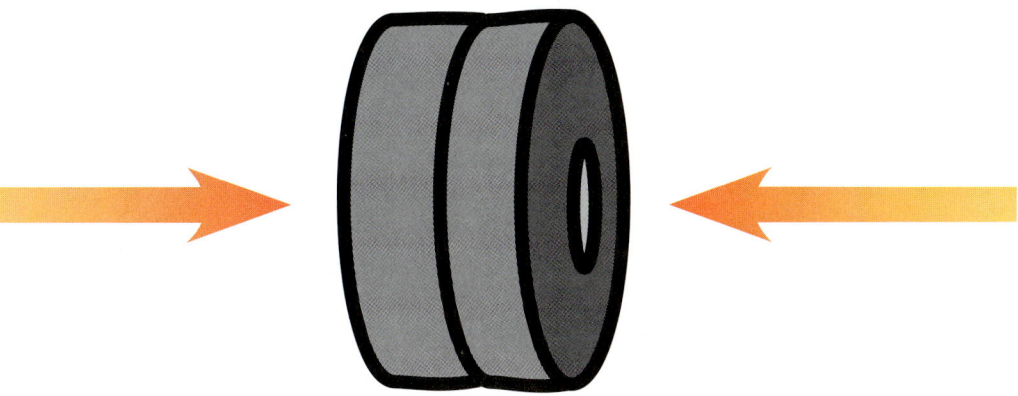

**Two magnets attracting**

At other times, magnets push each other apart. When they push apart, we say they **repel**. Why do you think they repel?

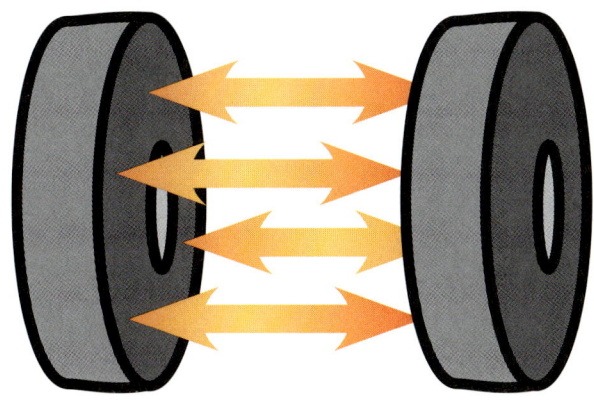

**Two magnets repelling**

## Magnetic Poles

Every magnet has two different sides or ends called **poles**. One pole is called the **north pole**, and the other is called the **south pole**. A simple bar magnet has its two poles on opposite ends. A horseshoe magnet has a pole on each end of the horseshoe. The doughnut magnets you worked with have poles on the two flat sides. Magnets always have a north pole and a south pole.

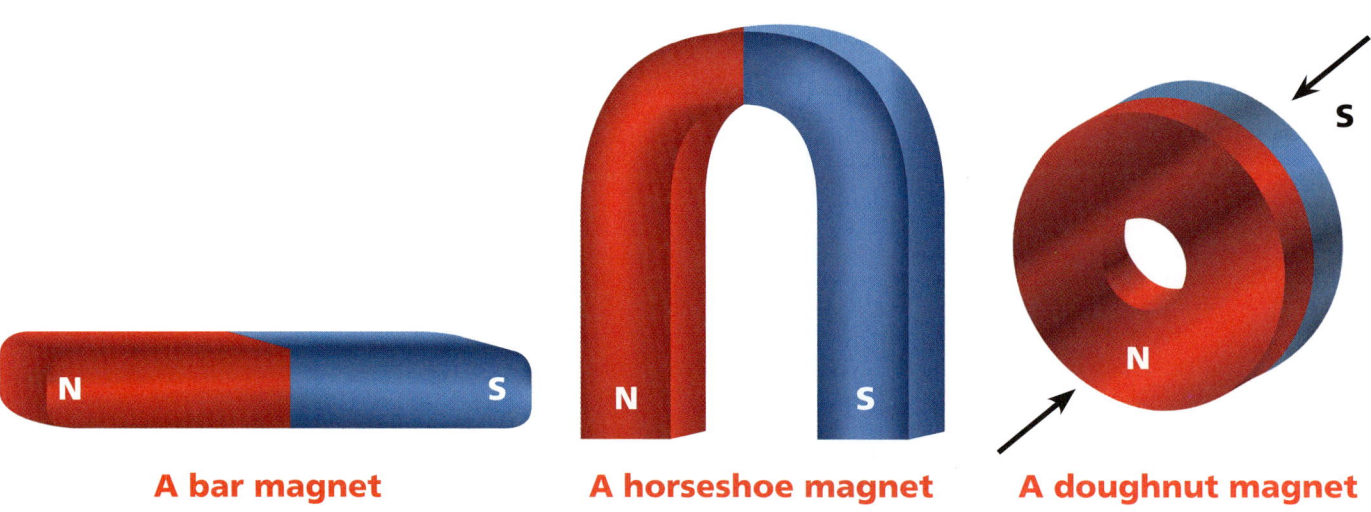

**A bar magnet**   **A horseshoe magnet**   **A doughnut magnet**

You might wonder what happens when a bar magnet breaks. Do you have a magnet with just one pole? No, both pieces still have a north pole and a south pole. The same is true for all other magnets. No matter how many pieces you cut a magnet into, each piece still has a north pole and a south pole.

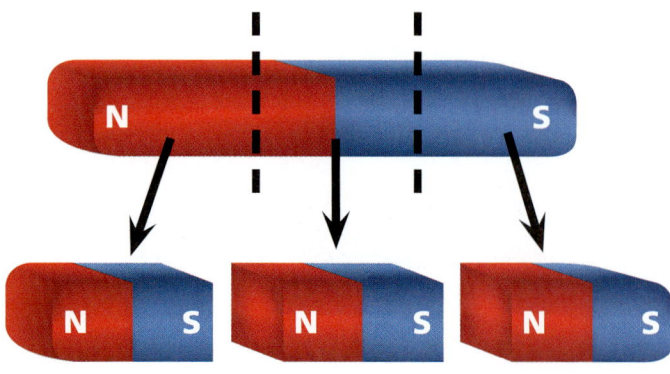

**Cut a long bar magnet into three pieces. Each piece has a north pole and a south pole.**

What happens when two magnets come close to each other, and you can feel them repel? How are the poles **oriented**? Do the magnets repel when two south poles come together? Do the magnets repel when two north poles come together? Or do they repel when one south pole and one north pole come together?

Here are four pairs of bar magnets being held together. Which ones will push apart when they are released?

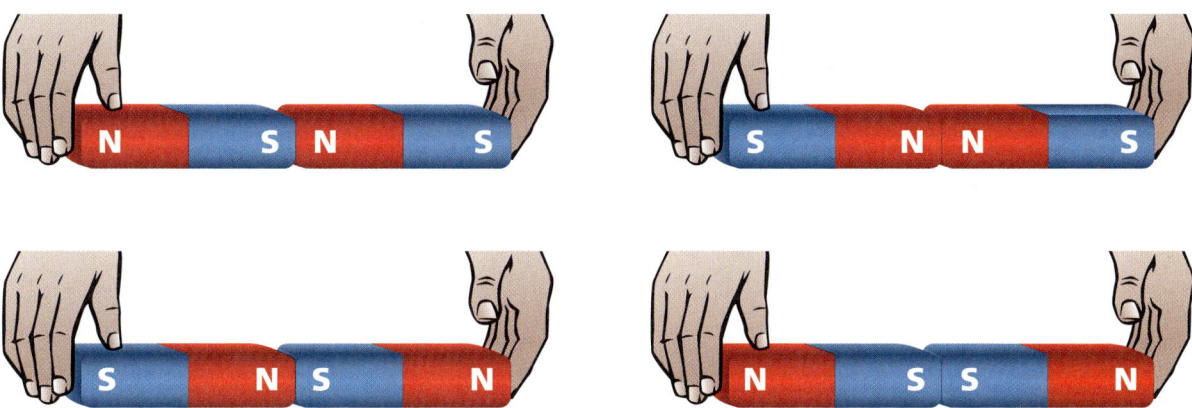

This is what happens when the magnets are released. The two pairs of magnets on the left attract each other. The two pairs of magnets on the right repel each other.

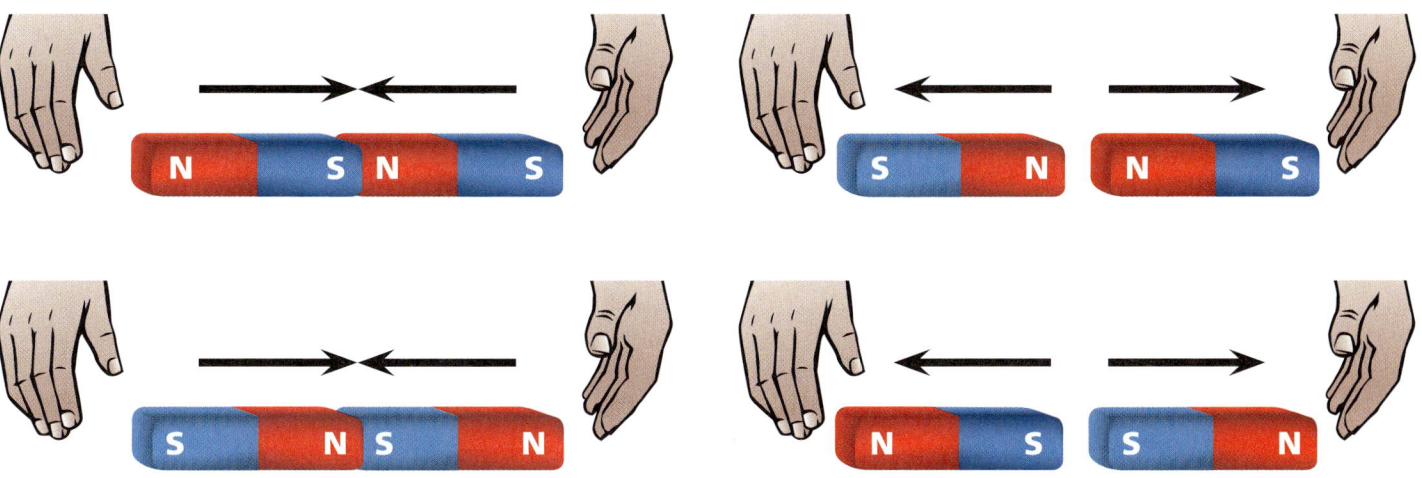

Two north poles always repel each other. Two south poles always repel each other. We can state a general rule. *Like poles repel.*

A north pole and a south pole always attract each other. It doesn't matter which magnet has the north pole and which has the south pole. We can state another general rule. *Opposite poles attract.*

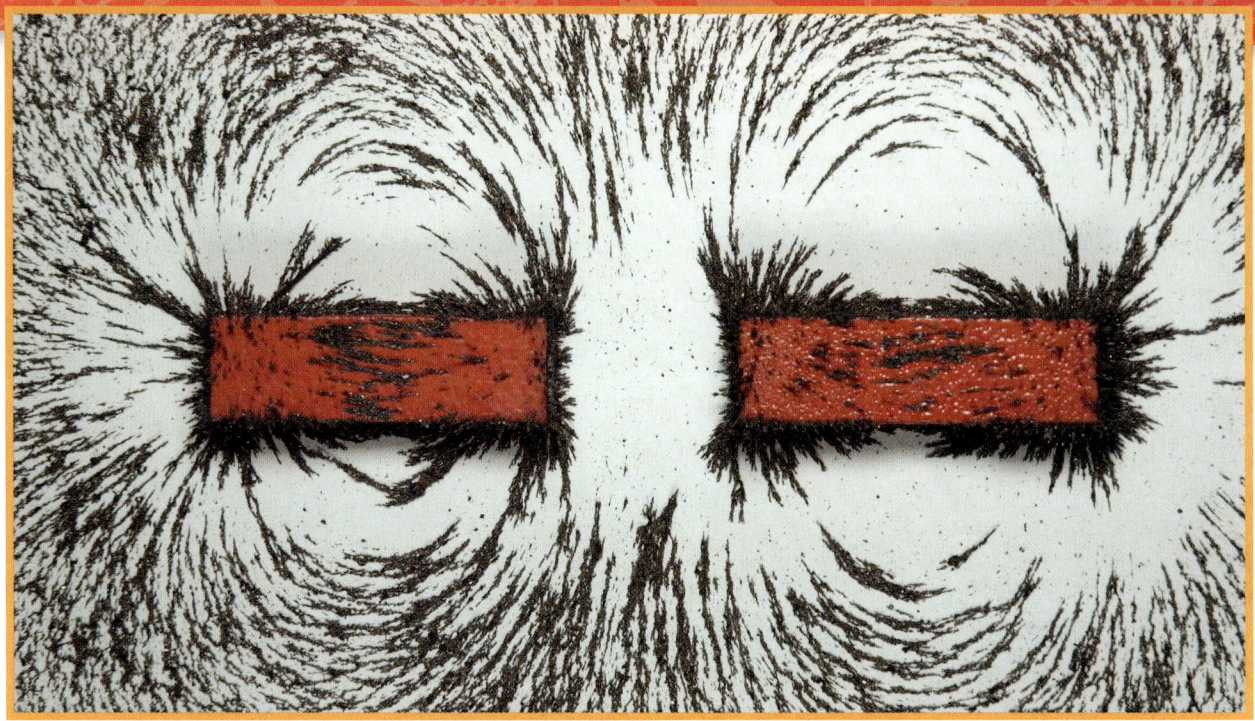

**Using iron filings, you can see magnetic fields around magnets.**

## The Magnetic Force

**Magnetism** is a **force**. A force is a push or a pull. You can feel the magnetic force when you pull two attracting magnets apart. In the same way, you can feel the magnetic force when you push two repelling magnets together. The force of magnetism is what makes magnets act the ways they do.

## How Magnets Stick to Iron

If opposite poles attract, why does a magnet stick to a piece of iron? Magnetism extends out from a magnet in an invisible area called a **magnetic field**. When a magnet comes close to a piece of iron, such as a steel nail, the magnetic field **interacts** with the iron in the nail. The nail becomes a **temporary magnet**. The end of the nail becomes one pole of a magnet. The magnet then sticks to the temporary magnet. So magnets don't really stick to iron. Magnets stick to other magnets.

The magnetism in the iron is called **induced magnetism**. Induced magnetism happens only when a magnet is close by. If you bring the south pole of a magnet close to the head of a nail, what pole will the head of the nail become? Just apply the rule. Opposites attract. (The nail head will become a north pole.)

## The First Magnets

The first magnets were pieces of a naturally occurring mineral called magnetite. Magnetite sticks to magnets because it contains a lot of iron. The black rock in your set of test objects is magnetite. When magnetite is by itself, it is called lodestone.

Legend has it that shepherds found bits of rock sticking to the iron nails in their sandals more than 2,000 years ago. One area rich with lodestone was a part of present-day Turkey. This region was called Magnesia. The word *magnet* may come from the name of this ancient region.

Magnetite is also found in a number of locations in the United States. Some of the major sources are shown on the map below. Can you find the major magnetite source closest to where you live?

**Magnetite**

**Lodestone was found in Magnesia.**

**Where is magnetite found in the United States?**

37

## Reviewing Magnets

Magnets are objects that stick to iron and steel. All magnets have two poles, a north pole and a south pole. Like poles repel. Opposite poles attract.

### Thinking about Magnetic Interactions

1. Why does magnetite stick to a magnet?

2. What causes magnets to attract each other at some times and repel each other at other times?

3. The magnets shown below have one pole labeled. Which pairs of magnets will attract, and which will repel?

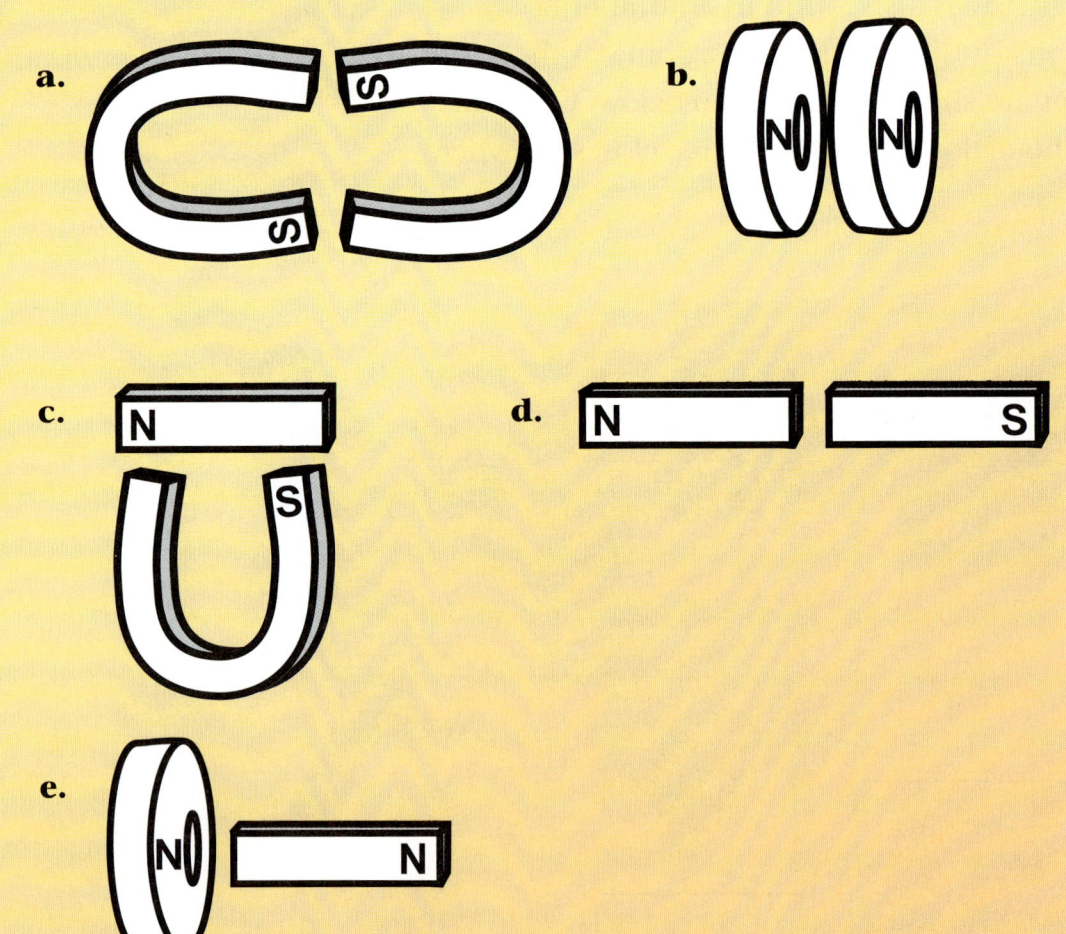

# Magnificent Magnetic Models

The ancient Romans and Egyptians used magnets to create artwork. They did not understand magnetic force. But they knew how to use it to do wonderful things with magnets. The Romans used magnets to suspend a figure of the god Mercury in midair in one of their temples.

The Egyptians hung iron and lodestone figures from ropes. The figures would repel and attract each other so that they appeared to dance. You can make models of these statues. Look on the next pages for plans.

**Roman and Egyptian artwork using magnets**

# Dancing Statues

## What You Need

- 2 Small plastic containers
- 14 Doughnut magnets
- 1 Ruler or pencil
- String
- Scissors

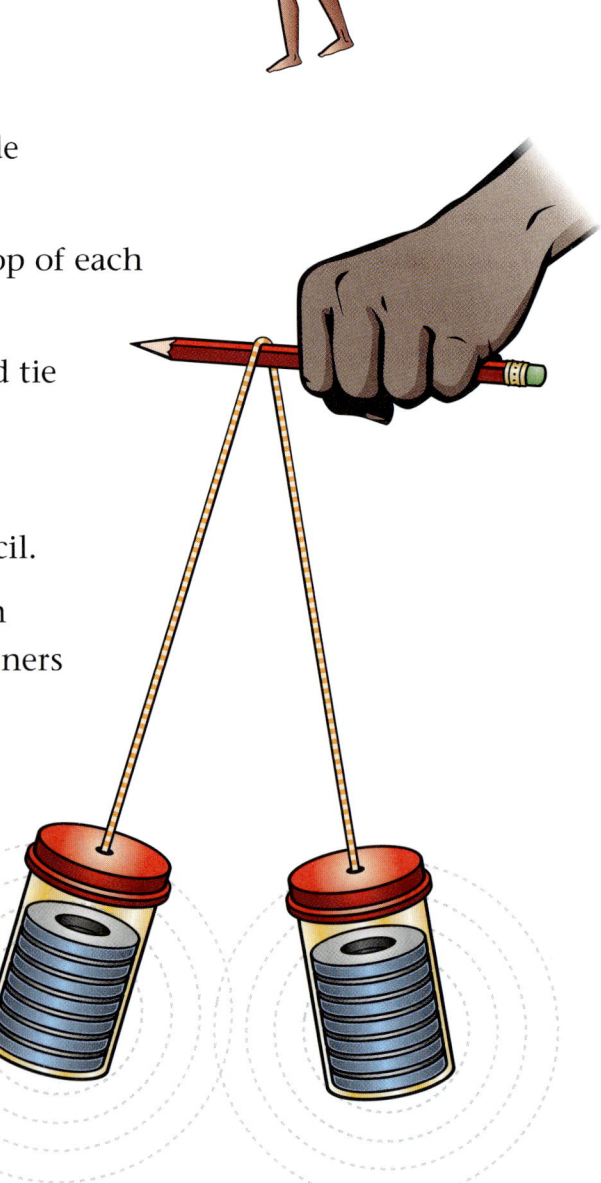

## What You Do

1. Place seven doughnut magnets inside each container.
2. Use the scissors to cut a slit in the top of each container, from side to center.
3. Slide the string through the slits and tie knots to hold the string in place.
4. Put the tops on the containers.
5. Hang the string from a ruler or pencil.
6. You may have to flip the magnets in one container over if the two containers do not repel each other.

## What Happens

The containers dance around each other and never touch.

# The Suspended Statue

## What You Need

1 Glass jar with a steel screw-on lid
1 Steel paper clip
1 Magnet
- Tape
- Thread

## What You Do

1. Stick the magnet to the underside of the jar lid.
2. Tie the paper clip to one end of the thread.
3. Be sure the thread is the right length. The paper clip should almost reach the lid when the thread is taped to the bottom of the jar.
4. Tape the other end of the thread to the bottom of the jar.
5. Hold the jar upside down. Screw on the lid. Then turn the jar upright again. The paper clip should not touch the magnet.

## What Happens

The paper clip floats mysteriously at the end of the thread.

## Discuss Your Ideas

1. Explain why the containers filled with magnets act the way they do.
2. Why doesn't the paper clip fall to the bottom of the jar?
3. If you wanted to have three containers of magnets dance around one another, how would you orient the magnets?

# Make a Magnetic Compass

You can make a **compass** just like the one a hiker might use to keep from getting lost. Here's how to do it.

## What You Need

- 1 Bar magnet
- 1 Ruler
- 1 Piece of thread about 30 centimeters (cm) long
- 1 Store-bought compass
- Masking tape

## What You Do

1. Tie one end of the thread to the middle of the magnet so that the magnet hangs level.
2. Tie the other end of the thread to the end of a ruler.
3. Tape the ruler at the edge of a table so that the magnet hangs in midair. Make sure the magnet is not close to any steel. (Do you know why?) Your compass is done!

A compass made with a bar magnet, a ruler, and a piece of thread

## What Happens

When the magnet comes to rest, it will point north and south because it is a compass. But which end points north? You will need a store-bought compass to find out.

The painted end of the store-bought compass needle will point north. Now you should be able to figure out which end of your bar magnet is pointing north.

You can make sure by slowly bringing the store-bought compass up to one end of your hanging bar magnet. Do the compass needle and the magnet point in the same direction? If the answer is yes, then both magnets are pointing north.

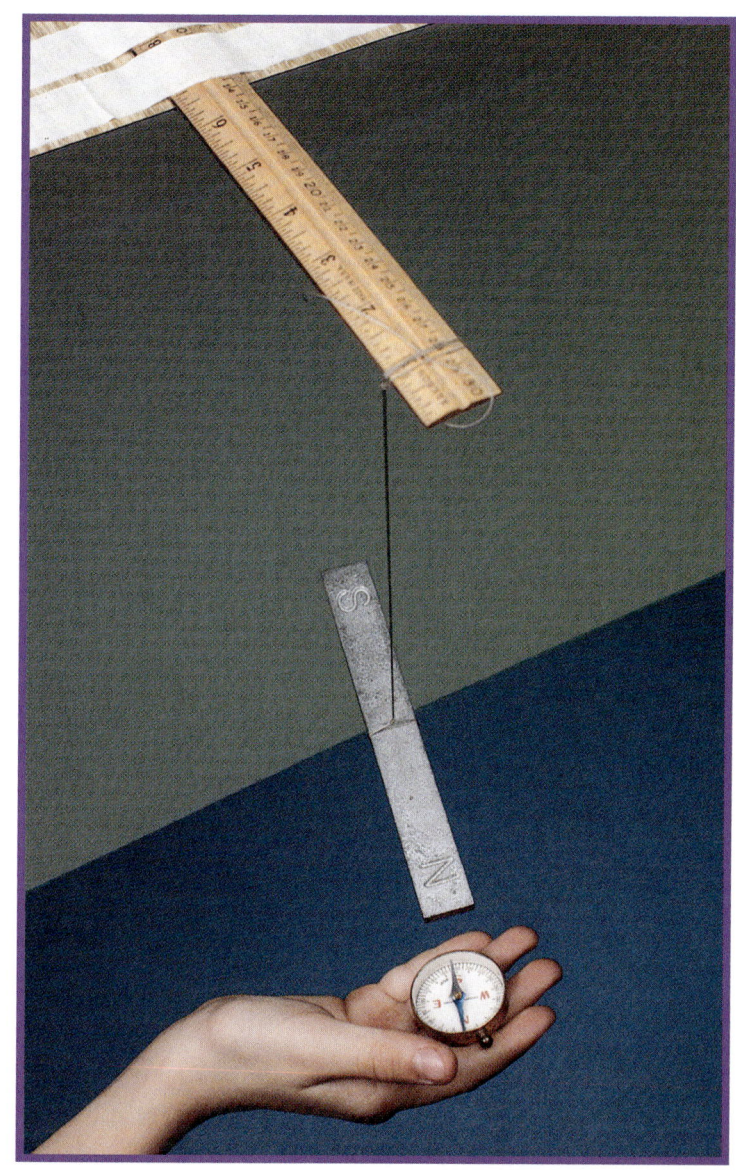

**A store-bought compass next to a homemade compass**

## Magnetic Fields

Every magnet has a magnetic field around it. Think of a magnetic field as many invisible lines that loop from the north pole to the south pole of a magnet, and then through the magnet. When two magnets interact, it is actually the magnetic fields of the two magnets that interact.

Earth is a giant magnet. Magnets all over the planet line up with Earth's magnetic field. The north pole of every free-rotating magnet points to the magnetic north pole of Earth. That's why a compass is a good tool for keeping track of direction. A compass needle will point toward Earth's magnetic north pole.

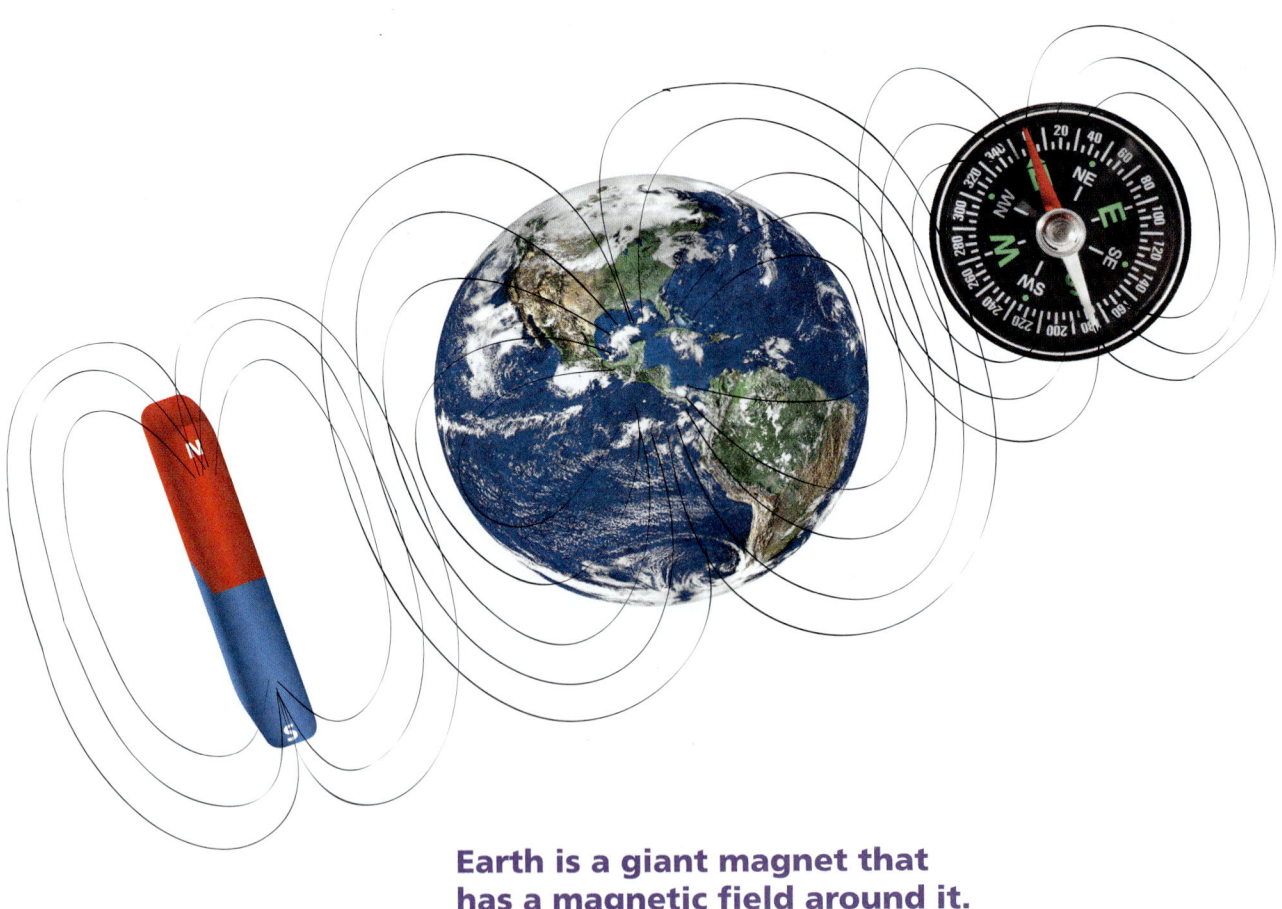

**Earth is a giant magnet that has a magnetic field around it.**

# Make Another Homemade Compass

You can make another simple compass by turning a sewing needle into a permanent magnet. Here's how to do it.

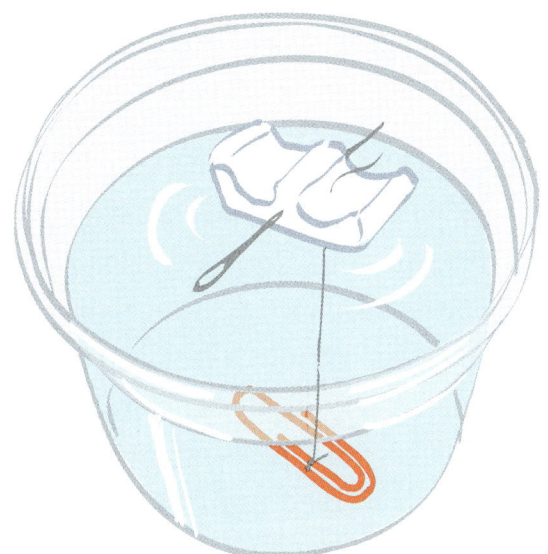

## What You Need

1 Steel sewing needle
1 Permanent magnet
1 Steel paper clip
1 Piece of plastic foam or cork
1 ½-liter container or cup
- Water
- Thread

## What You Do

1. Tie one end of the thread to the paper clip.
2. Tie the other end of the thread around the piece of plastic foam or cork.
3. Using a permanent magnet, rub the sewing needle several times in one direction. Now the needle has two poles, just like every magnet.
4. Push the needle through the piece of plastic foam or cork.
5. Put the needle-and-paper clip system in the center of the container of water.

## What Happens

The needle will float in the cup of water and rotate to line up with Earth's magnetic field. The needle is a compass!

The paper clip acts as an anchor so that the needle can freely rotate and won't get stuck on the side of the container.

# Electricity Creates Magnetism

## Oersted's Discovery

**Hans Christian Oersted**

Hans Christian Oersted (1777–1851) was born in Denmark. As a young child, he lived with a family in Germany. He learned to read and became skilled in math, even though he never attended a school. By the time he was 11 years old, Oersted returned home and worked in his father's pharmacy. There he learned the basics of chemistry.

By the time he was 17 years old, Oersted passed the exam to enter the University of Copenhagen in Denmark. He studied chemistry, astronomy, physics, and math. After he graduated, he became a physics professor at the university.

Like many scientists of his time, Oersted was fascinated with the discovery made by Alessandro Volta (1745–1827) in 1800. Volta invented the battery, which was the first source of electric current. The D-cell we use today is a direct result of Volta's discovery. Oersted conducted lots of experiments with electric current.

In 1820, Oersted was giving a lecture demonstrating that electric current makes wires hot. When he closed the electric circuit, a compass needle that happened to be on the lecture table rotated. Some people think he was planning to show the relationship between electric current and magnetism that day. Others think it was just a lucky accident. We will never know for sure.

Here's what might have happened. Oersted had a thin wire connected to a battery and a switch. A compass needle was right under one of the wires forming the circuit.

When the circuit was closed to deliver electric current to the thin wire, the compass needle rotated.

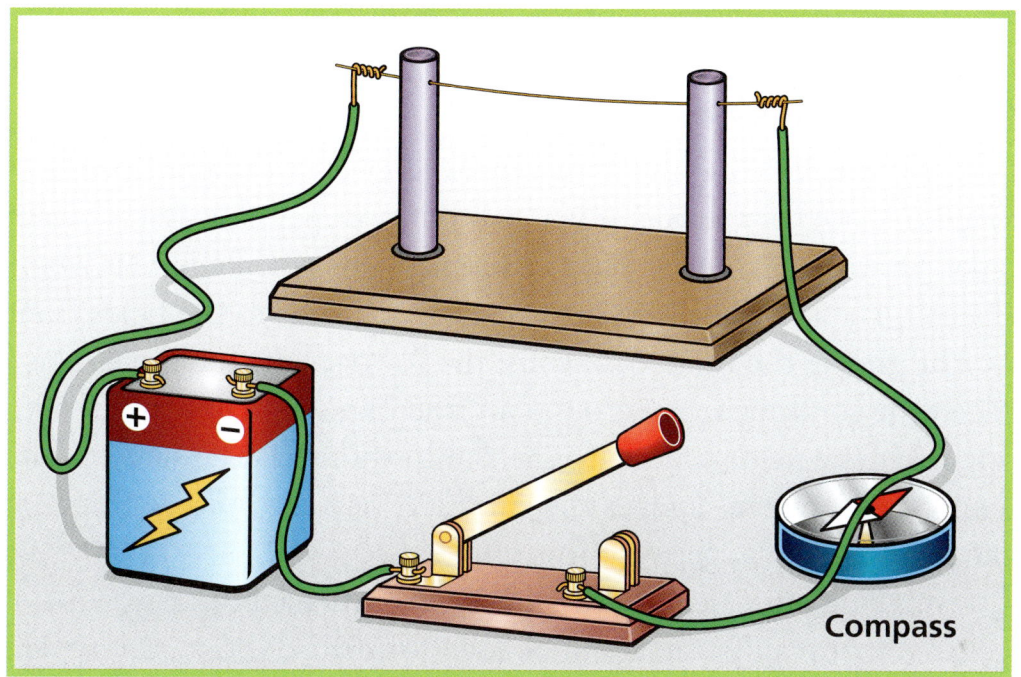

Oersted's demonstration with the switch open

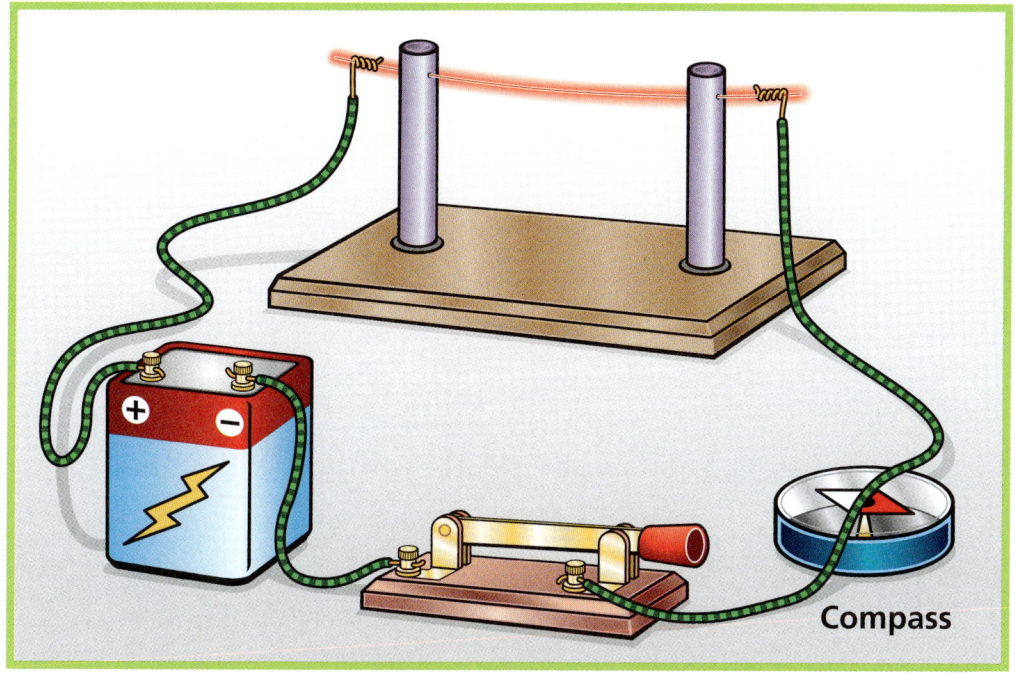

Oersted's demonstration with the switch closed

Oersted must have been excited, but he didn't announce his discovery at that time. He conducted more experiments. Four months later he wrote a report of his finding. His conclusion was that a flow of electric current produces a magnetic field.

This important discovery resulted in hundreds of inventions in the years that followed. One was the **electromagnet**, a magnet that can be turned on and off.

## Magnetic Fields

The magnetic field around a wire that has electric current flowing through it is not very strong. If you can put two magnetic fields together, the magnetism will be stronger. That's what happens when a wire is wound into a coil. The magnetic field around each coil adds to the fields from other coils. The greater the number of coils, the stronger the total magnetic field is.

When the coil is wrapped around an iron or a steel **core**, like a rivet, the strong magnetic field induces magnetism in the steel. The steel becomes a temporary magnet as long as the current is flowing. And, with a flip of the switch, the magnetism turns off.

It wasn't long after Oersted's discovery that Michael Faraday (1791–1867) discovered that magnetism could be used to create electric current. From that time on, there was no doubting that one force was responsible for both magnetism and electricity. That force is the electromagnetic force.

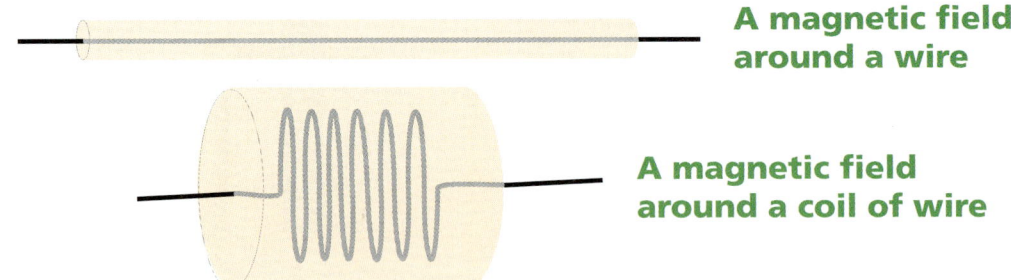

**A magnetic field around a wire**

**A magnetic field around a coil of wire**

## Thinking about Electromagnetism

1. What was Oersted's historic discovery?
2. How does an electromagnet work?
3. Why did Oersted's compass needle rotate when he ran electric current through the thin wire?

# Using Magnetic Fields

The wire you have been using to make circuits is made of copper. Copper wire is not magnetic. There is no magnetic field around a copper wire. You can confirm or prove this by bringing a compass close to a copper wire. The compass needle does not move.

Things change when you connect a copper wire to a source of electricity, such as a D-cell. While electric current is flowing through the wire, a magnetic field surrounds it. When you bring a compass close to the wire, the compass needle will rotate. When the circuit is broken, the magnetic field disappears, and the compass needle points north again.

The fact that a current produces a magnetic field can be used to make a very useful device. This device is an electromagnet. An electromagnet is a magnet that can be turned on and off with the flip of a switch.

The magnetic field surrounding a current-carrying wire is not very strong. The strength of the field can be increased by coiling the wire. When two coils are next to each other, the magnetic fields add together. This makes the magnetic field stronger.

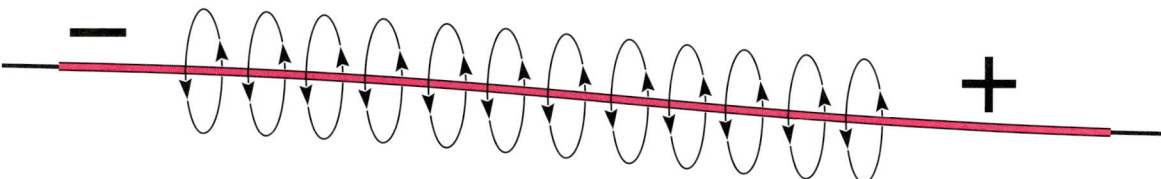

**A magnetic field around a current-carrying wire**

**A magnetic field around a coil of current-carrying wire**

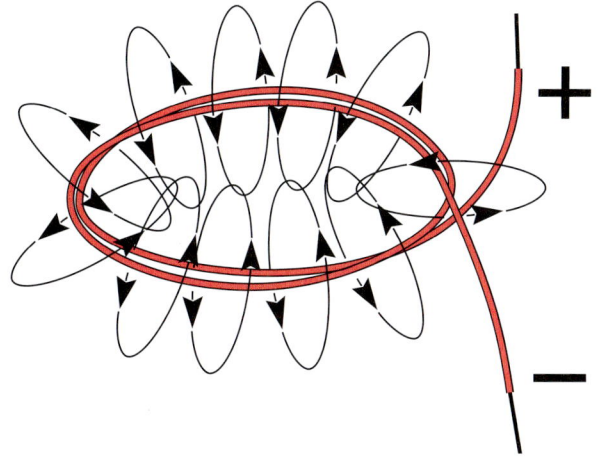

As you add more coils, the magnetic field gets stronger and stronger. If you put an iron core, like a rivet, in the center of the coils, the strong magnetic field will induce magnetism in the iron. That is how electromagnets are made.

There are several ways to make an electromagnet stronger. More coils of wire is one way that you have already learned about. The more wire you wrap around the core, the stronger the magnetism.

Another way to make an electromagnet stronger is to increase the amount of electric current flowing through the wire. You used one D-cell. Two D-cells increase the magnetism a lot. What if you had ten D-cells in series? Or 100 D-cells in series? Now we're talking about some strong magnetism.

A third way to make an electromagnet stronger is to wrap thicker wire around the core. Thicker wire can conduct more current. The thicker the wire is, the stronger the magnetic field, and the stronger the electromagnet.

There are a couple of other things you always need to think about. The wire must be insulated. (Do you know why?) And the coils of wire must all be wound around the core in the same direction. It doesn't matter which direction as long as they all go in the *same* direction.

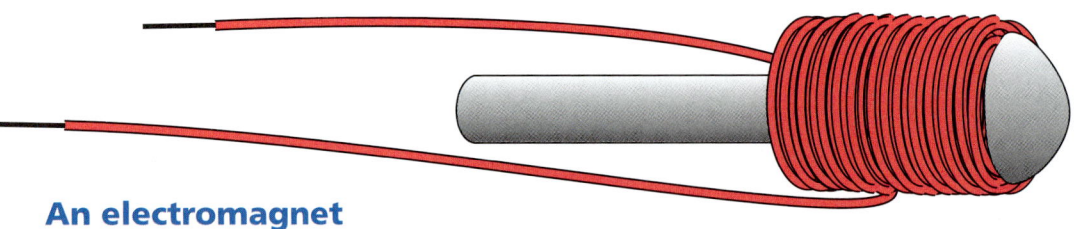

**An electromagnet**

## Discuss Your Ideas

1. What is one way to tell if a wire has current flowing through it?
2. How do you make an electromagnet?
3. How can you make an electromagnet stronger?

# Electromagnets Everywhere

## Motors

A motor that runs on a D-cell is a direct-current motor. A direct-current motor has two main parts. They are permanent magnets and electromagnets.

A simple motor is like a tin can with two permanent magnets stuck inside. In the center of the can, there is a shaft that has two or more iron cores attached. A lot of wire is wrapped around each of the cores to make electromagnets.

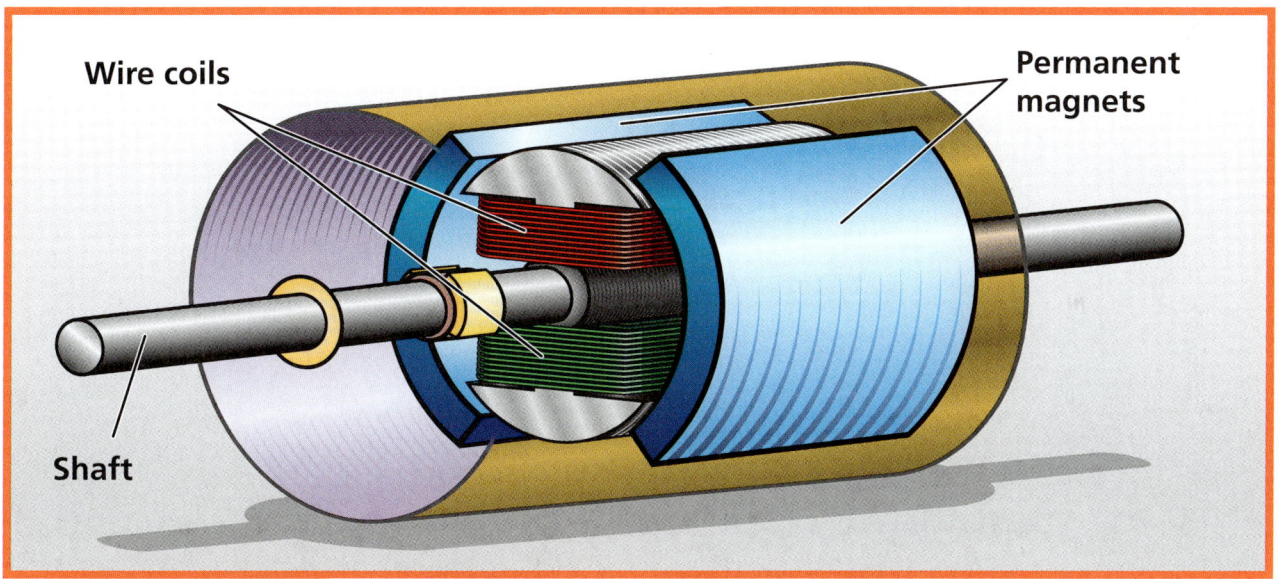

**The parts of a simple motor**

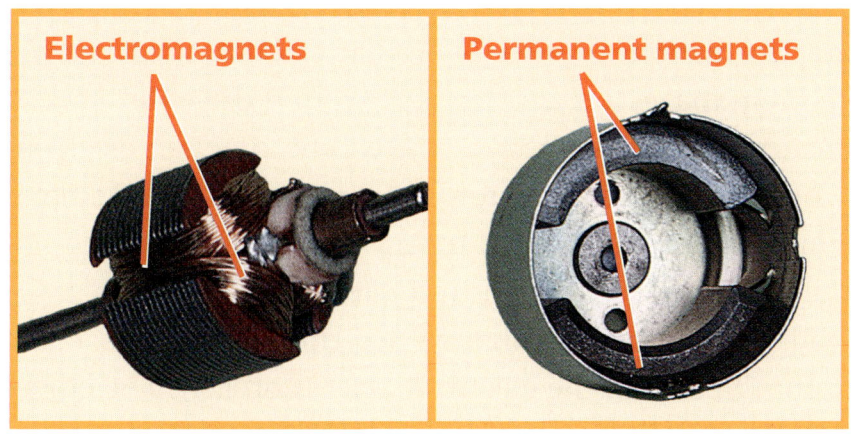

Imagine taking the permanent magnets and shaft out of the can. Take off all but one of the wire coils. The simplified motor would look like the one below.

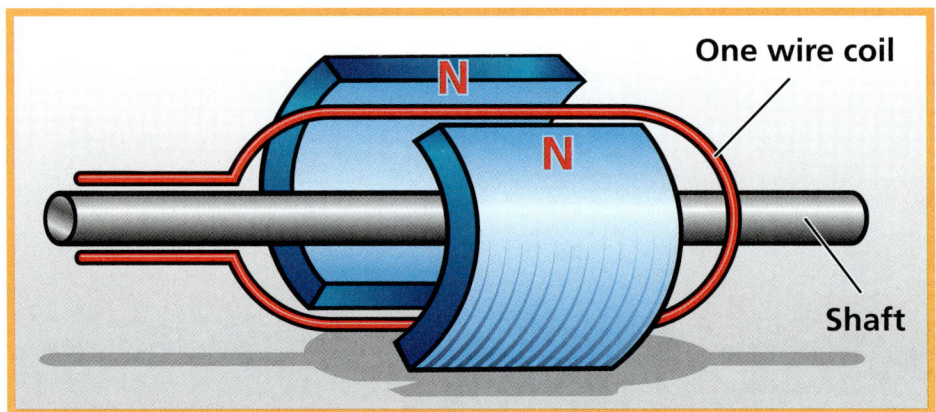

**A simplified motor with two permanent magnets and only one wire coil**

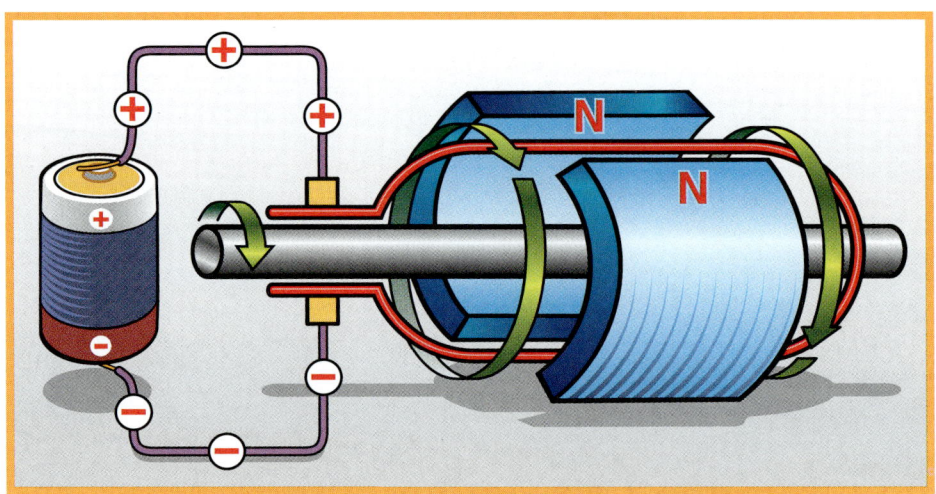

**The wire coil becomes an electromagnet when it is connected to a D-cell.**

Connect the wire to a source of electric current, such as a D-cell. The flow of current makes a magnetic field around the wire.

When current flows in the coil, the coil becomes an electromagnet. The magnetic field of the electromagnet is repelled by the fields of the permanent magnets. (Like poles repel.) This pushes the electromagnet away. The push causes the shaft to rotate.

But there is more to the design. When the shaft rotates, contact between the D-cell and the electromagnet is broken. The current stops flowing in the coil. The **electromagnetism** stops briefly.

As the shaft rotates a little farther, contact is made again. This creates the electromagnetic field in the coil again. The coil gets another magnetic push to keep the shaft turning.

The shaft gets hundreds of little magnetic pushes every second. The motor uses electric current and magnetism to produce motion.

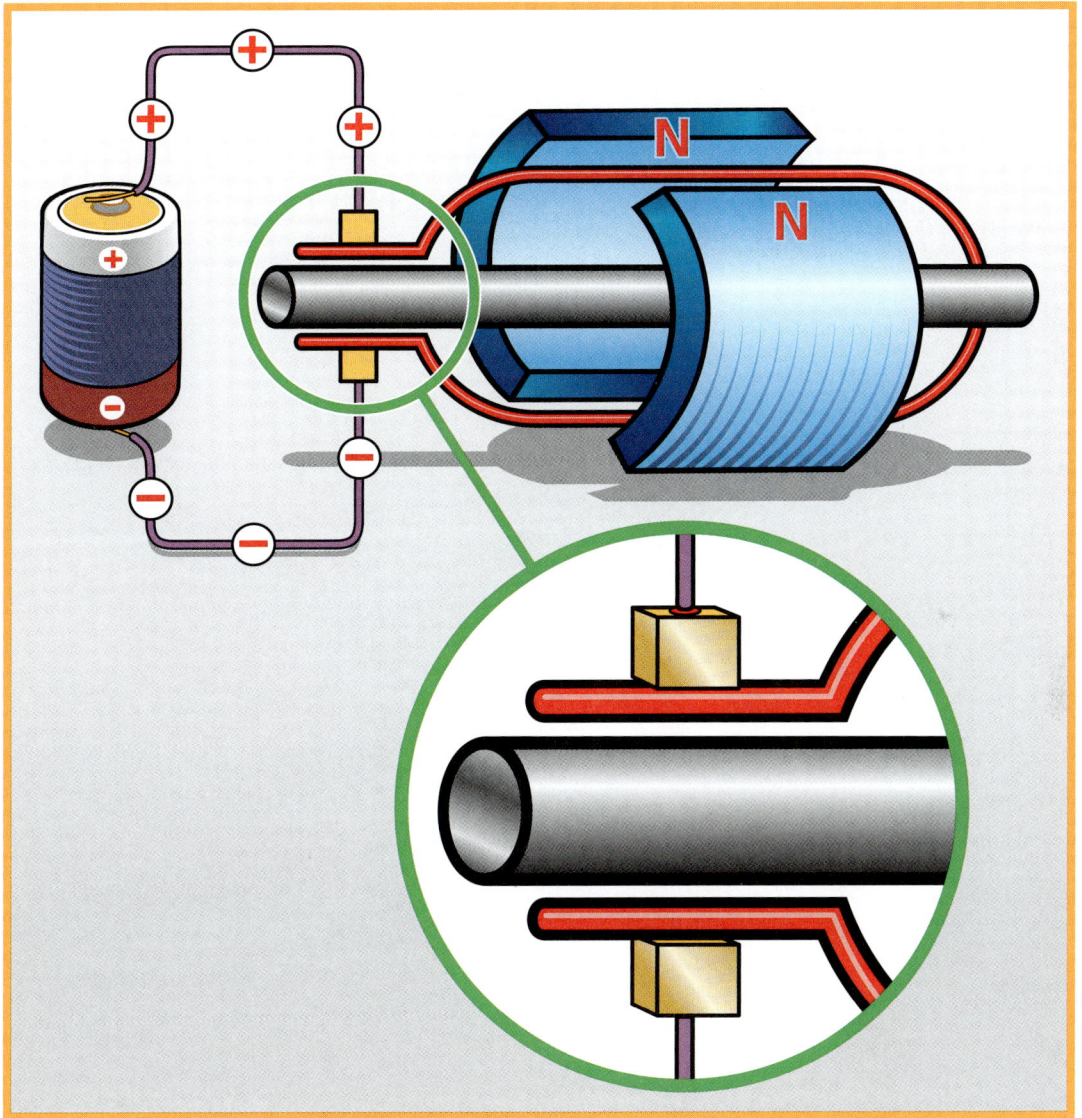

**As the shaft rotates, contact between the D-cell and the coil is broken. As the shaft rotates a little farther, contact is made again.**

## Generators

You know how to use electricity to make a flashlight work. You put some D-cells in it. But where does the electricity in your home come from? It does not come from batteries. The electricity in your home comes from a generator. Generators use motion to produce electric current.

A generator has two main parts. They are permanent magnets and wire coils. They are the same parts found in a motor. A direct-current generator is a motor running in reverse.

When you put electricity into a motor, you get motion. When you rotate the shaft of the motor, you get electricity. Here's how it works.

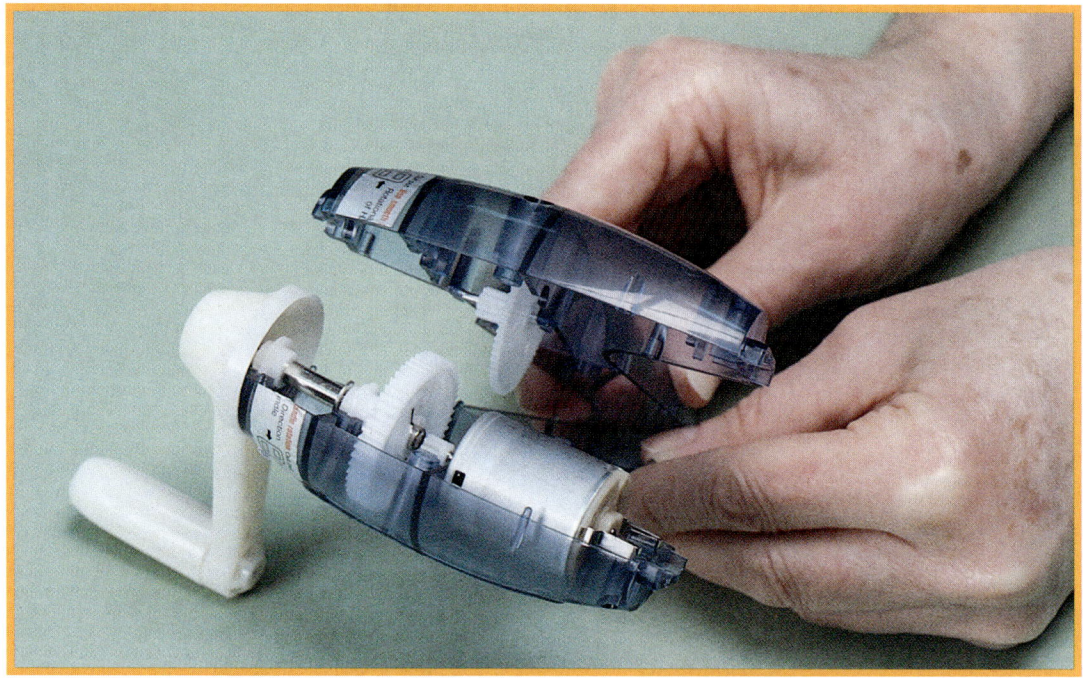

**A simple hand-operated generator**

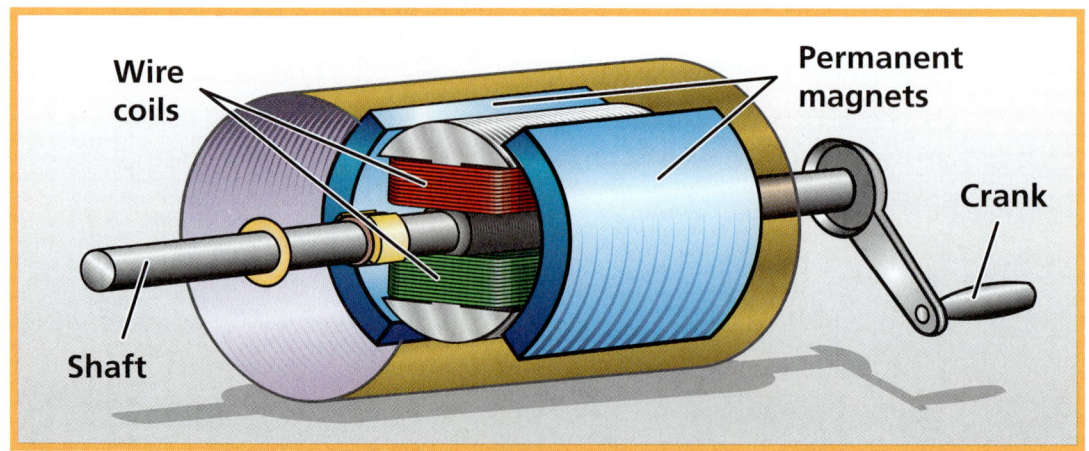

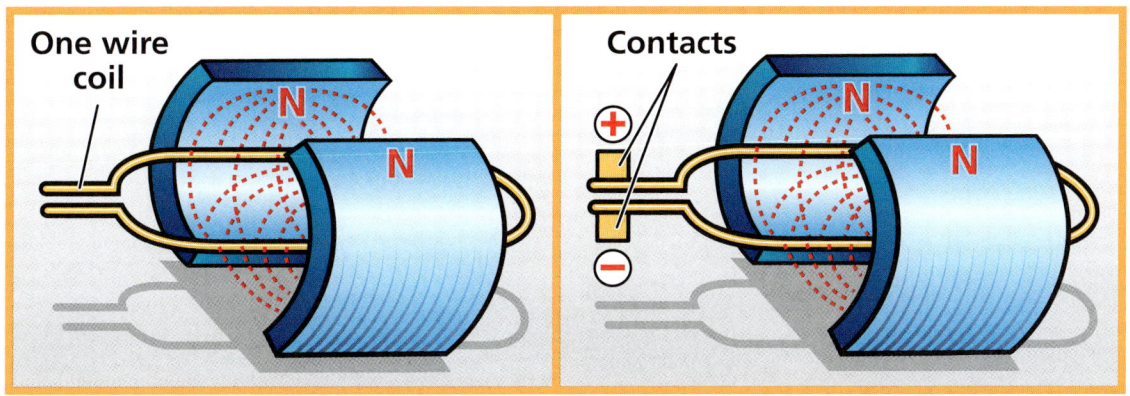

**When a wire coil turns in a magnetic field, an electric current is created in the wire.**

**Electricity flows from the generator when contact is made with the end of the wire coil.**

There is a magnetic field between the poles of the permanent magnets. Set a shaft with wire coils between the magnets. Take off all but one of the wire coils. The simplified generator would look like the diagram above.

When a wire passes through a magnetic field, an electric current is created in the wire. If you rotate a wire coil in a magnetic field, it will pass through the field hundreds of times in a second. This makes a continuous flow of electric current.

What turns the wire coil in the magnetic field? It could be many things. A windmill can be attached to the shaft. Wind can then rotate the coil. Water flowing downhill, steam from a boiler, or a gas engine can also be used to rotate the coil.

As a last resort, you can put a crank on the end of a generator shaft. A crank lets you turn the wire coil by hand to generate a little electricity.

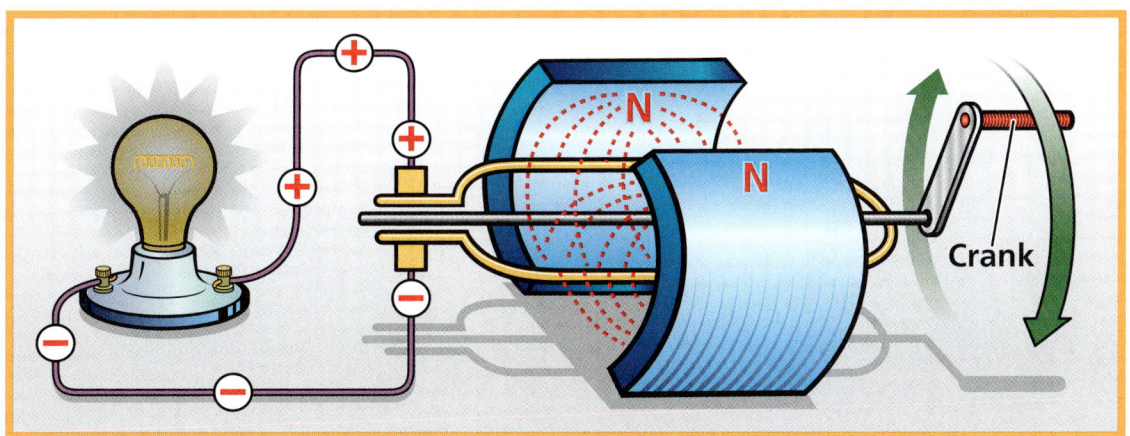

**With a crank on the end of the shaft, you can generate electricity by hand.**

# Doorbells

When you press a doorbell button, it completes a circuit, and you hear the loud "r-r-r-r-r-ing." The button is a switch. The sound comes from a bell being hit by a little hammer. The hammer is called a striker. But the striker does not hit the bell just once. It hits the bell dozens of times a second. How does a doorbell work?

A doorbell has a number of components that make a circuit. It has an electricity source, a doorbell button (the switch), a box terminal, a striker terminal, a movable striker, an electromagnet, and a bell connected to the box. Find these parts in the drawing below.

The box terminal is attached to the box holding the bell. The striker terminal is attached to the striker. When no electric current is flowing through the circuit, the box terminal and striker terminal touch.

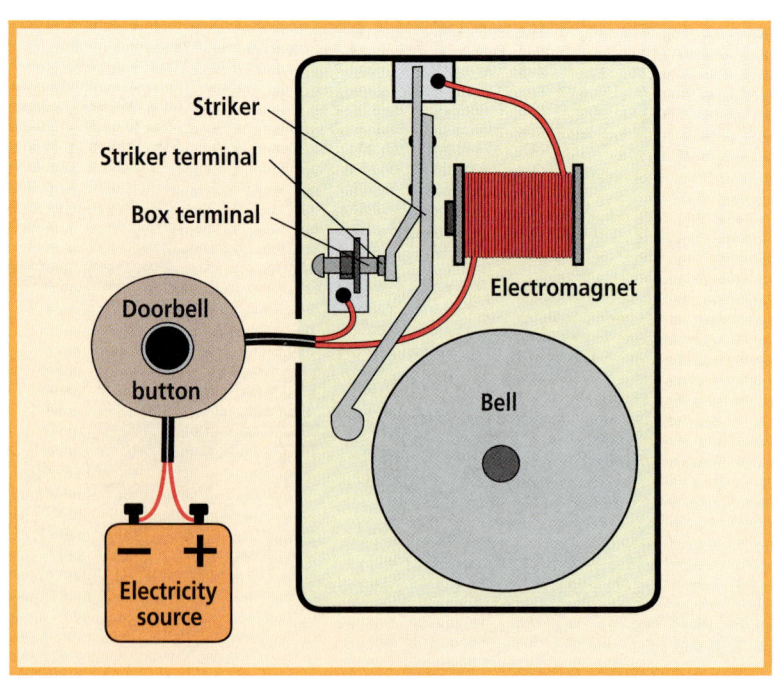

**Components in a doorbell**

When you press the doorbell button, current flows from the electricity source through the contact between the box terminal and the striker terminal. Then current flows through the striker, to the electromagnet, and back to the electricity source. The dotted lines show the circuit.

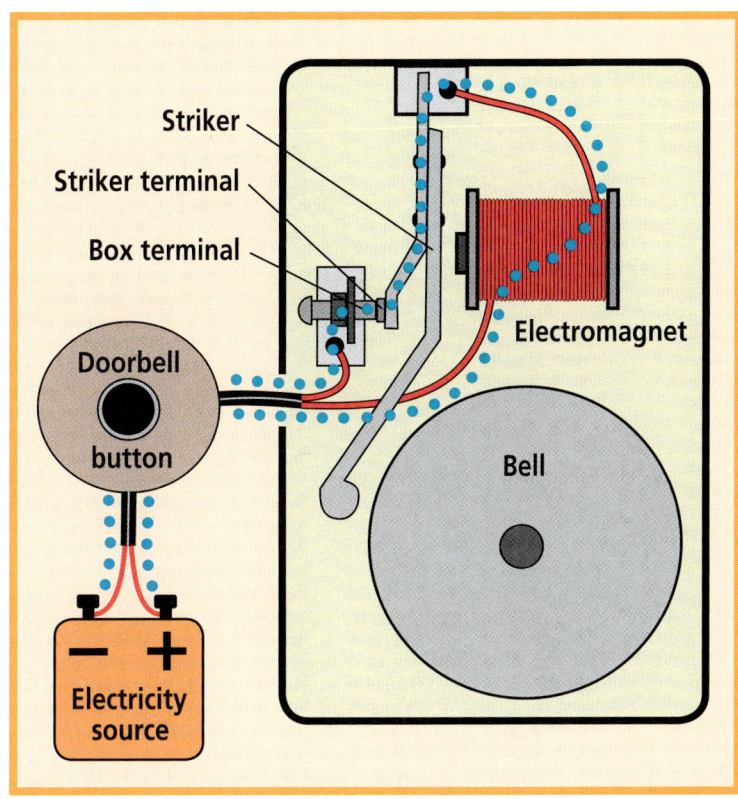

**Current flows in the doorbell circuit and turns on the electromagnet.**

When current flows, it activates the electromagnet. The electromagnet attracts the steel striker, and two things happen. The striker hits the bell. And the striker terminal pulls away from the box terminal. This breaks the circuit. When the circuit is broken, the magnetism goes away. The striker returns to its starting position. That brings the terminals back together so that the circuit is complete. The whole process starts over. The bell ding-ding-dings as long as you hold the button.

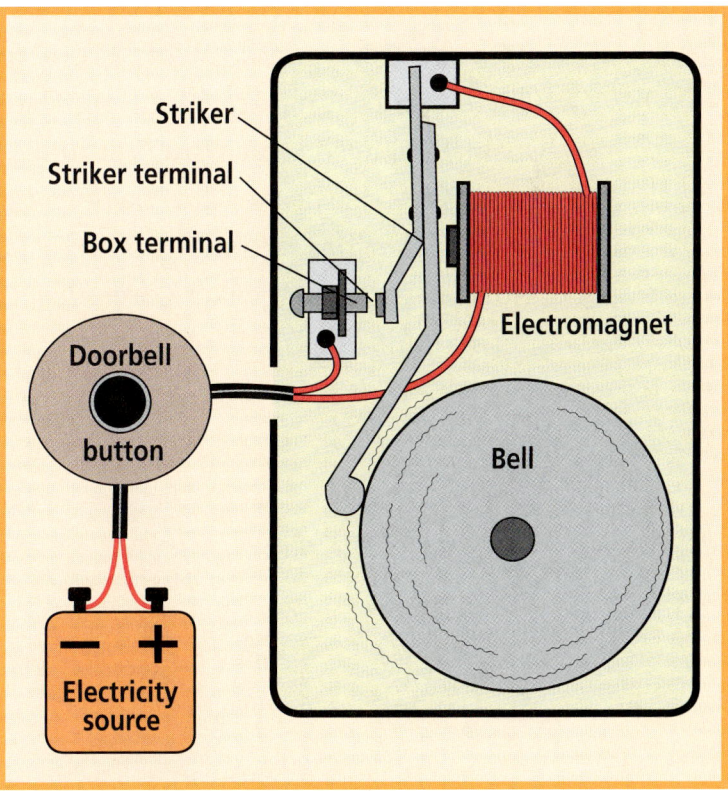

**The electromagnet attracts the striker. The bell rings. The striker terminal gets pulled away from the box terminal. The circuit is broken. The magnetism goes away.**

57

## Speakers and Earphones

Speakers use electric current to produce motion. You might have felt the **vibrations** from speakers when music is playing. How does a speaker produce motion from an electric current?

Sound from a radio starts in the form of electricity. The electric signal travels along a speaker wire to the speaker. The speaker wire is actually two wires. The sound signal travels to the speaker and back to make a complete circuit.

A speaker has two main parts. Part 1 is a coil of insulated wire glued to a paper speaker cone. Part 2 is a permanent magnet. The permanent magnet is placed in the center of the cone.

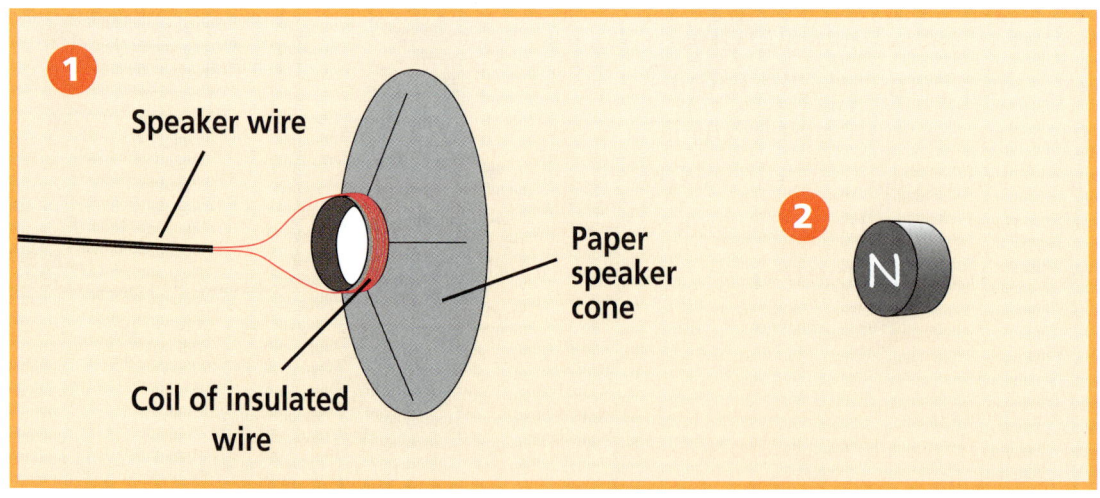

1. Speaker cone and coil
2. Permanent magnet

When a pulse of electricity flows through the coil, it creates a magnetic field. The magnetic field of the coil and the magnetic field of the permanent magnet repel. Because the coil is glued to the speaker cone, the cone moves. The movement of the cone pushes on air. This produces sound.

If you put two little speakers in the ear cups of a headset, you have a pair of earphones. If you put two tiny speakers into your ears, you have earbuds.

What if current flowing in a wire did not produce a magnetic field? How would your life be different without electromagnets?

## Thinking about Electric Devices

1. How does a motor work?
2. How does a doorbell make a continuous ring?
3. How does a speaker work?

# Morse Gets Clicking

Imagine what it would be like without cell phones and computers. How would you keep in touch with your friends? That's the way it was 170 years ago. There were no phones, radios, or televisions. There were no computers for e-mail. People wrote letters. It could take weeks or months to receive a letter and respond to it.

**Samuel Finley Breese Morse**

In 1820, Hans Christian Oersted discovered that a wire carrying an electric current produced a magnetic field. In 1825, the electromagnet was invented. People knew that electricity moved fast through wires. Could words be changed into electricity to speed up communication?

Samuel Finley Breese Morse (1791–1872) had an idea about how to make electricity "speak." In 1835, Morse used an electromagnet, a switch, and long wires to send a long-distance message. The switch (called a **key**) and a battery were in one location. Long wires ran to an electromagnet far away. When the key was pressed to complete the circuit, the electromagnet attracted a piece of steel with a loud click. Those first clicks announced the invention of the **telegraph**.

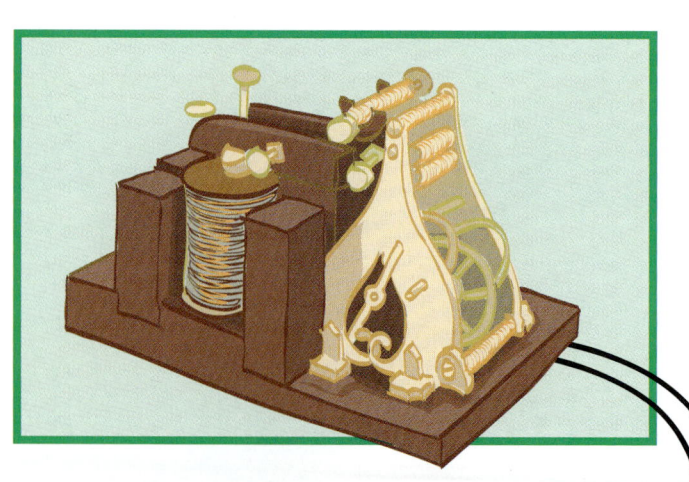

**The key used by Morse**

**The electromagnet used by Morse**

Morse knew his telegraph could change the way people communicated. But he had trouble finding others who agreed. Finally, 8 years later, he got a $30,000 grant to set up a telegraph line from the railroad station in Baltimore, Maryland, to the Supreme Court building in Washington, DC. The next year, in 1844, the first message traveled the 65 kilometers (km) between the two cities in a fraction of a second. In moments, the return message reached Morse. The telegraph was a success.

Morse's telegraph was not very different from the one you made in class. The key was similar to your switch. The batteries were stronger. The electromagnet had more winds of wire to make it stronger.

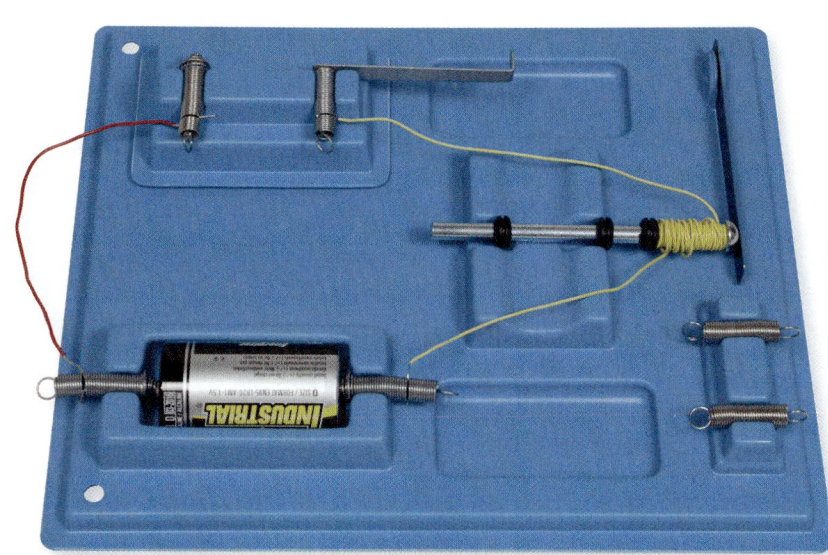

**The telegraph you made in class**

61

## Putting the Message into Words

There's one more important part to this story. Remember, the telegraph didn't send words, it just sent clicks. How can you make words out of clicks? Morse needed a **code** to translate clicks into words.

The first code Morse tried didn't work very well. The receiver had a pen attached to the electromagnet. When the circuit was closed, the pen moved and made a mark on a roll of paper. The dots and squiggles were too hard to decode.

Next, Morse developed a code where clicks stood for words. For example, one click might be the word *you*. Two rapid clicks might be the word *today*. Two widely spaced clicks might be the word *now*, and so on. The code book was huge. It took a long time to look up the words after a set of clicks was received.

The code that worked was developed by Morse and his partner, Alfred Vail (1807–1859), in 1838. It used short and long sounds, called dots and dashes, to stand for letters of the alphabet. You might wonder how Morse got his telegraph to make short and long clicks. He didn't. The short and long "sounds" were actually the pauses between the clicks. The telegraph receiver heard the short and long pauses between clicks as the dots and dashes.

**A modern high-speed key uses code to send messages in dots and dashes.**

After the first successful message was sent in 1844 from Baltimore, Maryland to Washington, DC, the telegraph became popular. Every major city had a central telegraph office. Businesses, newspaper offices, and governments depended on the telegraph for the fast delivery of news. The telegraph changed how the world communicated.

The code was modernized in 1848 and became known as the International Morse Code. Even though advances in communication soon made Morse Code and the telegraph obsolete for everyday use, the code still has some important uses more than 160 years after its invention. For years, airplane pilots and ship captains have been required to learn the code so they could communicate and respond to coded messages sent by automatic location identifiers at sea and on land. Navy ships can also communicate with one another silently by sending Morse Code using flashing lights, if they need to avoid detection by enemy ships. The international distress signal SOS is communicated even today by Morse Code and is understood all over the world. Dit–dit–dit; dah–dah–dah; dit–dit–dit is the sound that declares "I need assistance immediately." The SOS message can be sent in a number of ways, such as by flashing a **mirror**, by turning a flashlight on and off, or by keying a radio on and off.

| | | | |
|---|---|---|---|
| A .– | J .– – – | S … | 1 .– – – – |
| B –… | K –.– | T – | 2 ..– – – |
| C –.–. | L .–.. | U ..– | 3 …– – |
| D –.. | M – – | V …– | 4 ….– |
| E . | N –. | W .– – | 5 ….. |
| F ..–. | O – – – | X –..– | 6 –…. |
| G – –. | P .– –. | Y –.– – | 7 – –… |
| H …. | Q – –.– | Z – –.. | 8 – – –.. |
| I .. | R .–. | | 9 – – – –. |
| | | | 0 – – – – – |

Period .–.–.–
Comma – –..– –
Colon – – –…
Question mark ..– –..

Apostrophe .– – – –.
Hyphen –….–
Slash –..–.
At sign (@) .– –.–.

Right parenthesis –.– –.–
Left parenthesis –.– –.
Quotation marks .–..–.

**Here is the present-day International Morse Code.**

## Beyond the Telegraph

**Alexander Graham Bell**

The telegraph system developed by Morse was very successful. It did have one limitation. Only one message at a time could be sent over a telegraph line. With very few lines, only a few messages could be sent in a day. Several people tried to develop a way to send multiple messages along the line at one time. One of the people working on this problem was Alexander Graham Bell (1847–1922).

Bell's idea was that pulses of electricity of different frequencies could share the line at the same time. In his efforts to create electrical pulses of different **frequency**, Bell applied his knowledge of music to the problem. He was experimenting with methods to send pulses of electricity at high **pitches** and low pitches at the same time. What he needed was a device to produce electrical pulses in response to sounds of different frequencies.

In his efforts to develop such a device, he realized that the human voice could produce the range of frequencies he needed. The device that he developed produced electric currents of different intensities depending on the vibrations of the pitch of the note directed into the device. It occurred to Bell that if he could develop a second device to receive the pulses of electricity and convert them back into vibrations, he could transmit the human voice over a wire.

In 1876, Bell and his assistant Thomas Watson (1854–1934) successfully transmitted the human voice over a wire. The telephone was invented! The invention of the telephone also marked the beginning of the end for the telegraph. Speaking words was much more desirable than sending dots and dashes.

**This model of Bell's first telephone is a duplicate of the one through which speech sounds were first transmitted electrically.**

**Guglielmo Marconi and his invention**

# Communication Leaves the Wires

In 1888, Heinrich Hertz (1857–1894) was demonstrating that electric impulses could be transmitted through the air. He developed a device that generated electric sparks. This device created electromagnetic radiation that traveled out in all directions. This radiation is now called radio waves.

A young Italian inventor, Guglielmo Marconi (1874–1937), took an interest in Hertz's discovery. Marconi began developing an apparatus to send messages over long distances without wire. He assembled a transmitter, which was little more than a spark generator. He added an antenna to capture the electromagnetic pulses from the air. And he added a receiver to turn the electromagnetic pulses into sounds that could be interpreted. Before long, Marconi's system was able to send and receive messages over a distance of more than 1 km. By 1897, Marconi was able to send messages more than 6 km. In 1902, he successfully sent a wireless message across the Atlantic Ocean. By 1915, a new technology allowed audio transmissions. Now the airwaves could be used for radio transmissions of human voice and entertainment programming.

## Radio Meets the Telephone

The familiar cellular telephone carried by just about everyone these days was first conceived in 1947. At that time, mobile telephones were installed in cars because the phones needed a large, reliable supply of electricity. The phones were limited because they only worked near a transmission tower. The tower would receive the signal from the phone and send it to another phone, but both phones had to be near the same transmission tower.

The cellular idea was to develop a network of small service units, called cells, all over the country. A cellular phone user would always be in one cell or another. The phone user has only to communicate with the transmission tower in the small cell. The cell transmitter then communicates with the cell tower in the next cell. The signal gets relayed from cell to cell until it arrives at the receiver phone. It might be a block away or across the country.

Cell phones use radio waves to transmit signals. So your phone is a radio transmitter and radio receiver. Instead of music or sports, your radio receiver sends and receives only the conversation you want to have with your friend. It's as if you have your own personal radio station. Text messages travel the same way, but letters of the alphabet are sent instead of spoken words.

# Energy
## Burning Fuel

Energy is present in many different places. Energy comes from an energy source. One source of energy is fuel. Fuel is material that has stored energy. People burn fuel to release the stored energy. How can you tell that energy is released when fuel burns? You can see the light and feel heat. Wherever there is light and heat, there is energy.

Candle wax is a fuel. When candle wax burns, the energy of the wax can be observed as heat and light. Coal is a fuel. When coal burns, the stored energy of coal is released as heat. Burning coal produces heat to boil water in a steam train. The steam from the boiling water turns the train wheels. The energy of coal puts the steam train into motion. Wherever there is an object in motion, there is energy.

Natural gas is another kind of fuel. When gas burns, the energy of the gas produces heat. Heat from the burning gas can do many things. Can you think of some ways to use this heat?

**Candle wax is an energy source.**

**Coal is the fuel that makes steam to power this train.**

**Burning natural gas makes heat.**

**Cars, trucks, and buses use fuel to move on a road.**

Oil, gasoline, and wood are also fuels. Burning oil releases heat. People use heat to warm homes and make electricity.

Burning gasoline releases energy to make cars and trucks move. The energy of oil and gasoline produces heat and motion.

People burn wood to provide heat for homes. And heat from burning wood in a campfire can cook food.

**Heat from a campfire cooks food.**

**Food is the fuel that provides energy for people.**

## Food Is Fuel

A slice of pizza or a piece of fruit tastes good. Pizza and fruit are examples of food. But do people eat food only for the taste? No, food is the fuel that makes life happen.

Food has stored energy, just like other kinds of fuel. Living organisms "burn" fuel to release energy. The food doesn't really burn with a flame, like wood or coal. Animals digest food, and the stored energy is released.

Animals, including people, use food to produce motion and heat. Sled dogs digest food to provide energy to run, pull the sled, and keep warm. What do you do with the energy of food?

**All animals eat food to get the energy they need to live.**

**Food gives you energy to play sports.**

69

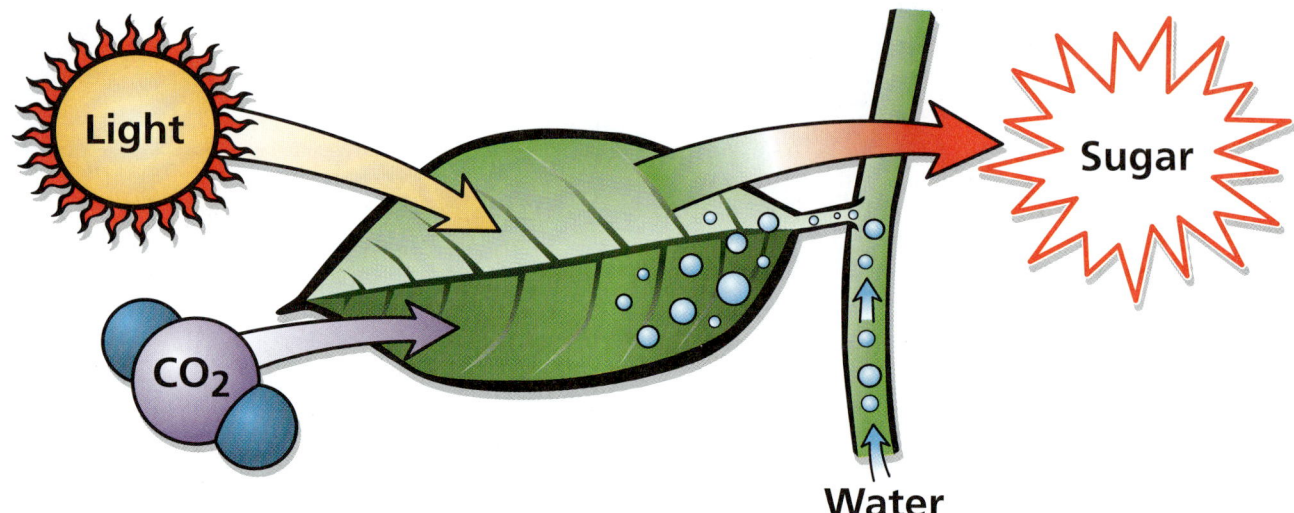

How does energy get into food? You might be surprised to know that the energy of food comes from the Sun.

Light is one way that energy moves. Light from the Sun shines on plant leaves. The leaves **absorb** energy.

The leaves take up water from the soil and carbon dioxide ($CO_2$) gas from the air. Plants make sugar from the $CO_2$, water, and energy of the Sun's light. Sugar is food.

Energy stored in food is released when you eat and digest food. So really, it is energy from the Sun that keeps you warm, lets you run, and makes all your other activities possible.

**Food has stored energy.**

**It takes energy to stand, point, look, and think.**

## Motion

Did you transfer any energy today? The answer is yes. Every second of every day, you are transferring energy. The action of lifting a pencil takes energy. The action of looking at a picture takes energy. The action of thinking about what to eat for lunch takes energy. Every action requires energy.

The energy for lifting, looking, moving, and thinking comes from food. The energy of food is stored in chemicals. As food breaks down in your body, energy produces heat and motion, and even electric currents. Electric currents send messages throughout your brain and along your nerves. Heat, movement, and electric impulses are important ways that energy moves to keep you and your friends alive.

## Making Sound

Sound is another way to observe that energy is present. When objects vibrate, they produce sound. A vibration is a fast back-and-forth movement. A vibrating object pushes on air. That back-and-forth motion pushes on the air and makes waves that create sound.

The sound waves travel through air. They carry the energy created by the vibrating (moving) object. The sound waves hit your ear. The energy carried by the sound waves moves the little bones in your ear. You hear the sound.

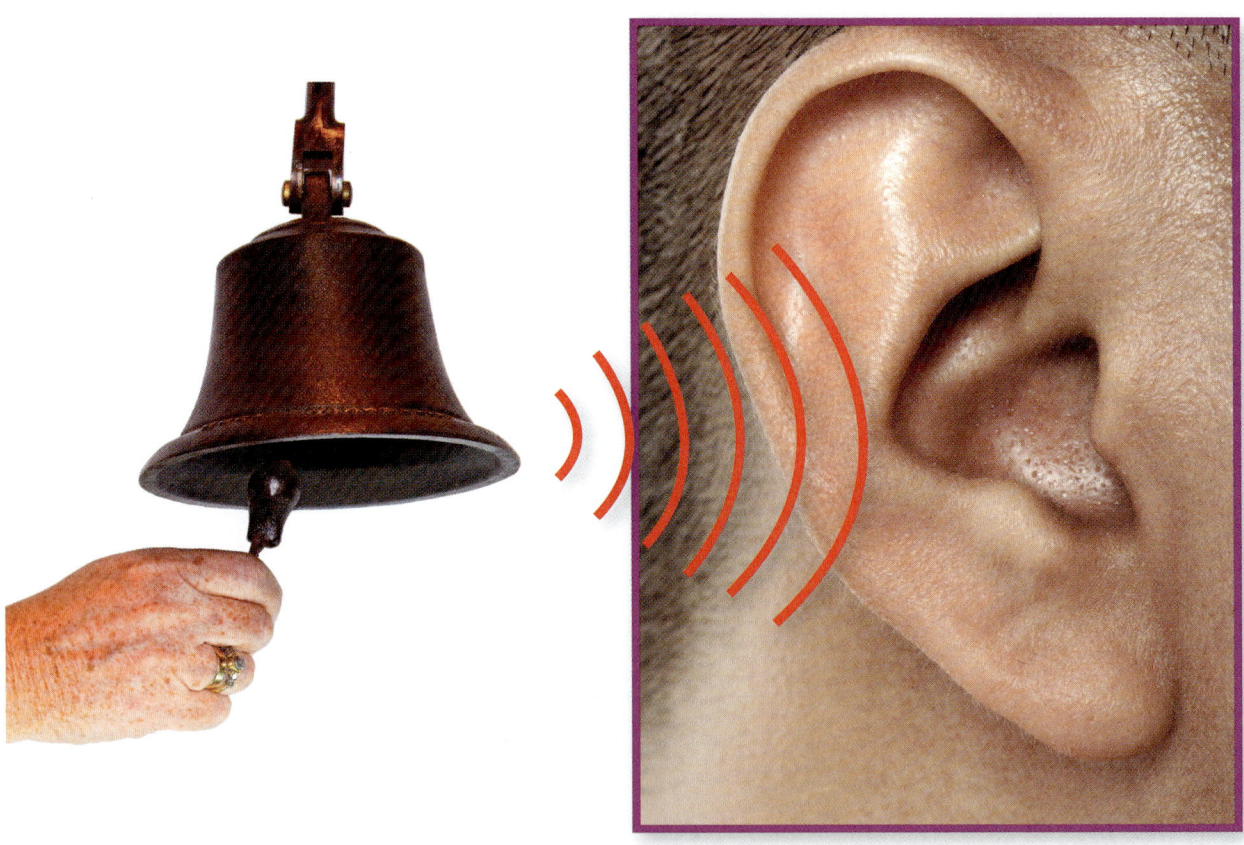

**Waves carry sound from a bell to your ear.**

**A fern fossil**

# Fossil Fuels

Do you know what a fossil is? You may have seen fossils of leaves, shells, or bones. They are usually found in layers of rock. Fossils are the preserved remains of organisms that lived long ago. We know that dinosaurs lived on Earth 65 million years ago. That's because we have fossils of dinosaur bones that we can study.

Oil, coal, and natural gas are called **fossil fuels**. Scientists think that fossil fuels started as organisms that lived a long time ago. For millions of years, these organisms died and piled up on Earth's surface. Over time they got buried deep underground. Slowly, the organisms changed into oil, coal, and gas. That's why they are called fossil fuels. They are the ancient remains of organisms.

Fossil fuels are made of chemicals. The chemicals in fossil fuels can be burned to produce useful energy. Burning fossil fuels produces heat.

How do we use fossil fuels? People everywhere use oil for transportation. Cars, buses, trucks, ships, trains, and airplanes burn fuels made from oil to make them move.

Coal is used a lot in the midwestern and eastern United States. Coal is burned to generate heat and electricity. Coal is also burned to make steel.

In the western part of the United States, people use a lot of natural gas to generate electricity. The burning gas heats water to make steam. The steam turns generators to make the electricity used in homes and schools.

**Oil is a fossil fuel.**

**Coal is a fossil fuel.**

**Natural gas is a fossil fuel.**

# Observable Evidence of Energy

Stored energy is useful to people when it produces heat, light, sound, and electric current, and puts objects in motion. Heat, light, sound, electric current, and objects in motion are evidence that energy is present and available to do work.

The energy of food produces heat and motion in our bodies when digested.

The energy of fuel produces heat and light, and can sometimes produce motion.

The energy of batteries produces electric currents in a complete circuit. Electric currents can produce heat, light, motion, and sound.

Look at the table below. The left-hand column lists sources of stored energy. The right-hand column lists the evidence of energy the source can produce.

| Stored-energy source | Produces observable evidence of energy |
|---|---|
| corn | heat and motion |
| turkey | heat and motion |
| carrot | heat and motion |
| wood | heat and light |
| wax | heat and light |
| oil | heat and light |
| natural gas | heat and light |
| coal | heat and light |
| battery | heat, light, sound, and motion |

# Thinking about Energy

1. What evidence shows that energy is present?
2. How are food, fuel, and batteries alike?
3. What is the source of most of the energy used by people?

# What Causes Change of Motion?

A wagon is a useful tool for moving a large **load** around more easily. Suppose you have a wagon sitting motionless with a load of watermelons in it. To take the watermelons with you, you will need to put the wagon into motion. How can you do that? You have two options. You can get behind the wagon and push it. Or you can get in front of the wagon and pull it. The wagon will not move by itself. The wagon will move only if a force acts on it. Pushes and pulls are forces (red arrows show force). Forces make things move (blue arrows show direction of motion).

**Pushes and pulls are forces (red arrows). Forces make things move (blue arrows).**

If you apply a force to get the wagon moving, it will keep rolling. Oops! You don't want the moving wagon to crash into something. How can you stop it? It takes force to change the motion of a moving object. Again, you have two options. You can get in front of the wagon and apply a pushing force to slow or stop its motion (a). Or you can get behind the wagon, grab onto it, and apply a pulling force to slow its motion (b). To bring a moving object to a stop, you need to apply a force in the opposite direction of the motion. To change the motion of an object, a force is needed.

Each wagon was moving to the right (blue arrow). A force in the opposite direction (red arrow) caused each wagon to stop.

a. Push to stop

b. Pull to stop

If the rolling wagon of watermelons is moving too slowly, how can you make it move a little faster? You can use more force. If you get behind the wagon and give it another push, the wagon will move faster. The wagon will move faster if you get in front of it and give it another pull, too. More force in the same direction will make the wagon move faster.

If the wagon starts moving too fast, you can use a push or a pull to slow it down. Force can be used to change the **speed** of a moving object.

If the wagon starts to roll to one side, how can you make it roll straight again? You need to apply a force. But this time, you need to apply a force to the side of the wagon in order to change its direction of motion. Any change of motion of an object, such as starting, stopping, change of speed, or change of direction, requires a force.

A force applied to the side of a wagon will change its direction.

# Gravity

Think about a ball resting motionless on a table. A gentle push on the ball will put it into motion. The ball will roll across the table. What will happen when the ball comes to the edge of the table? The ball will roll off the edge and fall to the ground. The ball's motion changes when it rolls off the edge of the table. It moves in a different direction and starts to move faster.

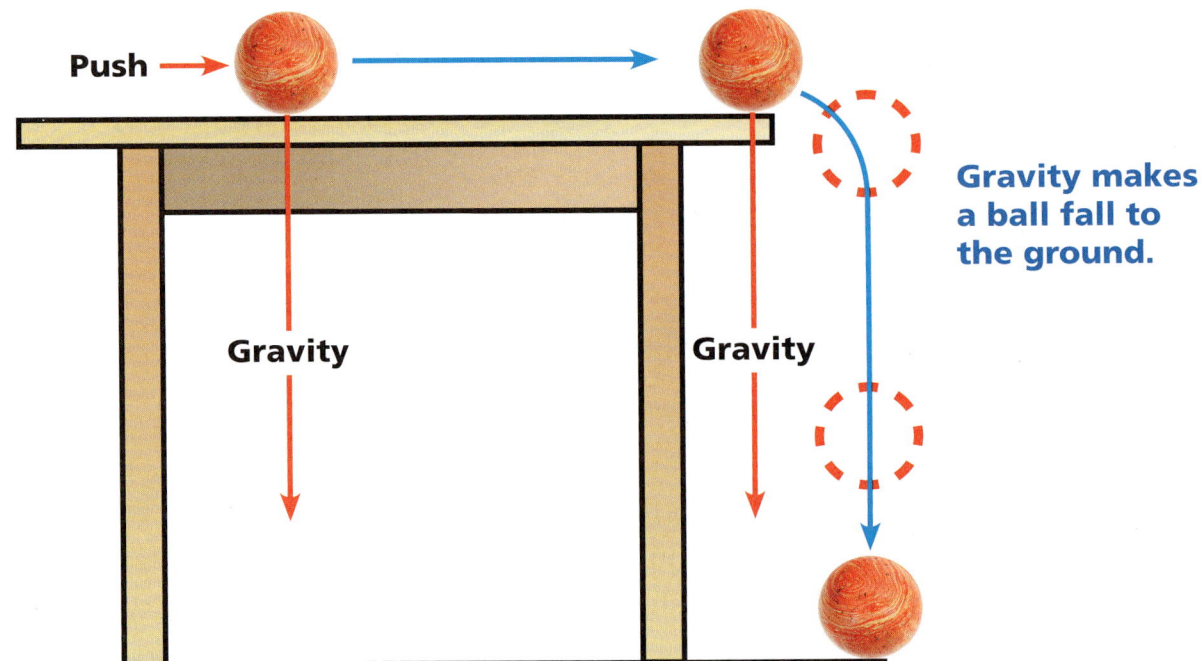

Gravity makes a ball fall to the ground.

What causes this change of motion? That's right, force. What force makes the ball move toward the ground? The force that makes the ball fall to the ground is **gravity**. Gravity is a pulling force between two objects, and it draws them toward each other. The bigger the objects, the stronger the gravitational force between them. Earth is a huge object, so it pulls strongly on all other objects. It is the force of gravity that pulls objects to Earth's center.

When you toss a basketball through a hoop, gravity pulls the ball to the ground.

If you return the ball to the flat tabletop, it will again rest there motionless. Why doesn't the ball fall to the ground? The ball doesn't move because the forces acting on it are balanced. There are two forces. First, the table is pushing upward on the ball. Second, gravity is pulling the ball downward toward Earth's center. When two equal forces act on an object in opposite directions, the forces are balanced. When the forces acting on an object are balanced, the object's motion does not change.

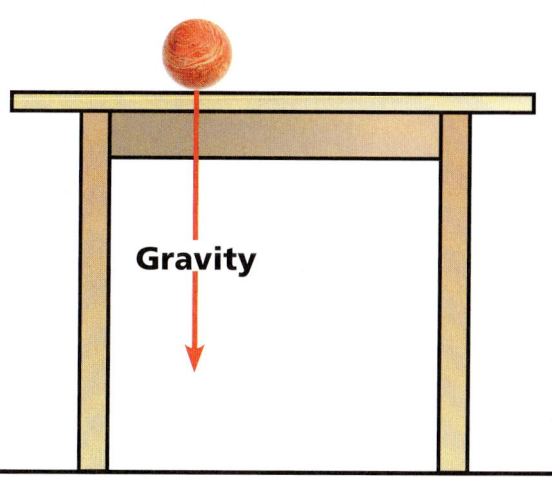

But what happens if you tip the table? The ball starts to roll down the table. For the ball to start moving, a force must act on the ball. Tipping the table unbalances the forces. The forces are no longer opposite and equal. Gravity pulls the ball downhill toward Earth's center. The round ball rolls across the table, over the edge, and down to the ground. When you're on a slide, can you feel the moment when the forces become unbalanced and gravity pulls you down?

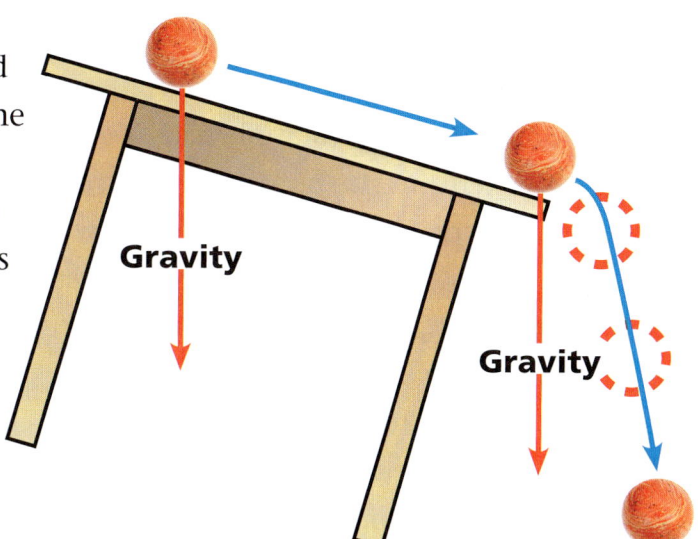

**The force of gravity pulls the ball to the ground.**

# Thinking about Motion

1. How do you get an object to start moving?
2. How do you get a moving object to stop?
3. Starting and stopping are two changes of motion. What are some other changes of motion?

# Bowling

Bowling is a sport in which a player rolls a heavy ball from one end of a hardwood runway (called a lane) to the other end, where ten wooden pins stand. The object of the sport is to have the ball knock down as many of the pins as possible in two turns.

How does the bowler move the ball down the lane? The trick is to use the force of gravity to apply force to the ball in order to get it moving. Bowling does require the bowler to use some muscle force, too. The bowler holds the ball by placing her thumb and two fingers into three holes in the ball. As the bowler moves toward the release line, she lifts the ball behind her, much like raising a pendulum bob into position to put it into motion. As the ball swings forward, driven by the force of gravity, the bowler applies small forces to the ball to adjust the direction of the swing. By doing so, she accurately guides the ball down the lane toward the pins. Just as the ball reaches its lowest position and its greatest speed, she releases the ball.

# Force and Energy

**Sir Isaac Newton**

Sir Isaac Newton (1642–1727) was one of the greatest scientific minds of all time. He was born on a sheep farm 150 kilometers (km) north of London, England. In those days, most children from farming communities did not go to school for more than a few years. Newton's teachers were so impressed by his ability to learn, they encouraged him to attend the University of Cambridge.

After completing his studies, Newton became a mathematics professor at the university. It was at this time in his life that he had one of his most important ideas. While he was at his family's farm, resting in the apple orchard, an apple fell from a tree and landed near him. The simple act of a falling apple made Newton wonder why apples fall straight down to Earth's surface instead of falling in different directions.

Newton had already figured out that a force applied to an object causes it to **accelerate**, or travel faster and faster, as long as the force is applied. Newton observed that the apple accelerated as it fell from the limb of the tree and traveled toward the ground. He reasoned that there had to be some kind of force acting on the apple to cause it to accelerate. That falling force was an invisible attraction between objects and Earth's center. The force was the result of gravity, the natural attraction between masses. The gravitational attraction between the apple and Earth produced the force that accelerated the apple directly toward Earth's center. Newton reasoned that the force of gravity extended over a great distance. Apples at the top of the tree fall to Earth just as certainly as apples on the lowest limbs.

81

Newton reasoned that if the attraction between masses extended up to the Moon, the pulling force of gravity could explain how Earth kept the Moon from flying off into space. Newton's theory was later confirmed through experimentation. Carefully designed experiments showed that the strength of the force of attraction between two masses is determined by the size of the masses and the distance between them. The larger the masses are and the closer they are to one another, the stronger the gravitational attraction between them. Since Earth is so large, it pulls on all masses with a tremendous force.

**Earth pulls on all masses with a lot of force.**

When you set a ball on a slope, the force of gravity pulls down on the ball. The slope pushes the ball sideways or at an angle. The unbalanced forces put the ball into motion. Because the ball started above the ground, the force of gravity will continue to pull on the ball as it rolls down the slope. The longer a force acts on an object, the faster the object moves. A ball that starts high up on a slope will be going faster when it reaches the bottom of the slope than a ball that starts lower on the slope. We know that the faster a ball moves, the more **kinetic energy** (energy of motion) it has. So a ball that starts high on a slope has more energy than a ball that starts lower on a slope. The more energy an object has, the more work it can do when it collides with something else. Faster-moving objects hit with more force and do more work when they collide with another object.

**The slope pushes the ball sideways.**

**The ball rolls down the slope.**

**Gravity pulls the ball down.**

82

# Measuring Force

How much force is needed to move something? To find out, you can measure the force with a tool called a spring scale. A spring scale is a simple piece of technology designed to measure the strength of the force needed to do work. The most important part of a spring scale is the spring. A spring is an object made of tough steel wire wound in a coil. At rest, the loops of the spring do not touch.

If you put your hands on the two ends of the spring and apply a small pushing force, you can compress, or squeeze, the loops a little closer together.

The harder you push, the more the spring will compress.

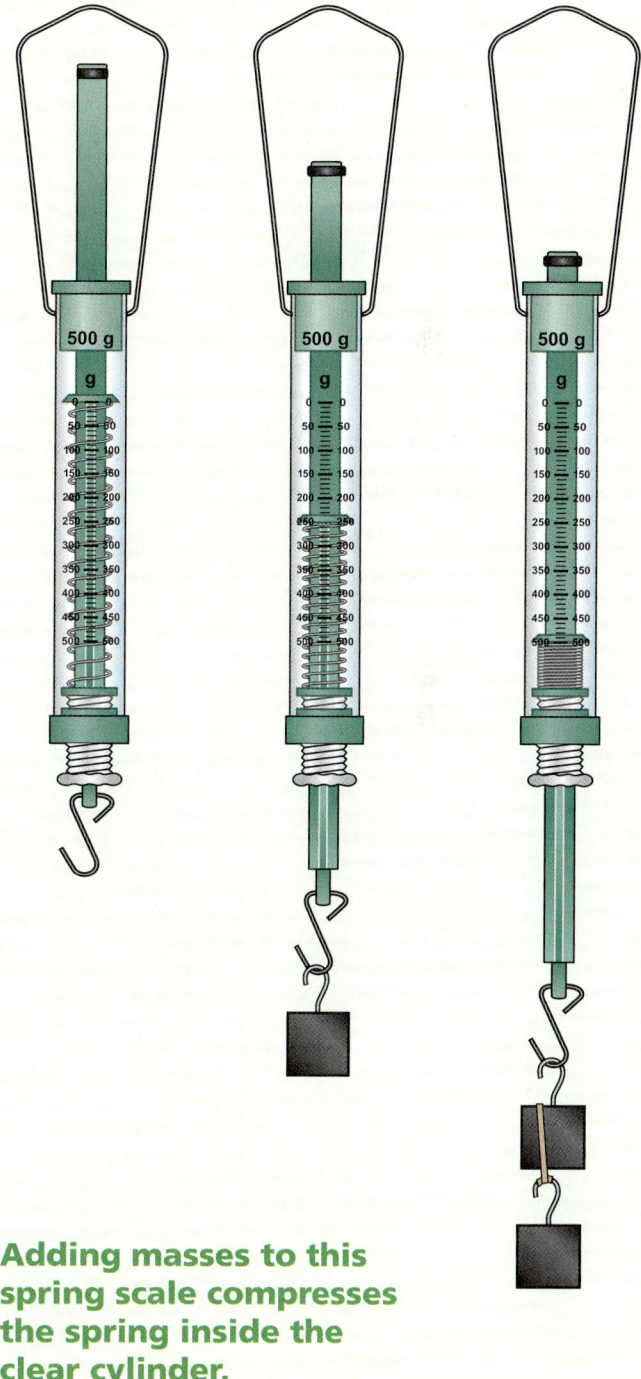

**Adding masses to this spring scale compresses the spring inside the clear cylinder.**

83

The spring is mounted in a clear cylinder. A shaft with a stop ring is passed through the center of the spring. The stop ring is attached to the central shaft. The spring can now be compressed by pulling down on the hook at the bottom of the central shaft or pushing down on the top of the central shaft. Every little bit of force applied to the spring compresses it a little more.

The standard unit of force is the **newton (N)**. A 100-gram (g) mass will exert a force of 1 N when pulled by the force of gravity. So if we put a number scale on the side of the spring cylinder, and put a 100 g mass on the hook, we can write 1 N by the stop ring. After adding another 100 g to the hook, we can mark the 2 N location on the cylinder. By adding more and more 100 g masses on the hook, we can find the compression locations for forces up to several newtons. Then we can use the spring scale to determine the strength of unknown forces in newtons.

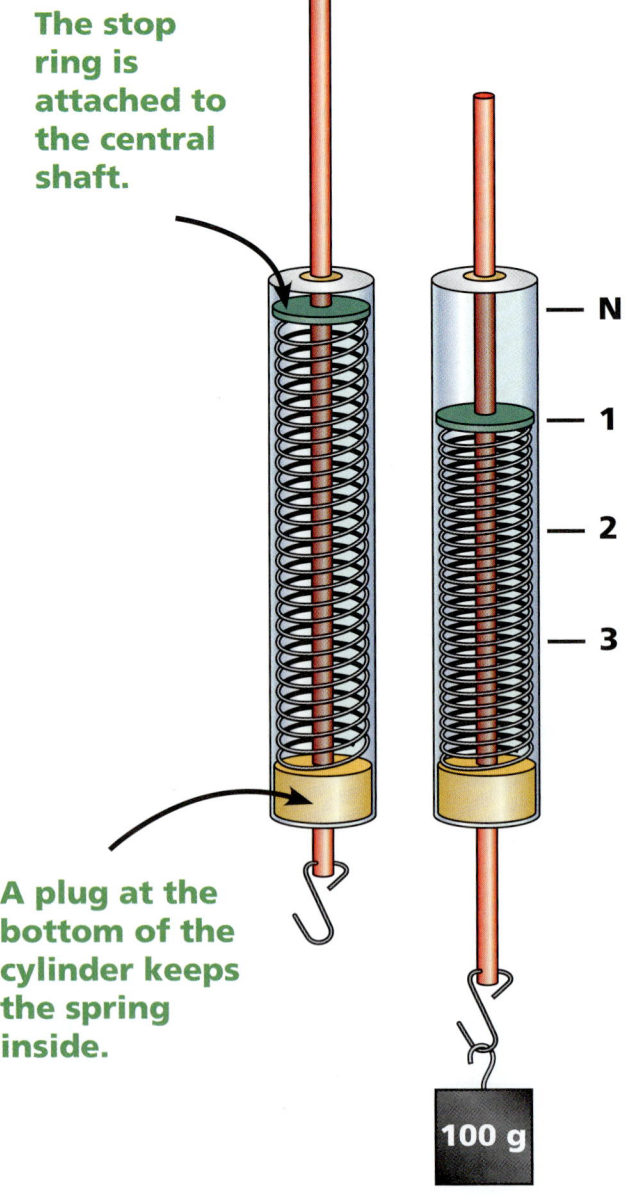

**The stop ring is attached to the central shaft.**

**A plug at the bottom of the cylinder keeps the spring inside.**

**Moving boxes is work.**

**Mowing the lawn is work.**

# Potential and Kinetic Energy at Work

You know what work is. Something that makes you strain, either physically or intellectually. Mowing the lawn can be hard work. Completing a difficult set of math problems can be hard work. In science, work is about moving masses (objects) around. Work is defined as the amount of force needed to move a mass from one place to another, or to change it in some way. You do work when you lift a mass from the ground onto a table. It takes work to move boxes from a delivery truck to a home. It takes work to hit a baseball from home plate into the outfield. Doing work always involves applying a force, either to move an object a certain distance or to change the object in some way.

A baseball bat can be used to do work. Doing work on a baseball by using a bat sends the baseball into the air. Doing work on a watermelon by using a bat breaks the watermelon and scatters the pieces all over. Doing work on a lump of clay by using a bat will change the shape of the lump of clay. The distance the baseball travels, the damage done to the watermelon, and the amount of reshaping of the clay depend on how much force is applied to each object. The amount of force applied is the amount of kinetic energy in the bat as it hits the other object.

Sometimes the kinetic energy of a moving object can cause the object to change. A baseball in a high position has a lot of **potential energy** (energy of position). As the baseball falls, the force of gravity gets it moving really fast. When the baseball nears the ground, it has a lot of kinetic energy. When the baseball hits the ground, the force of the impact deforms (flattens) the baseball. As the baseball changes shape, the kinetic energy of the moving baseball is transferred to potential energy. When the energy stored in the deformed baseball is released, and the ball reforms, the energy pushes the baseball back up into the air. This kind of energy transfer is called bounce.

**A baseball bat can be used to do work.**

If a watermelon is dropped from the same high position, the kinetic energy of the watermelon hitting the ground will apply a lot of force throughout the watermelon. The force will be too strong for the structure of the watermelon. The watermelon will break into many pieces. Juice and seeds will scatter in all directions.

**Using a baseball bat to do work on a watermelon breaks the melon into pieces.**

If you drop a ball of clay from the same high position, the force resulting from its impact with the ground will deform the ball of clay. Unlike the baseball, the energy changes the shape of the clay without loading the clay ball with potential energy. The clay ball flattens out and stays flat. In each case, the ground did work on the falling object, causing a change. The work caused the baseball to bounce, the watermelon to break, and the clay to change shape.

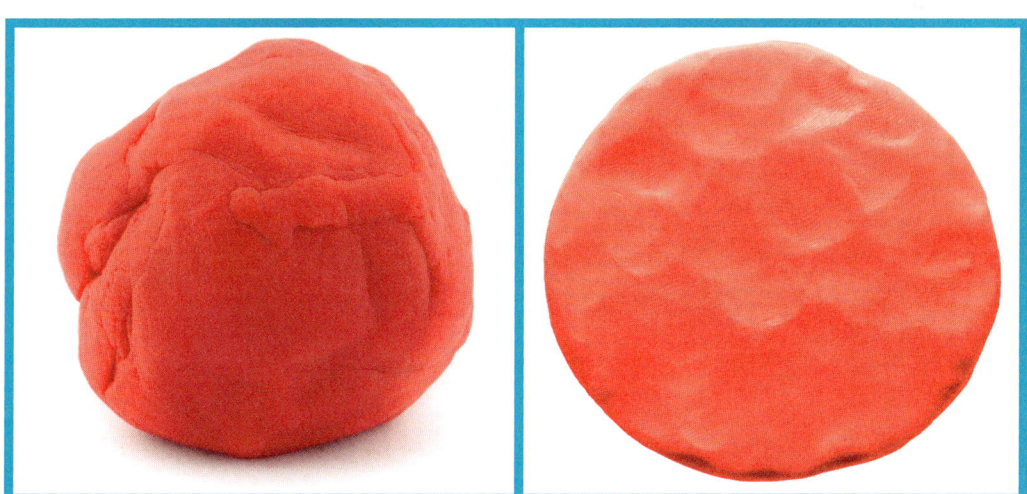

## Thinking about Potential and Kinetic Energy at Work

Describe what *work* is using scientific vocabulary. Give some examples of doing work.

# Waves

Wind is moving air. Moving air has a lot of kinetic energy. When wind blows across the surface of the ocean, energy transfers from the air to the water. The result is waves in the water. The energy wave moves across the ocean. What happens to that energy when the wave reaches a beach?

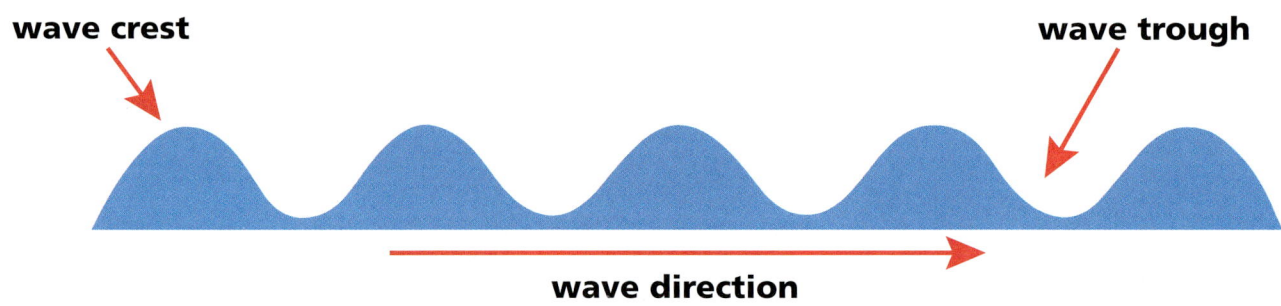

When a wave runs into a ship at sea, the wave passes right under the ship. The wave's energy lifts the ship and then lowers it into the **trough** behind the wave. You can observe this same motion with a ball floating in a basin of water. As the wave moves across the basin, the ball bobs up and down.

The moving wave transfers energy to floating objects. Energy lifts the ball to the **crest** of the wave. After the energy surge passes, the ball settles back in the same spot. The motion up and down is an **oscillation**.

# Energy Transfer

An ocean wave is a repeating pattern of motion in water. The water's energy can be graphed. The shape of the graph is called a **sine wave**. The high points on the wave graph are called **peaks**. Peaks of energy match the crests of the ocean wave. The lowest points are called troughs. The graph shows how the motion of the ocean wave transfers energy through the water. When the wave breaks on the shore, it transfers all its energy to the beach.

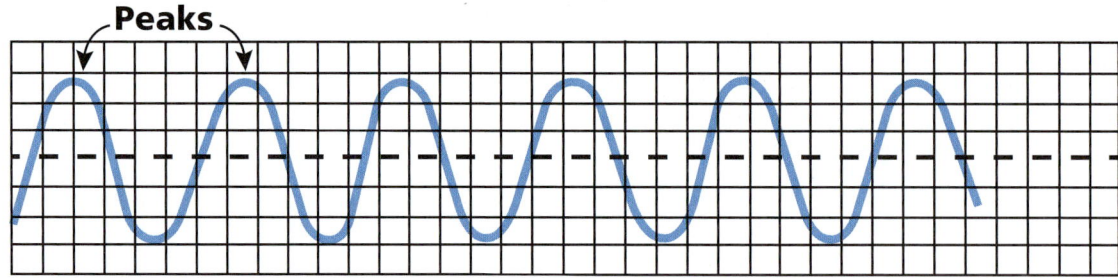

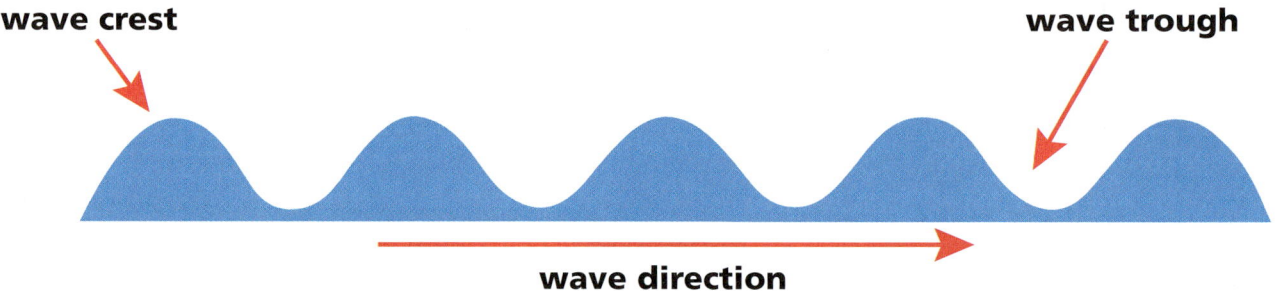

Energy waves show up in many places. When you shook the end of a rope, waves ran along the rope. Moving your hand smoothly back and forth made a regular sine wave.

What happened when you snapped the rope? A large wave surged along the rope. Supplying more energy made a larger wave. The size and shape of a wave depend on how energy transfers to the wave medium. In the ocean, water is the medium. In the rope, the fibers of the rope are the medium.

# Sound Waves

Vibration is another kind of oscillation. Sound comes from a vibrating source. It travels through a medium in energy pulses. A sine wave can represent sound pulses. Repeated energy pulses are represented by this sine wave of the sound of a bell.

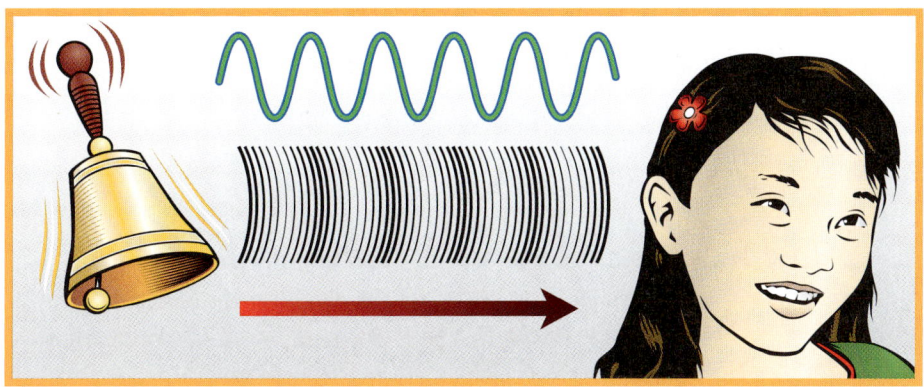

**Waves carry sound from a bell to your ear.**

This kind of wave is like the motion of the spring toy. The energy pulse traveling along the spring is like the energy pulse sent out through the air by a vibrating object. The pulse creates a series of compressions. The compression pulses are the peaks of the sound-wave pattern.

Sound has two important properties. They are volume and pitch. If a sine wave represents a sound, can we tell how loud it is and how high or low it is? Yes!

The peaks of the wave show how loud the sound is. Their height is the **amplitude** of the wave. In sound, amplitude equals volume. Here are wave graphs of two sounds that are the same pitch. Which sound is louder?

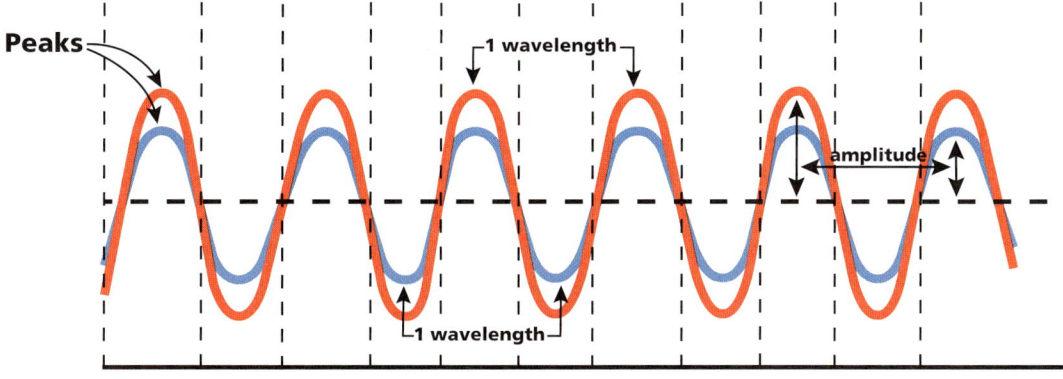

The sound graphed in red is louder. Its amplitude is greater than the amplitude of the blue sound.

91

What does the graph tell us about pitch? The distance between the centers of two peaks (or troughs) is the **wavelength**. A sound's wavelength determines its pitch. The shorter the wavelength, the higher the pitch. In the last graph, the two sounds are the same pitch because their wavelengths are the same. But the red sound is louder.

Look at the sound waves graphed on this page. What can you tell about the pitch and volume of these two sounds?

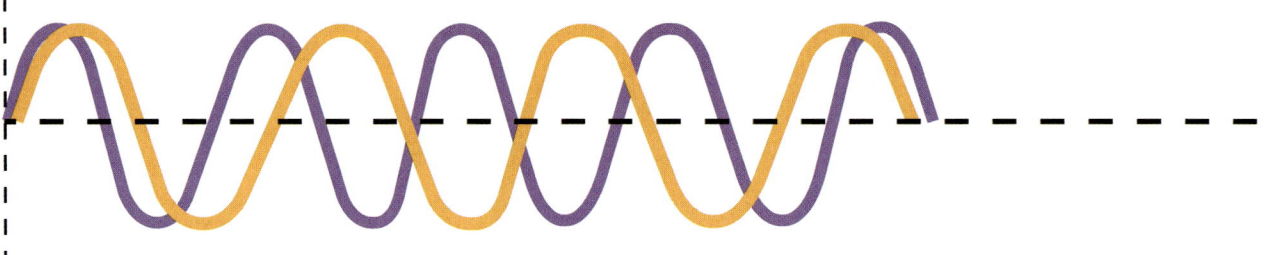

The amplitudes of the two waves are about the same. So these two sounds are about the same volume. What about the wavelengths? The wavelength of the orange wave is longer than the wavelength of the purple wave. The orange wave graph represents a lower-pitched sound.

# Thinking about Waves

1. How do waves transfer energy in the ocean?
2. What patterns describe the energy of waves?
3. How does the amount of energy affect a wave pattern?

# More about Sound

We often describe sounds as high or low. A small bird's chirp is a high sound. A big dog's deep bark is a low sound. *Pitch* is the word that we use to describe how high or low a sound is. Most birds make high-pitched sounds. Truck engines make low-pitched sounds.

Pitch is related to the frequency of the vibrations of a **sound source**. Vibrations are a kind of oscillation. High-frequency oscillations produce high pitches. Low-frequency oscillations produce lower pitches. Changing the oscillation of a sound source to produce a certain pitch is called tuning.

**A big dog's bark is a low sound.**

**Tuning pegs on a violin**

**A violin player changes the length of the vibrating strings.**

## Getting in Tune

Most musical instruments make sounds in one of three ways. String instruments, such as guitars and violins, make sound with vibrating strings. Musicians pluck or bow the strings to make them vibrate. They tune the strings by tightening or loosening tuning pegs. Each string is tuned to a certain pitch.

A player can make other pitches by pressing fingers on the strings. This makes the strings shorter. Shorter strings make higher-pitched sounds.

Flutes and trombones are wind instruments. They produce sound from a vibrating column of air. Different lengths of a column of air produce different pitches.

A player's fingers cover holes on the flute body. This lengthens the column of air that vibrates inside the flute.

A trombone player's lips vibrate against the mouthpiece when the player blows. The player tenses and relaxes the lips to produce different pitches. The player also moves a slide back and forth. This changes the length of the column of air inside the trombone.

Drums are percussion instruments. Striking a drum surface makes sound. Pitch depends on the tightness of the drum surface. The kettledrum can be tuned to various pitches. The player presses on a foot pedal to loosen or tighten the drumhead.

**A flute**

**A trombone**

**A kettledrum**

## Big Sounds, Small Sounds

Tuning varies the pitch of an instrument's sound. The size of the instrument is important also. Big instruments generally vibrate more slowly than small ones and produce lower-pitched sounds. Smaller instruments vibrate faster and produce higher-pitched sounds.

The column of air vibrating inside a flute is smaller than the column inside a tuba. The flute makes a higher-pitched sound. A cello has a bigger body and longer, thicker strings than a violin. The cello makes a lower sound. Bongo drums make higher sounds than bass drums.

**A flute has a smaller column of air than a tuba.**

## Seeing Sound

Everything around you is made of atoms. You cannot see them, but they are everywhere around you. Solid objects are made of atoms. So are liquids and gases. The air you breathe is a gas. Sound energy can move only through the atoms of a solid, liquid, or gas. In the study of sound, solids, liquids, and gases are called mediums.

When you ring a hand bell, the bell vibrates. The vibrating sound source pushes on the air atoms close to it. These atoms get pushed close together. When the compressed air expands, the moving atoms compress the air atoms close to them. The compression and expansion produce a wave of energy transfer. Energy rushes out from the source in all directions.

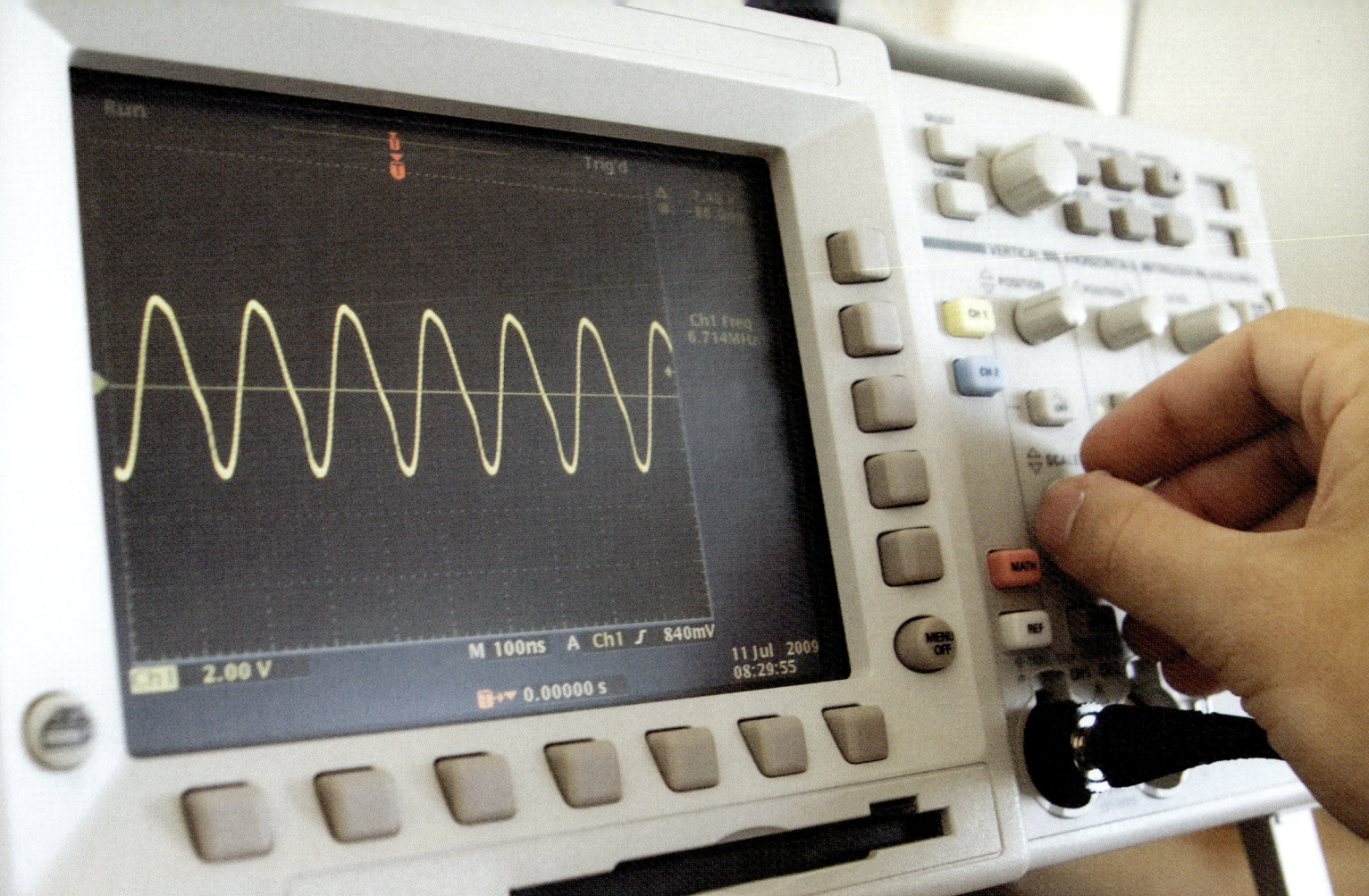

**An oscilloscope displays sound as a wave form.**

The energy wave in the air is invisible because we can't see air. But scientists and engineers have developed instruments to represent sound. One instrument is the microphone. A microphone turns sound vibrations into electric energy pulses. These electric pulses can travel to an amplifier, which makes the sound much louder. Or they can travel to an **oscilloscope**. This instrument displays representations of electric pulses on a screen. The result is a picture, called a wave form, of the sound.

## Measuring Waves

The wave forms on the oscilloscope are not real sound waves. They are electronic images of sound. The oscilloscope screen has a center line running left to right. Each wave on the screen has peaks above the line and troughs below the line. The peaks represent the compressions in the real sound wave. The troughs represent the expansions in the real sound wave. The distance from the center line to the peak is the sound's amplitude. The distance from one peak to the next is the sound's wavelength.

An oscilloscope can count how many wavelengths pass a point in 1 second. That number is the sound's frequency. The fewer wavelengths that pass, the lower the frequency. A low-pitched sound, such as the bark of a big dog, might have a frequency of 500 wavelengths per second. A high-pitched sound, such as a bird call, might have a frequency of 20,000 wavelengths per second.

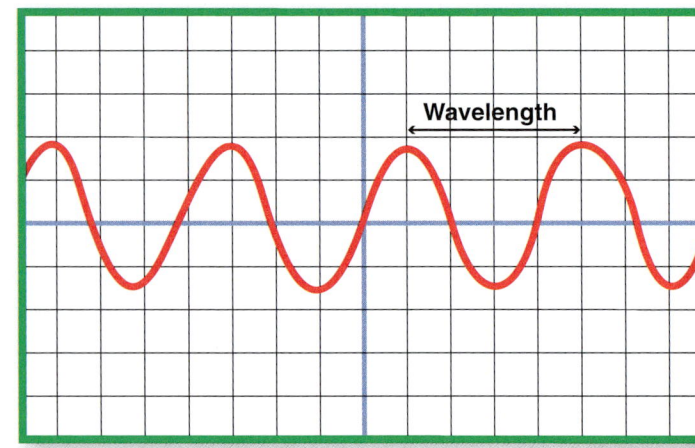

**An example of wavelength**

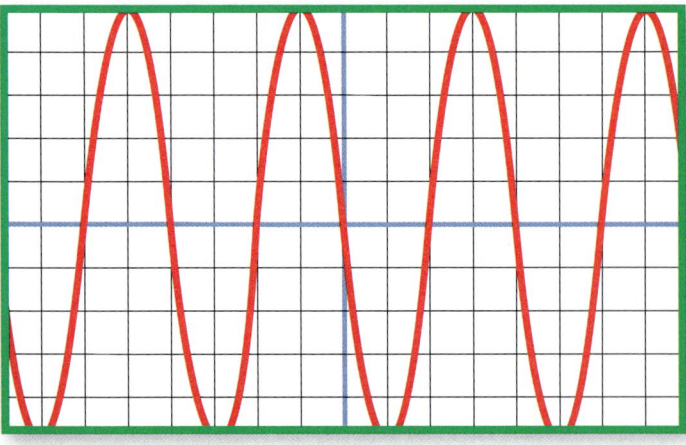

**High-frequency waves**

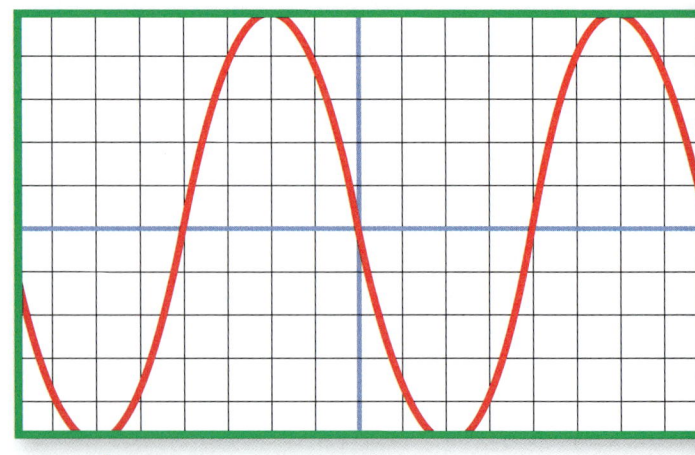

**Low-frequency waves**

Frequency is one **property** of a sound wave. Amplitude is another property. A loud sound has a wave with a high amplitude. A softer sound of the same pitch has a lower amplitude.

Two sound waves could have the same wavelength, but different amplitudes. Or the waves might have the same amplitude but different frequencies.

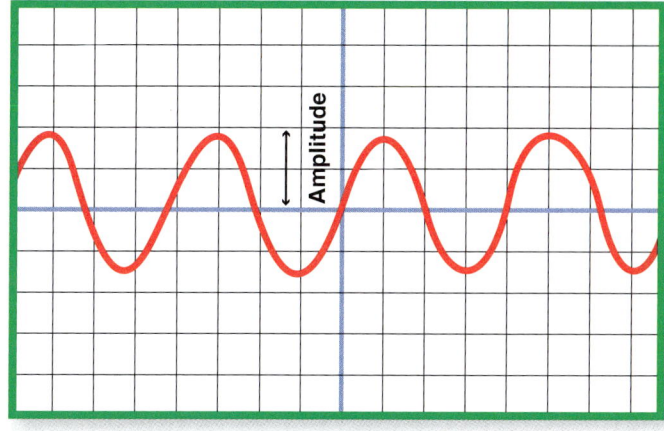
An example of amplitude

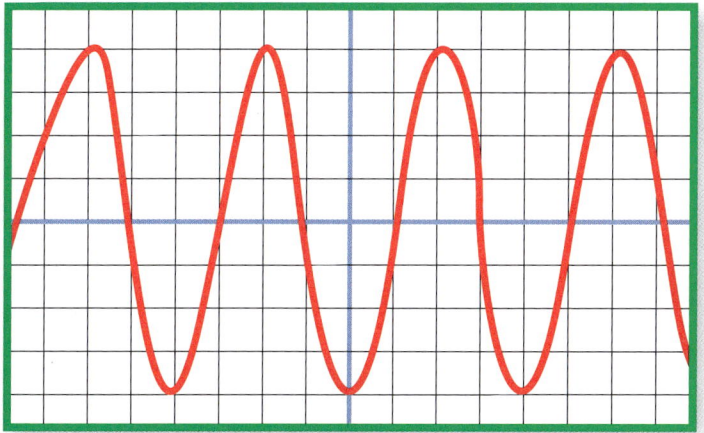
High amplitude

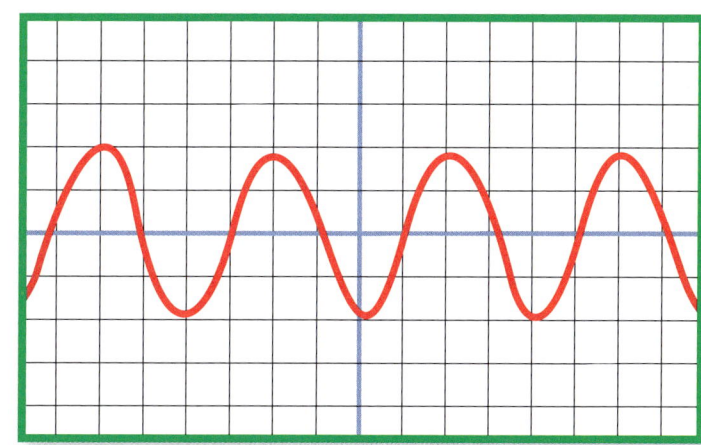
Low amplitude

## How Loud Is Loud?

Any sound, from a whisper to a roar, can be measured to see how soft or loud it is. Sound volume is measured in decibels. A noise of 20 decibels is 100 times louder than a 10-decibel sound. A noise of 30 decibels is 1,000 times louder than a 10-decibel sound.

| Sound | Decibels |
| --- | --- |
| Rustling leaves | 10 |
| Whisper | 20 |
| Normal conversation | 65 |
| Car without a muffler | 100 |
| Live rock concert | 120 |

99

You can see changes in a sound source on the oscilloscope. Say a musician bangs one key on a piano. The sound wave for that musical note has a high amplitude. Gradually, the note grows softer. The oscilloscope shows that the amplitude of the wave for the note becomes shorter. The frequency stays the same.

What if a trombone player blows evenly while moving the slide? The tone's volume stays the same, but its pitch changes. The oscilloscope shows that the wave frequency changes. The wave amplitude stays the same.

When you hear voices, both the volume and the pitch change constantly. This image shows what speech might look like on the oscilloscope.

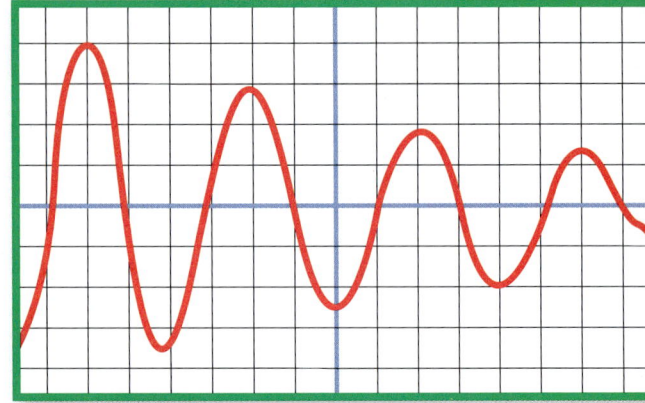

**Same frequency, decreasing amplitude**

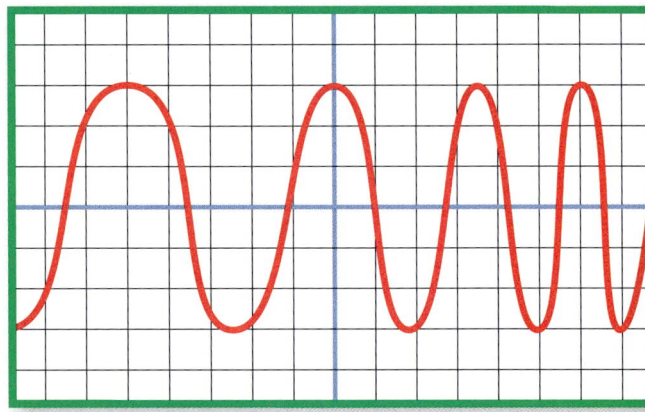

**Increasing frequency, same amplitude**

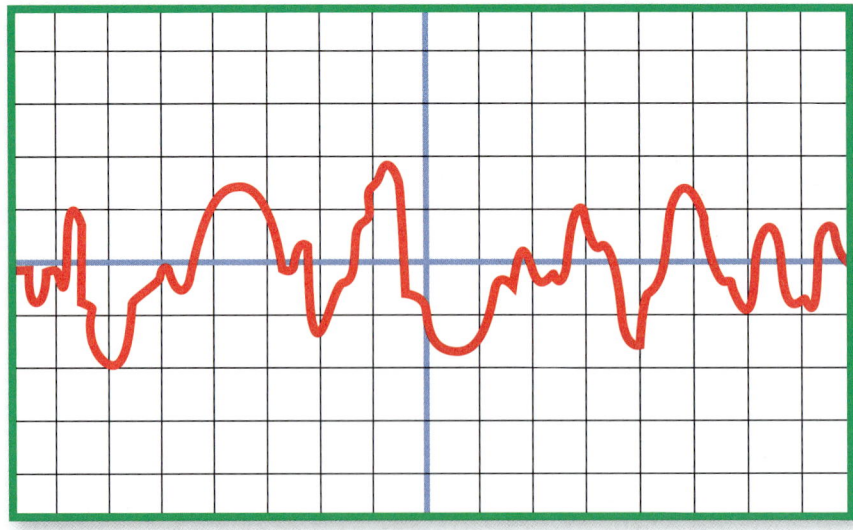

**Noise**

Scientists measure the frequency of sound waves in hertz (Hz). One Hz has a frequency of one wavelength per second. A sound with 1,000 wavelengths in 1 second has a frequency of 1,000 Hz, or 1 kilohertz (kHz). Radio waves are measured in megahertz (MHz). One MHz. has a frequency of 1 million Hz.

## Getting in Range

All animals can hear a certain range of frequencies. This chart shows the range, measured in hertz, for various animals. Which animal has the greatest range of hearing? Which has the smallest? How many animals from the chart can hear sounds humans can't hear?

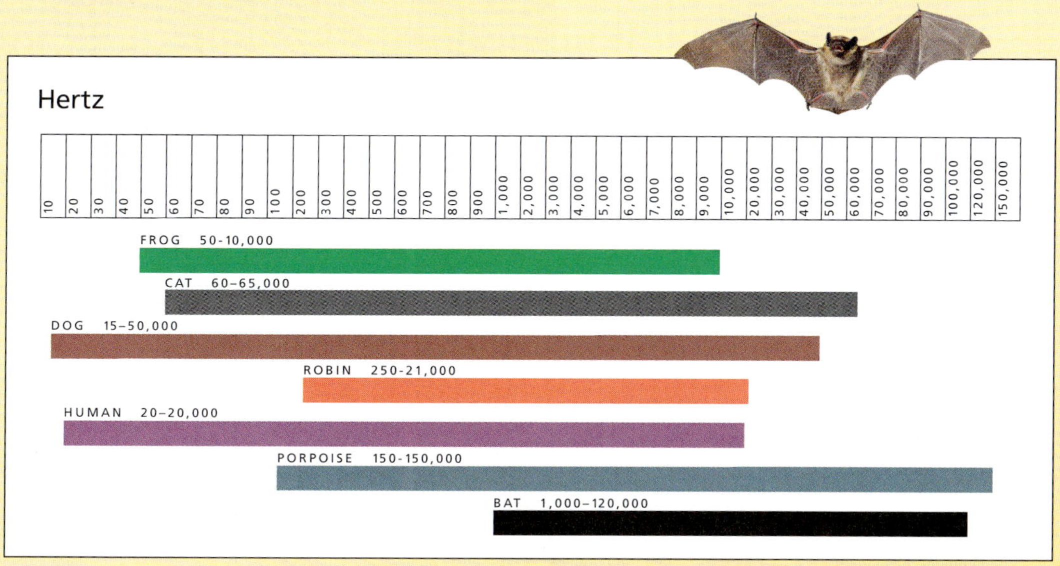

Hertz
10
20
30
40
50
60
70
80
90
100
200
300
400
500
600
700
800
900
1,000
2,000
3,000
4,000
5,000
6,000
7,000
8,000
9,000
10,000
20,000
30,000
40,000
50,000
60,000
70,000
80,000
90,000
100,000
120,000
150,000
FROG 50-10,000
CAT 60–65,000
DOG 15–50,000
ROBIN 250-21,000
HUMAN 20–20,000
PORPOISE 150-150,000
BAT 1,000–120,000


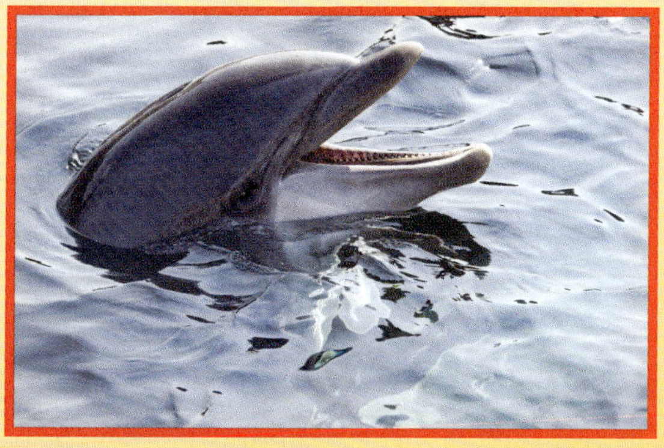

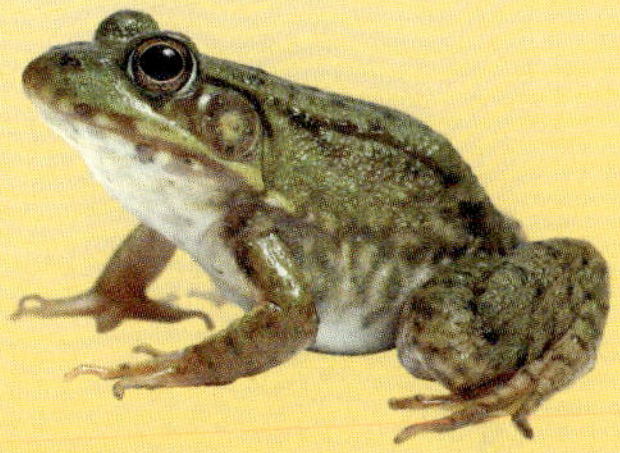

# Light Interactions

Light is evidence of energy. Light comes from a light source. The Sun is a light source. A lightbulb is a light source. A flame is a light source. Anything that makes light is a light source. Can you think of any other light sources?

Light travels in rays. Light rays travel from a light source in straight lines in all directions. Light rays don't curve around things. They just travel straight. And they will travel forever if they don't run into anything.

A candle is a small light source. It is safe to look at a candle. When light rays from a candle flame enter your eyes, you can see the flame. If light rays from the flame don't enter your eyes, you can't see the flame. You can only see something if light travels from it into your eyes.

## Reflected Light

Can you see the picture of a candle on this page? If you can, light must be traveling from the picture into your eyes. But the picture of the candle is not making light. Where is the light coming from?

Look around. Are the lights on in the room? Is there a window where light can come in? That's where the light is coming from. Light from lightbulbs and the Sun is traveling to the candle picture. Then the light bounces off the picture into your eyes. Light bouncing off a surface is called **reflection**.

A lightbulb is a light source. Light rays travel from the source in straight lines. Some of the light rays strike the candle picture. The light rays reflect off the picture. When the light reflects, it changes direction. But it still travels in a straight line. When light from the candle picture reflects into your eyes, you see the picture.

**A candle flame is a light source.**

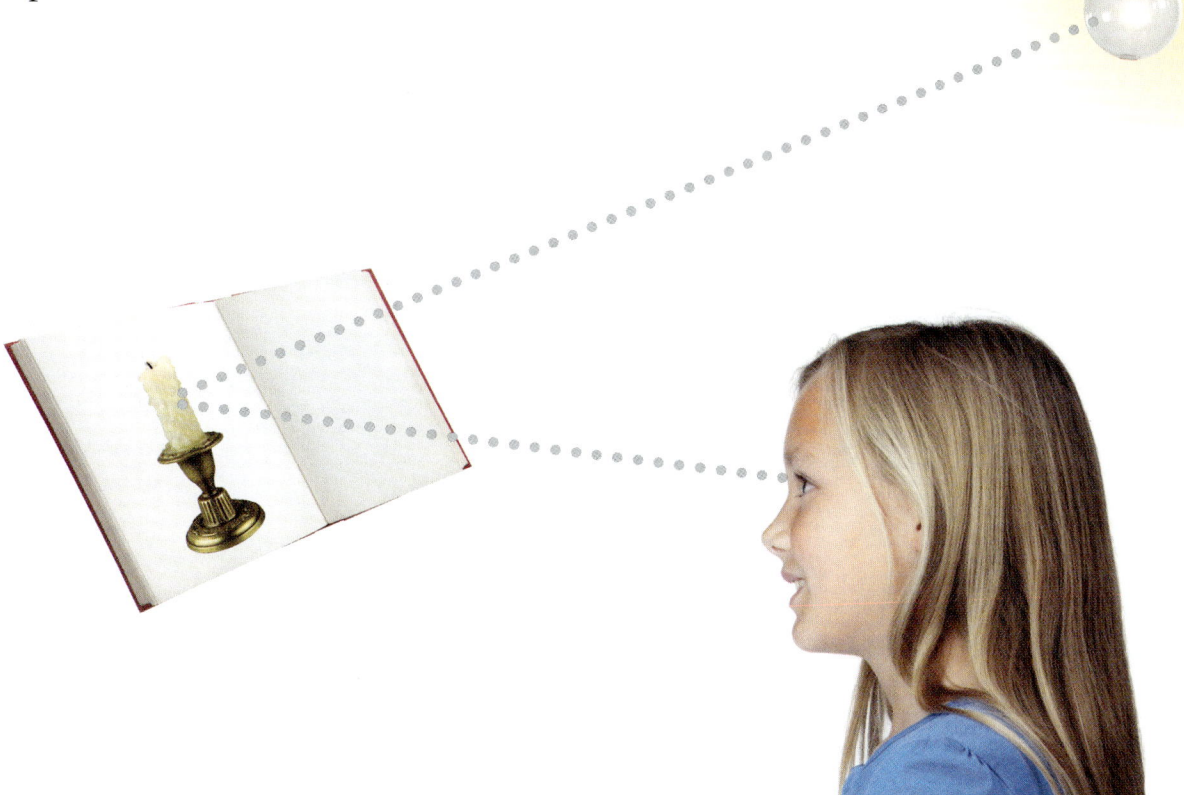

A duck and its reflection in a mirror

A mirror can show what is behind you.

## Mirrors

What do you see when you look in a mirror? Often you see yourself, but not always. You can hold a mirror to see things in other directions. In fact, if you hold a mirror just right, you can see objects behind you. It's like having eyes in the back of your head.

Mirrors are shiny surfaces that reflect light. You can use a mirror to reflect light into your eyes. That's how you are able to see yourself in a mirror. That's how drivers can see what's going on behind them. And that's how sailors in submarines look around the ocean's surface. They use a device with two mirrors called a periscope.

A submarine periscope can show what is above you.

Mirrors can also be used to change the direction of a beam of light. Mirrors can direct light around an object.

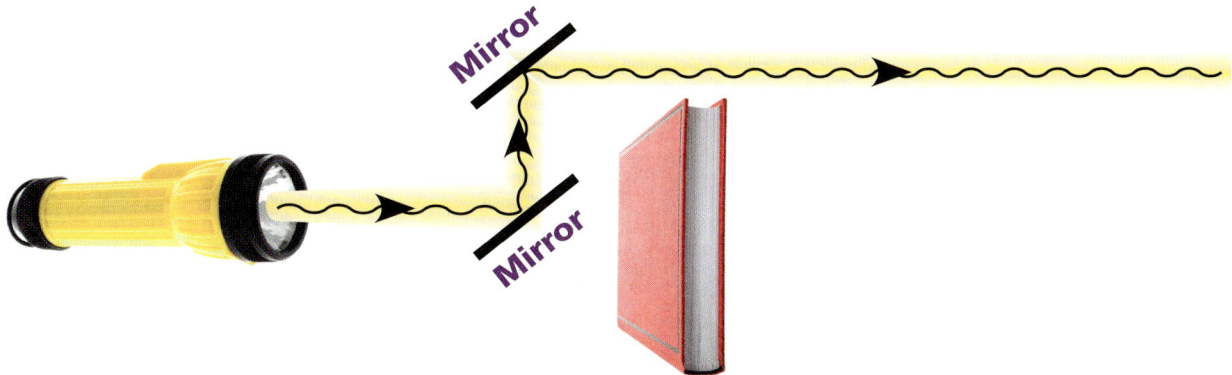

Two mirrors can direct light back to the source.

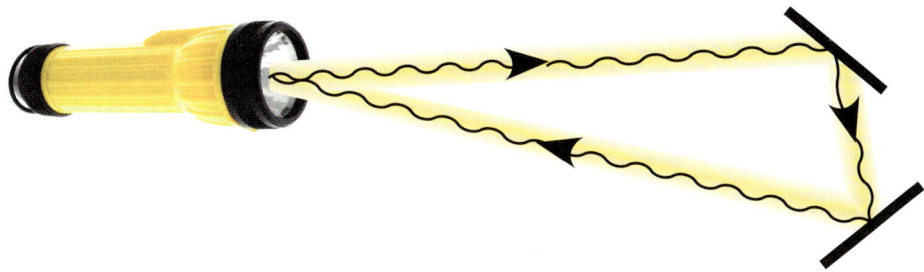

With four mirrors, you can make it look like light shines through a solid object.

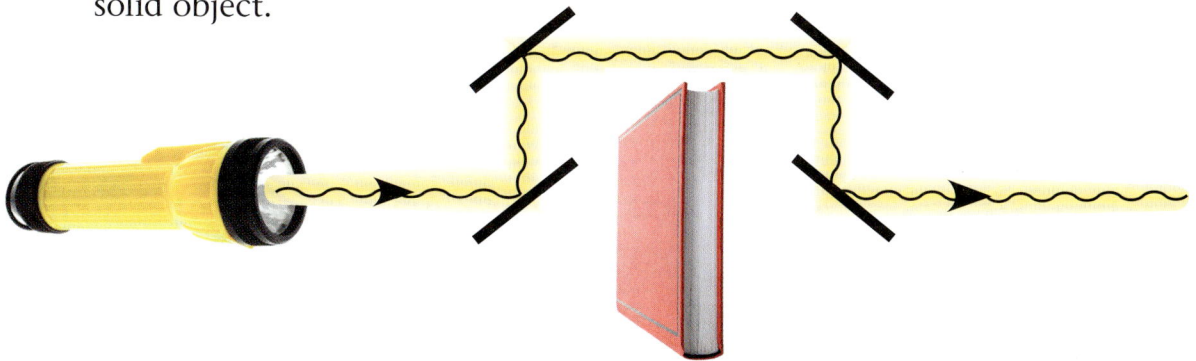

Two mirrors can be used to reflect light in two directions at the same time.

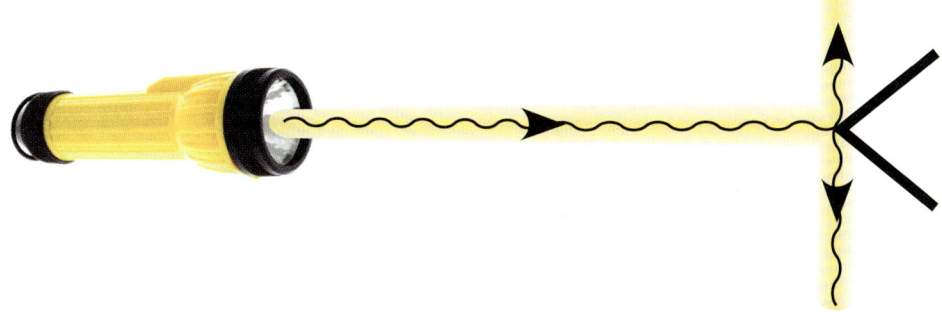

**Smooth water reflects light.**

Other smooth, flat surfaces can act like mirrors. Sometimes you can see your reflection in a glass window. The surface of a calm lake can reflect light, too.

Did you ever look at your reflection in a shiny spoon? Something funny happens. On the back of the spoon, you look tall and skinny. In the bowl of the spoon, you look small and upside down. Curved surfaces reflect light in interesting ways.

**Spoon reflections are fun.**   **Glass reflects light to show this cat's reflection.**

# Refraction

Light travels at different speeds. It moves very fast through air, but it moves slowly through things that are more dense than air. The more dense the substance, the more slowly light travels through it. That's why a light ray moving through water, plastic, or glass seems to bend. These materials are more dense than air. We call this bending of light rays **refraction**.

A hot surface can change the density of air just above it. When that happens, light is refracted where the hot air meets a layer of cooler air. The refraction makes you think you see something that is not there. This illusion is called a mirage. On some days, you might see a mirage that looks like a pool of water above a hot, paved road that is completely dry.

**Straws in a glass of water look broken because of refraction.**

## Reflecting on Light

1. What must happen for you to see an object?
2. What happens when light reflects?
3. What kinds of surfaces reflect light?
4. What can you use a mirror for?
5. What happens when light refracts?

# Throw a Little Light on Sight

Sara's class was on a field trip at the Lawrence Hall of Science.

They were studying light. Sara was excited when she saw an exhibit called "Throw a Little Light on Sight!"

A helper was standing by the open door.

"Would you like to come in and learn about light and vision?"

"Yes, we are studying light in class."

"Good! Let's go into this dark room. It has no windows and no lights. I am closing the door."

"What do you see?"

"I can't see anything."

"I am putting two objects in front of you on the table. We will wait 5 minutes."

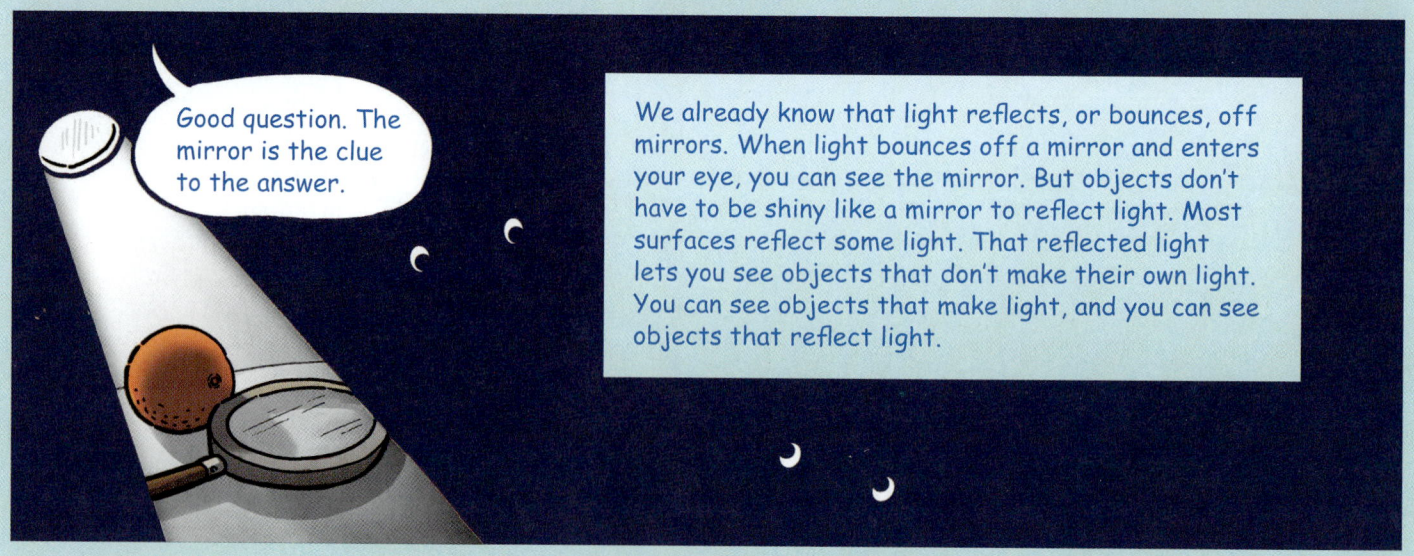

## Later That Week...

Sara tried some experiments at home. She got some clear blue plastic, some green plastic, and some yellow plastic. With these she could shine blue, green, and yellow light with her flashlight. With an orange and a lime from the kitchen, she was ready.

When she shined blue light on the orange and lime, they both looked black.

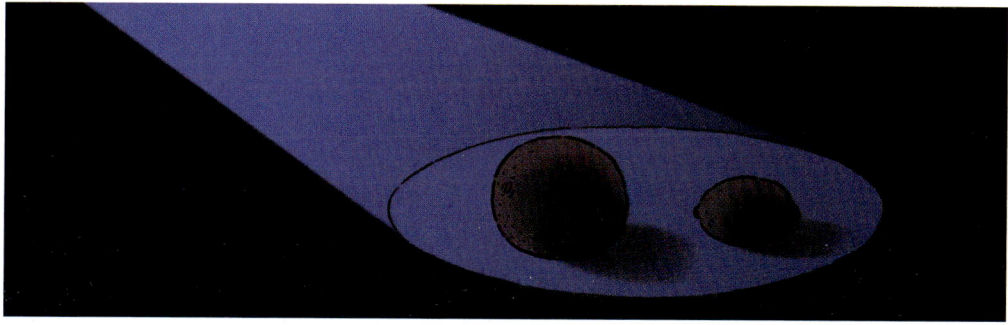

When she shined green light, the orange looked black and the lime looked green.

And when she shined yellow light, the orange looked yellow and the lime looked black.

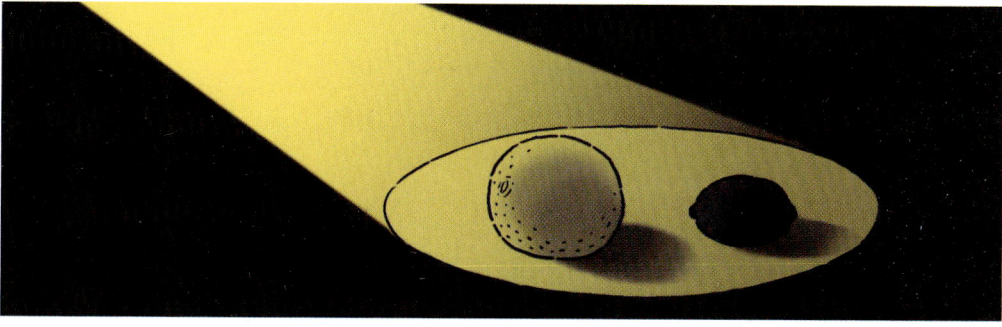

Sara remembered something she learned in class. White light is all colors of light mixed together. White light has yellow light, red light, green light, and all the other colors. A triangle of glass called a prism can separate the colors.

**A prism separates white light into the colors of the rainbow.**

When white light strikes an object, the object absorbs light or it reflects light. Objects like paper, snow, and cotton reflect almost all the light that hits them. That's why they look white. Objects like charcoal, pencil lead, and truck tires absorb almost all the light that hits them. That's why they look black.

When white light hits an orange, almost all the colors of light are absorbed except orange. Orange is reflected. That's why oranges look orange. All of a sudden Sara knew why the orange looked black when blue light shined on it. There was no orange light for the orange to reflect.

Sara thought, "I bet I can predict the appearance of a red apple in green light. And what if I had some red plastic for my flashlight? I could predict the appearance of the lime in red light."

# Thinking about Light

1. Why couldn't Sara see anything when she first went into the exhibit at the Lawrence Hall of Science?

2. Why did Sara's orange appear black in blue light?

3. Why did Sara's lime appear green in white light?

4. How will Sara's lime look in red light? Explain why.

# More Light on the Subject

Energy from the Sun comes to Earth as light. Energy of batteries can produce light. Energy of fuel can produce light. Anything that produces light is a light source.

Light travels from a light source in rays. The rays travel in straight lines. A light ray will travel forever in a line unless it hits an object. When light hits an object, two things can happen. The object might absorb the light. Or the object might reflect the light.

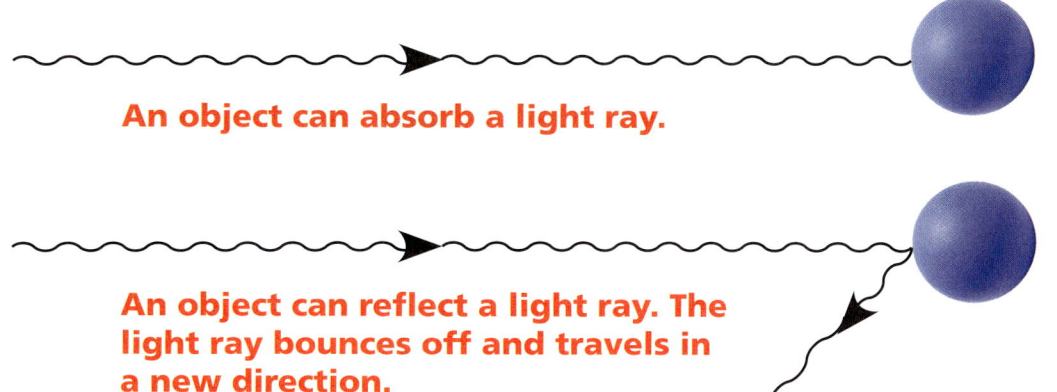

**An object can absorb a light ray.**

**An object can reflect a light ray. The light ray bounces off and travels in a new direction.**

Light that is absorbed is no longer light. This absorbed light can be changed into heat. Light that is reflected is still light. Reflected light bounces off an object and continues on its way. Reflected light travels in a new direction.

## Mirrors

A mirror is a shiny surface. Light reflects from a mirror. A mirror can change the direction of light coming from an object. This property is useful when the light is coming from behind you. A mirror can change the direction of the light so that you can see what is going on behind you.

A flashlight makes a beam of light. A beam is millions of light rays. A mirror can be used to change the direction of a beam of light. Two mirrors can reflect light into a dark room down the hall and around the corner.

Most objects reflect light. That's how we are able to see them. Rays of light from a light source or rays of reflected light enter our eyes. When we see an object, we are actually seeing the light that travels from that object into our eyes. If no light enters our eyes, like when we are in a dark room, we see nothing.

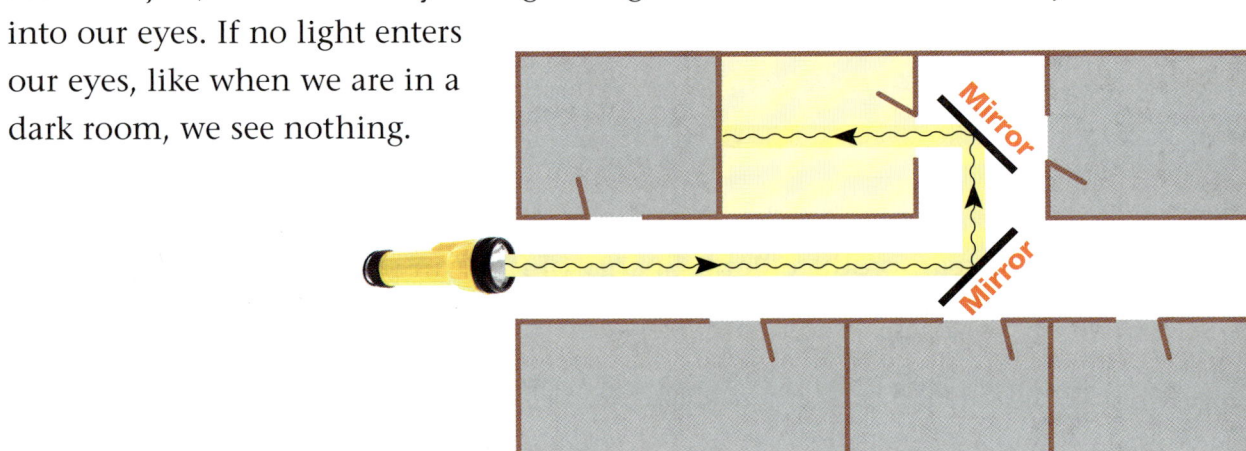

**Drivers use a rear-view mirror to see behind them.**

# Seeing Color

Light from the Sun and from lightbulbs is called white light. But white light is really a mixture of all the colors of the rainbow. In fact, when you see a rainbow, you are seeing all the colors in white light. When conditions are right, tiny drops of water separate the colors.

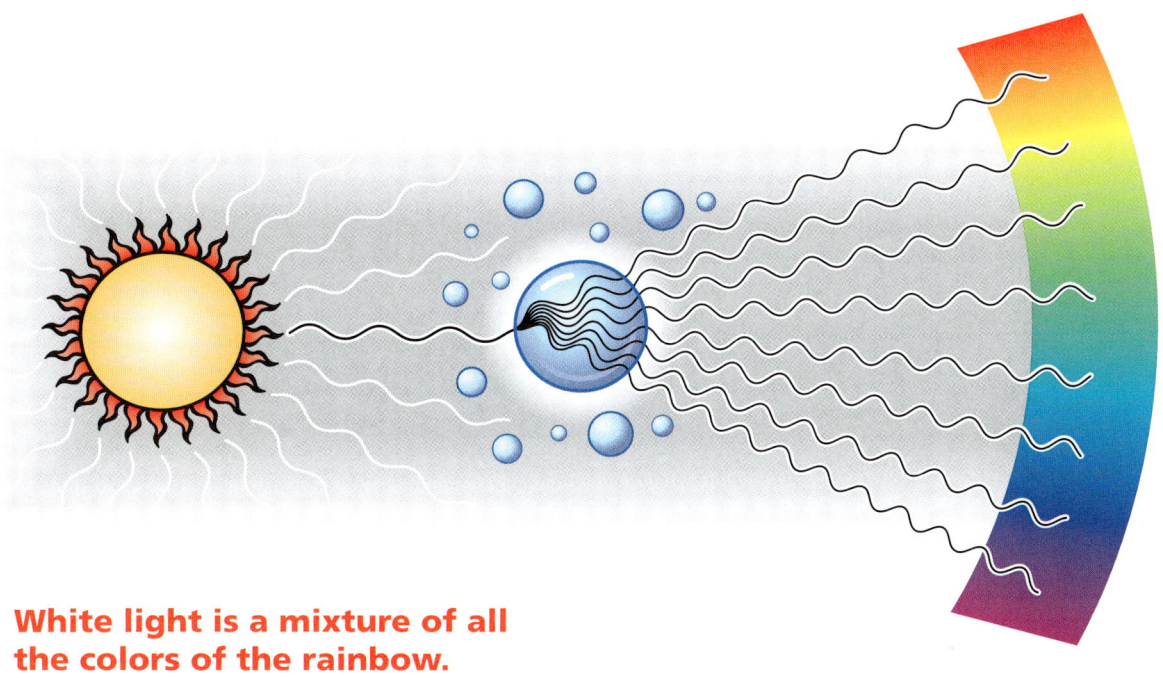

**White light is a mixture of all the colors of the rainbow.**

When white light strikes an object, some colors are absorbed and some are reflected. When white light shines on a red apple, all the colors of light except red are absorbed. Only red light is reflected. When the red light goes into your eyes, you see that the apple is red.

What will you see if you shine blue light on the same red apple? The apple will appear black. The blue light is absorbed by the apple. No light is reflected.

The color of light striking an object affects the way you see the object.

**The apple appears red because it reflects only red light. Other colors of light are absorbed by the apple.**

115

A house generating electric energy with solar panels

# Alternative Sources of Electricity

People use electricity. We use it to light classrooms, to run computers, and to toast bread.

Most of our electricity comes from power plants that burn fossil fuels. Oil, coal, and natural gas are burned to heat water. The steam from the water moves rapidly and spins turbines. The turbines generate electricity. This electricity is expensive to produce. Burning fossil fuels is not good for the environment. And fossil fuels will not last forever.

Remember when you took a solar cell outside to run the motor? You were using an alternative energy source to produce electricity. Sunshine is a renewable resource. If you connected the motor to a battery and let it run, the battery would soon die. You would probably recycle the dead battery and buy a new one. If you set up the same motor with a solar cell, it would keep going for years. Could these little solar cells be used on a larger scale? You bet!

Let's look at a few ways to produce electricity using alternatives to fossil fuels. These natural sources of energy are renewable. Renewable resources are replaced as we use them. We will not run out of renewable resources. And using renewable resources is much better for the environment.

## Solar Power

When people want to use solar energy to generate electricity, they use solar cells that are wired together to create a solar panel. Sometimes they are called photovoltaic cells. Often the solar panels are wired in series circuits. Then they are placed on the roofs of schools, businesses, and homes to generate electricity. There are even solar-cell power plants in deserts that help generate electricity for cities.

**An apartment building using solar panels to generate electricity**

Solar cells absorb the Sun's light and change it into electricity. Electricity is used to power lights, computers, and appliances, and even to heat our homes. If you have a lot of photovoltaic cells and a sunny day, you can create a lot of electricity. Sometimes these solar panels make more than enough electricity for the building on which they are installed. The extra electricity can be sold to power companies.

**A solar power plant**

117

**Wind turbines**

# Wind Power

Wind is powerful. During powerful storms, the wind is strong enough to knock down big trees. On milder days, wind can move large sailboats quickly across a bay. Do we use the wind's energy to create electricity? Yes, we do.

Wind turbines on tall towers use the strong winds above Earth's surface to generate electricity. Strong and steady wind makes the long blades spin. The spinning blades turn a generator to create electricity. Wind turbines are expensive to build. But the wind is free and clean. Wind farms are being built around the country where there is strong, steady wind on most days of the year.

## Geothermal Power

Some places in the world have vents leading from Earth's mantle, up through its crust, to the surface. Water can collect underground near a vent and heat up. When this happens, the steam and water shoot out in the form of geysers. Do engineers put the steam-generating geysers to work? Yes, they do.

A power plant captures Earth's heat to generate electricity. How does it do this? A power company drills into the vent until it reaches an area where the water collects. The steam that flows through the hole spins a turbine to generate electricity. The power company condenses water vapor gas back to liquid water by cooling it. The liquid water returns to the ground to get hot again and to generate more electricity.

**An engineer at a geothermal power plant**

# Hydroelectric Power

Have you ever seen a swollen river in the springtime after heavy rains? If you have, you probably know how powerful moving water can be. Hydroelectric power plants are built across rivers. They have turbines that spin as the water falls from a high point to a low point. The turbines are placed in the path of the falling water to generate electricity. Hydroelectric power is used across the country where rivers flow from mountains to valley floors.

Building a hydroelectric power plant across a river is not always good for the plants and animals that live there. We need to be careful about what we do to the environment. We need to make sure that the benefits of building a power plant are greater than the damage caused to the environment.

A hydroelectric power plant

Reading outside using natural light

## Saving Electricity

One of the best ways to make sure that we have enough energy is for everyone to use less electricity. Energy conservation is a quick and easy way for families and schools to save money. It also helps conserve Earth's natural resources. Here are just a few of the things you can do. When you're not using a computer, turn it off. When you're leaving a room, turn the lights off. When you need something from the refrigerator, decide ahead of time what you're going to get, open the door, and get it as quickly as you can.

Maybe someday you'll have a job working with alternative sources of energy. By then, maybe they will be our main sources of electricity!

# Ms. Osgood's Class Report

Our school is located on an island called Vinalhaven, in the state of Maine. If we want to go ashore to the mainland, we need to take a 12 kilometer (km) ferry ride from our home in Penobscot Bay. It is very expensive to buy electricity on the island because it travels so far underwater. We often lose power in the winter during big storms. On November 13, 2009, we went on a field trip. We went to watch the ribbon-cutting ceremony for three new wind turbines. The wind turbines will provide most of the electricity for two islands. We hope the wind turbines will make our electricity cost less.

It was very exciting when the towers and blades arrived. They came from the mainland on huge barges at high tide. None of us had ever seen towers that were so wide. Part of the excitement was watching how the workers got the parts off the barge and onto the trucks. The huge blades were transported to the site and assembled. They were lifted into the air by gigantic cranes and attached to the towers. We were surprised to see how big the turbines are up close.

Here are two of the wind turbines! Can you guess where the photographer was when he took this picture?

123

Earth Science
**FOSS Science Resources**

# Soil, Rocks, and Landforms

# Table of Contents

**Investigation 1: Soils and Weathering**
What Is Soil? . . . . . . . . . . . . . . . . . . . . . . . . . . . . . . . . . **129**
Weathering. . . . . . . . . . . . . . . . . . . . . . . . . . . . . . . . . . **132**

**Investigation 2: Landforms**
Erosion and Deposition . . . . . . . . . . . . . . . . . . . . . . . . **135**
Landforms Photo Album . . . . . . . . . . . . . . . . . . . . . . . **141**
Fossils Tell a Story . . . . . . . . . . . . . . . . . . . . . . . . . . . **149**
Pieces of a Dinosaur Puzzle . . . . . . . . . . . . . . . . . . . . **153**

**Investigation 3: Mapping Earth's Surface**
Topographic Maps . . . . . . . . . . . . . . . . . . . . . . . . . . . **157**
The Story of Mount Shasta . . . . . . . . . . . . . . . . . . . . **160**
It Happened So Fast! . . . . . . . . . . . . . . . . . . . . . . . . . **164**

**Investigation 4: Natural Resources**
Monumental Rocks . . . . . . . . . . . . . . . . . . . . . . . . . . **176**
Geoscientists at Work . . . . . . . . . . . . . . . . . . . . . . . . **181**
Making Concrete . . . . . . . . . . . . . . . . . . . . . . . . . . . . **186**
Earth Materials in Art. . . . . . . . . . . . . . . . . . . . . . . . **191**
Where Do Rocks Come From? . . . . . . . . . . . . . . . . . . **193**

# What Is Soil?

Have you ever dug a hole in the ground? What did you remove to make the hole? **Soil**. Sometimes people call it dirt, but a scientist calls the layer of diggable material that covers planet Earth soil.

What is soil? If you pick up a handful of soil and look at it closely you might be able to see and feel what soil is made of. Soil is mostly made of several sizes of **rock**. You might see pebbles and smaller pieces of gravel. Soil usually contains sand. **Particles** of sand are really tiny rocks. Some pieces of rock are even smaller than grains of sand. Smaller pieces are called **silt**. The smallest pieces of rock are clay particles. Clay particles are too small to see, but you can feel them. Clay feels slippery when it is wet.

So soil is a mixture of different-sized rocks (pebbles, gravel, particles of sand, and even smaller particles of silt and clay) along with water and air. Rocks, air, and water are **earth materials**. But there is more to soil than earth materials.

**Digging into soil**

**Soil is mostly made of rock in several sizes along with water and air.**

### Rock Size Chart

| Particle name | Average size |
|---|---|
| pebble | ⬭ |
| gravel | o |
| sand | ∘ |
| silt | . |
| clay | invisible to bare eye |

Soil also contains organic material. Organic material is the remains of dead plants and animals. Plants send their roots into the soil and animals dig into the soil. When plants and animals die, their remains become part of the soil. Plants and animals **decay** into tiny pieces called **humus**. Humus provides **nutrients** for plants. Humus also helps the soil **retain** water.

What is an animal that lives in soil? Worms! Worms are good for soil and help plants grow. Worms burrow through the soil. As they move, worms mix the soil and make passageways for air and water. Worm waste also adds nutrients that are good for soil and plants.

**A worm in soil enriched with humus**

Not all soils are alike. Some kinds of soil have more humus. Some soils have more clay. Some have more sand, pebbles, and gravel.

## Digging into Soils

1. What differences do you see in the soils shown above?
2. Where do you think these soils are found?

# Weathering

Pebbles and sand are pieces of rock. Pebbles are pretty big. You can count a handful of pebbles. Pieces of sand are tiny. You can't count the particles in a handful of sand. All pebbles and sand particles start out as huge masses of rock the size of mountains. How do mountains break down into pebbles and sand?

The answer is **weathering**. Weathering is the breaking apart of rocks into smaller pieces. Weathering happens to all rocks when they are exposed to water and air.

## Physical Weathering

Rocks break down in two ways. **Physical weathering** makes rocks smaller, but does not change the rocks in any other way. When a big rock falls from the side of a cliff, it breaks into lots of smaller rocks. All the **minerals** in the small rocks are the same as the minerals in the big rock.

When rocks get hot and then cold, they can crack. Sometimes water gets into cracks in rocks. Water expands when it freezes. It can expand enough to break big sections of rock along the crack. When ice melts, the rock may break into smaller pieces.

**Physical weathering of cliffs**

**A rock weathered by freezing and thawing of water**

Roots of trees and bushes can grow down into cracks in rocks. As roots grow, they make the cracks bigger. Sometimes the cracks get so big that the rock falls apart.

When rocks bang into one another, they get worn down. Rubbing, grinding, and banging is called **abrasion**. Abrasion is a kind of physical weathering. It happens when rocks fall in **landslides**, tumble in flowing water, or crash around in waves. Wind can blow sand against rocks. This sandblasting weathers the rocks.

**Tree roots grow and break rocks.**

**Sand abrasion on cliffs**

**Sand carried by wind can weather rocks into interesting shapes.**

# Chemical Weathering

**Chemical weathering** happens when minerals in rocks are changed by chemicals in water and air. The starting minerals change into new substances.

Many rocks contain iron. When oxygen in air comes in contact with iron, the iron in the rock can rust. Rust is iron oxide. Iron oxide is softer than other iron minerals. This causes the rock to break apart faster.

Carbon dioxide gas in the air **dissolves** in water droplets. This makes **acid**. The acid droplets can fall as rain. The acid causes the **calcite** in **limestone** and **marble** to make holes. This is a chemical change. Monuments, buildings, and gravestones made of marble or limestone change and weaken when exposed to acid rain.

Salt can cause chemical weathering. Salt water can **react** with minerals in rocks to make new minerals. When the new substances are softer than the original mineral, holes can form. The weak rock breaks and falls apart more easily.

**Chemical weathering of a rock containing iron**

**Chemical weathering of marble by acid rain**

**Chemical weathering of sandstone by salt water**

# Erosion and Deposition

A trip to the beach is fun. One of the best parts is playing in the sand. And there is so much sand. Where did it all come from? Was it made right there, or did it come from some other place?

Much of the sand on the beach came from mountains. **Erosion** moved the sand from the mountains to the beach. Erosion is the taking away of weathered rock. After rocks have weathered into small pieces, they can be carried away by gravity, water, or wind. Most of the sand shown here was carried to the beach by water flowing in rivers and streams.

As long as water keeps flowing, the bits of sand keep moving downstream. When the river enters the ocean, the water slows down. The sand settles to the bottom of the ocean. The settling of **sediments** is called **deposition**. Deposits of sand form beaches all over the world.

**A beach**

## Erosion

The beach sand might start on high mountain cliffs. Sometimes big chunks of rock fall off the sides of mountains. Gravity pulls rocks downhill. Other times landslides move rocks and soil downhill.

Rainwater moving over the ground erodes the broken rocks. Water **transports** rocks into creeks. Water flowing in creeks transports broken rocks downstream. This process is called erosion.

**Cliffs high in the mountains**          **Weathered rock in a mountain creek**

**Strong river currents move rocks downstream.**

Creeks flow into rivers. Rivers have strong currents. Rivers can carry many sizes of rocks. The rocks bang together and rub on the riverbed. The rocks break into smaller and smaller pieces. The smaller pieces are pebbles, gravel, sand, and silt. Erosion continues. The farther the rocks move in the river, the smaller they get. They also get smoother and rounder as they tumble along.

**Smooth, round pebbles along a river**

## Deposition

When the water flowing in a river slows down, the rocks are deposited as sediments. Large rocks are the first to settle to the bottom. Powerful **flood** waters move rocks of all sizes, even large boulders.

Where a river flows into a lake, a bay, or the ocean, the water slows down. Sand is deposited near the mouth of the river. The sand can form sandbars, deltas, and beaches. Farther out are deposits of silt and clay.

**Large and small sediments deposited after a flood**

**Can you see deposits of sand and silt where this river enters the lake?**

**Can you see meanders in the river?**

## Other Kinds of Erosion and Deposition

Wind blows sand and smaller pieces of rock from one place to another. Sometimes the wind blows hard enough to carry a lot of sand and dust. Wind can erode valuable farmland.

When the wind dies down, sand and dust are deposited far from their starting places. This is how sand dunes form. Death Valley in California and Great Sand Dunes in Colorado are two places where large sand dunes formed.

**Strong winds move earth materials from one place to another.**

**Great Sand Dunes National Park, Colorado**

**Sand dunes in Death Valley National Park, California**

**A U-shaped valley eroded by glaciers**

**Glaciers** are frozen rivers. Rocks can be frozen in glaciers high in mountain canyons. Glaciers flow slowly through canyons. The frozen rocks scrape the floor and sides of the canyon. Glaciers weather and erode V-shaped canyons into U-shaped valleys.

Thousands of years ago in the Western United States, glaciers scraped down mountain valleys. They crushed and ground up rock beneath them. At the same time, glaciers covered much of the Midwest. These sheets of ice were over 1.5 kilometers (km) thick. They changed much of the landscape by eroding the surface and depositing the rock material in new places.

What happens when sand finally makes it to the ocean? Is that the end of the erosion and deposition story? Not quite. Waves erode beaches and deposit sand in different places all the time. As waves crash on the beach, sand continues to weather. Sand gets finer and finer. Sand abrades the rocks and cliffs along the ocean shore. Erosion and deposition go on and on.

**Sand deposited on a beach around a weathered rock**

# Reviewing Erosion and Deposition

1. Describe and give examples of erosion.
2. Describe and give examples of deposition.

# Landforms Photo Album

## Landforms Formed by Weathering and Erosion

**Arch** A curved rock that forms when chemical and/or physical weathering weakens the center, and the rock erodes.

Arches can form on the land or near the coast where waves batter and erode the center of the rock.

**Butte** A hill with steep sides and a small, flat top. A butte is smaller than a mesa.

**Mesa** A single, wide, flat-topped hill having at least one steep side.

**Gorge** A narrow, steep-sided valley or canyon.

**Valley** A low area between mountains where a stream or glacier flows. Stream valleys are V-shaped. Glacier valleys are often U-shaped.

**Hanging valley** A valley floor above another valley floor. Glacial erosion causes hanging valleys.

**Canyon** A V-shaped gorge with steep sides eroded by a stream.

**Meander** A curve or loop in a river or stream.

**Hoodoo** A rock shaped like a mushroom or statue. Hoodoos are formed when weak rocks erode away and leave behind stronger rocks.

**Exfoliation dome** A dome formed when rocks like granite peel away at Earth's surface.

**Spheroidal rocks** Rounded rocks formed by physical and chemical weathering.

# Landforms Formed by Deposition

**Alluvial fan** A fan-shaped deposit of rocks formed where a stream flows from a steep slope onto flatter land.

**Beach** An area made of sand and other sizes of rocks between the low-tide and high-tide levels at the coast or a lake.

**Floodplain** Land covered by water during a flood. Small particles, like sand and silt, are deposited on a floodplain.

**Delta** A fan-shaped deposit of earth materials at the mouth of a stream.

**Sandbar** A long ridge of sand in shallow water, built up by river currents or ocean waves.

**Levee** A bank along a stream that may stop land from flooding. Levees can be natural or made by people.

**Moraine** The unsorted rocks and soil carried and deposited by a glacier.

**Outwash plain** A flat or gently sloping surface made of sorted sediments deposited by water from melting glaciers.

**Plain** A low area of Earth's surface that is often formed by flat-lying sediments.

**Sand dune** The sand deposited by wind in ridges, mounds, or hills.

**Landslide** The rapid downslope movement of earth material.

**Slump** A downward movement of a single mass of earth material.

# Landforms Formed by Eruptions

**Volcano** A place where lava, cinders, ash, and gases pour out through openings in Earth's surface.

**Caldera** A hole that forms when the top of a volcano blows off or when the magma below the volcano drains away.

**Cinder cone** A volcano formed from a pile of cinders and other volcanic material blown out in an explosive eruption.

**Composite volcano** A volcano built by alternating eruptions of lava, cinders, and ash. Mount Rainier and the other volcanoes in the state of Washington are composite volcanoes.

**Shield volcano** A volcano built of very fluid lava. It looks wider than it is tall. Shield volcanoes created the Hawaiian Islands.

# Landforms Formed by Crust Movements

**Fault** A break in Earth's crust where blocks of rock **fracture** and move. The San Andreas Fault has created a wide crack in Earth's surface.

**Plateau** A high, nearly level, uplifted area composed of horizontal layers of rock. The Colorado River has eroded the Colorado Plateau, forming the Grand Canyon.

**Mountain** A high, steeply sloped area where rock is uplifted along a fault or created by a volcano.

# Fossils Tell a Story

Earth scientists called **geologists** and **paleontologists** ask questions about the history of Earth. Geologists focus their studies on the structures of rocks and how they formed. Paleontologists ask questions about what life was like millions of years ago. These scientists can't travel back in time, so they look for answers to their questions in rocks. From the **evidence** they find, paleontologists build models to explain how they think plants and animals lived and what their world was like.

## Digging through the Layers

Over billions of years, Earth's surface has changed dramatically. Areas once covered by water are now dry. Continents have moved around on the globe. Large areas of Earth's surface were once covered by thick sheets of ice, which have now melted.

Through all these changes, layers of new rock have formed on Earth. Some layers were formed by molten **lava** that erupted from **volcanoes**, covered Earth's surface, cooled, and turned into solid rock. Other layers of rock formed from tiny particles of rock called sediments that settled in Earth's ocean, lakes, and swamps. After millions of years these layers of sediments changed into **sedimentary rock**. By digging through layers of sedimentary rock, earth scientists have determined the age of Earth and discovered the **organisms** that lived here at the time the sediments were deposited.

**Scientists dig through layers of soil and rock.**

A fern fossil

## Fossils Found

Scientists attempt to assign age to the rocks they study. They have several tools they use to determine the age of rocks. One technique is based on the **fossils** they find in them. Fossils are the remains of organisms preserved in rocks. Scientists know that some of the organisms represented by the fossils are much older than other fossils they find. This kind of information tells a scientist that one rock is older than another, based on the fossils found on them, but not how old either rock is in absolute terms. For determining the absolute age of rocks, geologists use other tools and techniques.

Fossils form in several different ways. Most form when a dead organism ends up at the bottom of a water environment (the ocean, a lake, or a swamp). The organism gets buried in mud and sediments. Most of the softer parts of the organism decompose, but the hard parts (bones, teeth, some shells) remain. Sediments carried by erosion continue to deposit on top of the remains. Over very long periods of time, the sediments are squeezed and compacted and eventually harden into rock. As buried bones age, minerals seep into the bones and bit by bit turn the bones into solid rock. A bone fossil is no longer bone but rock in the exact shape of the original bone. This is the same way a tree turns into **petrified wood**. A piece of petrified wood is a tree fossil, preserving the tree's wood grain and growth rings exactly.

A fish fossil

Sometimes a buried organism decomposes, leaving a space in the sediment where the organism was originally. Later, as the sediments continue to change into rock, the space in the sediments called a **mold** will fill with minerals. The minerals that fill the mold turn into a different kind of rock than the sediments surrounding the mold. After a long time, the minerals in the mold form an exact replica of the original organism. This kind of fossil is called a **cast**. Cast fossils of organisms, like clams, sea urchins, and snails, are fairly common.

**Look at the mold and cast of an ammonite fossil. Ammonites are extinct ocean animals that had spiral shells. They are excellent index fossils and are used to date the rocks.**

After years of studying fossils found all over the planet, paleontologists have discovered that some of the fossil organisms lived on Earth for only a short time, perhaps a few million years, and are very wide spread. A few are found all over the world, in the United States, Europe, Asia, and South America. Such short-lived, widespread fossils are known as index fossils. Index fossils help Earth scientists determine the absolute age of the rocks they are studying. When a scientist locates an index fossil in the rock layer she is studying, she knows a lot about that rock layer and when its sediments were deposited.

**Fossilized tree trunks**

## The Fossil Record

Together, all the fossils on Earth make up the **fossil record**. The fossil record is a valuable source of information about the history of life on Earth.

The fossil record also provides evidence of the environment in which ancient organisms lived. An important part of an organism's environment is climate, the average weather in an area.

We have learned from fossils that Earth's climates have changed over time. For example, fossils of plants that would have thrived in hot and humid areas (tropical jungle) have been found in areas that are deserts now. Such fossil evidence suggests that these areas were wetter millions of years ago than they are today.

Fossilized tree trunks can provide similar kinds of evidence. Most trees do not grow as fast when the temperature is cold and dry. A petrified tree trunk with narrow growth rings suggests that the climate was probably cool and dry when the tree was living. A petrified tree trunk with wide growth rings suggests that the climate was probably warm and moist during the tree's lifetime.

Sometimes a scientist finds fossils of ocean animals high up on a mountain. What do you think she might conclude about the history of that area? Why?

# Pieces of a Dinosaur Puzzle

Most dinosaur fossils date from 65 million to 225 million years ago. Fossils help scientists determine what dinosaurs looked like and how they lived. For example, a dinosaur's teeth reveal whether it ate meat or plants. The size of a limb can tell if the dinosaur walked on four legs or two.

When paleontologists find a complete skeleton, they can assemble it to show what a dinosaur looked like. The bones might come from more than one skeleton of the same type of dinosaur. They build a full model of the dinosaur's body based on the bones they have. They construct bones to replace the ones that are missing to make a complete skeleton. This process of filling in the gaps of missing bones is called a **restoration**. Many museums display dinosaur models that are restorations. Often the entire skeleton is not made of the real bones, but of copies of the original model.

**A scientist assembling dinosaur bones**

**A dinosaur skeleton restoration**

Paleontologists around the world continue to piece together models of dinosaurs based on newly unearthed fossils. New discoveries add information to our knowledge of past life on Earth.

One thing that paleontologists are interested in finding out is what dinosaurs ate. The earliest dinosaurs were small-bodied, fast-moving **predators** that hunted and ate other animals. They were **carnivores**, or meat eaters. But later, the fossil record shows that two other major groups of dinosaurs existed and these two groups were both **herbivores**, or plant eaters.

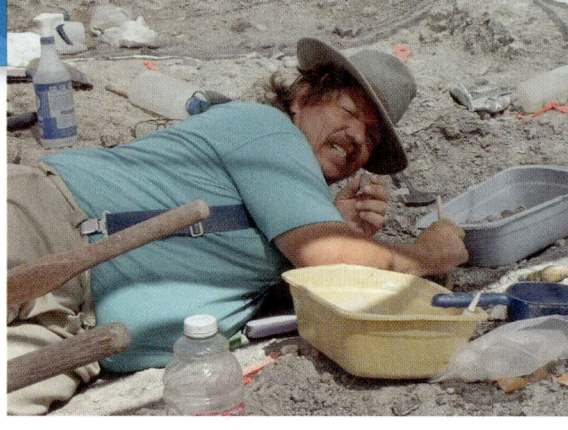

James Kirkland, a paleontologist and geologist, brushing off a fossil at a Utah site where scientists have found the fossils of hundreds of small dinosaurs

How did these plant-eating dinosaurs evolve from the early meat eaters? This was a mystery, and there was no fossil evidence to provide the answers.

In 2002, paleontologists began digging bones out of rocks in east central Utah. In one location, they found fossils of hundreds of medium-sized dinosaurs with long necks and long, clawed hands. They compared the dinosaur skeletons to existing dinosaur bones. When the new bones did not match, the scientists came to an interesting **conclusion**. They had discovered a new type of dinosaur. They published their finding in 2005.

The new dinosaur was about 4 meters (m) long, head to tail. It stood about 1.4 m tall and might have weighed about 225–450 kilograms (kg). It had sharp, curved claws that were 10 centimeters (cm) long. With almost 1,700 bones excavated between 2002 and 2005, scientists have about 90 percent of the dinosaur's bones.

Kirkland standing near a full-size model of the newly discovered dinosaur with sharp, curved claws

They named the newly discovered creature *Falcarius* (pronounced fal-cah-RYE-us), Greek for "sickle bearer" because of its claws. Based on the rocks where it was found, it lived in the early Cretaceous period about 125 million years ago. The sharp, curved claws indicate it hunted and ate small animals like its dinosaur relatives.

One thing that was so interesting about this new dinosaur was its teeth. They were shaped like tiny leaves. This would be a good shape for shredding plants. Meat-eating dinosaur relatives had blade-like teeth. *Falcarius* was different from its relatives.

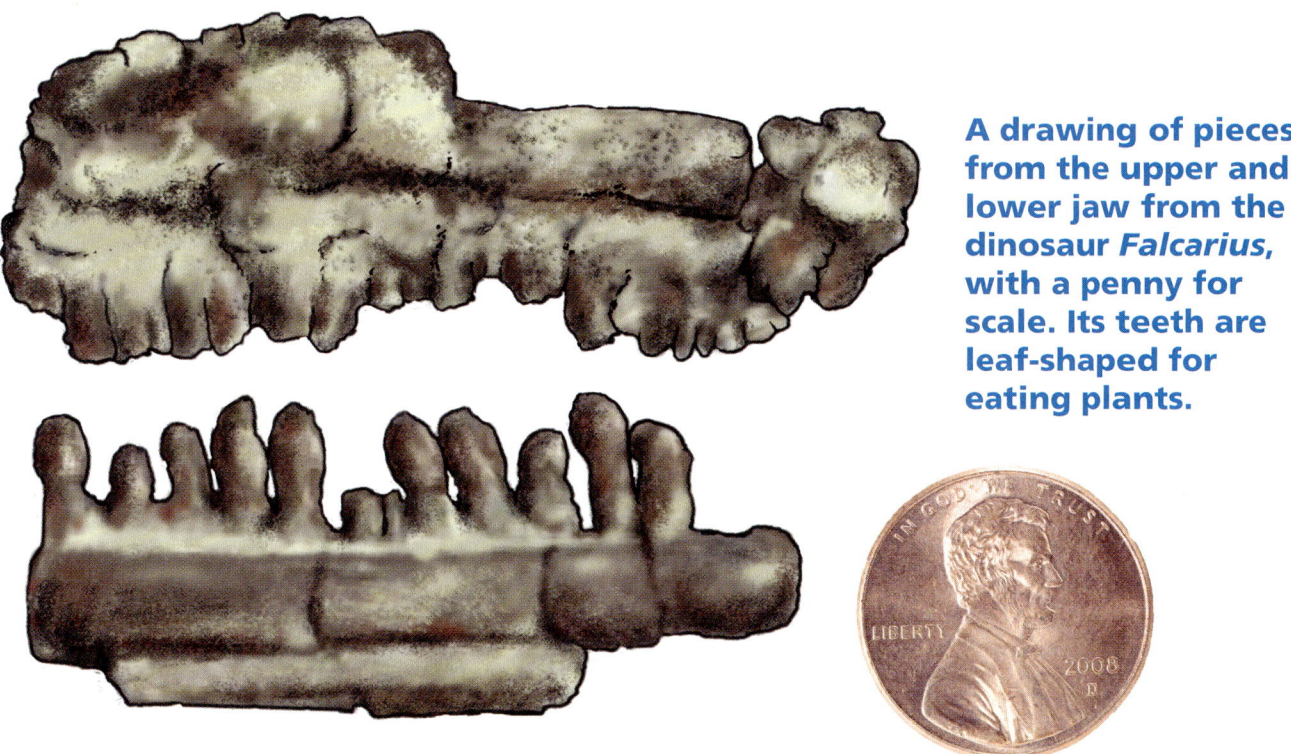

**A drawing of pieces from the upper and lower jaw from the dinosaur *Falcarius*, with a penny for scale. Its teeth are leaf-shaped for eating plants.**

Another interesting thing was the pelvic bone of *Falcarius*. The shape of that bone was broad, providing evidence that the dinosaur had a very large **digestive system**. A large gut would be needed if the animal ate plants.

The lower legs of *Falcarius* were stubby. It couldn't run very fast to catch prey. Compared with carnivorous relatives, *Falcarius*'s neck was longer and its forelimbs were more flexible. These features made it easier for the dinosaur to reach plants to eat.

All together, the analysis of these bones revealed something extraordinary. This dinosaur was not just a carnivore like other dinosaur relatives that lived in the Cretaceous period. It also ate plants. It represented a stage between carnivores and herbivores.

During dinosaur evolution, two major groups of dinosaurs shifted to plant-based diets. But fossils of dinosaurs that were both meat eaters and plant eaters hadn't been found. Scientists didn't have the information they needed to understand the plant-eaters' relationship to their meat-eating ancestors. The *Falcarius* fossils show this transition in action among one group of dinosaurs. That group is the birdlike meat-eating and plant-eating dinosaurs of the Cretaceous period.

The discovery of *Falcarius* was a very important piece of the larger puzzle of dinosaur evolution. The dinosaur dig in Utah will continue to provide more information for paleontologists in years to come. The site has fossils of *Falcarius* babies, juveniles, and adults. Scientists will be able to compare the structural differences between young and adult dinosaurs, and between males and females. Scientists will be able to develop more models about how fast the animals grew, at what age they became adults, and how they lived in the environment so long ago.

An artist's conception of the dinosaur *Falcarius*

# Topographic Maps

A map is a picture of Earth's surface. Although most maps are drawn on flat paper, Earth has many bumps and curves. These changes in elevation are difficult to show on a flat surface. A **topographic map** is a type of map that shows changes in elevation. At first, a topographic map may look like squiggles and blotches of color. However, the map can provide a great deal of information. First, you must understand how the lines and symbols are used.

The most obvious feature of a topographic map is the system of curved lines that covers the map. These lines are called **contour lines**, and they are usually brown. Each contour line represents a specific elevation. Elevations on US maps published by the US Geological Survey (USGS) are measured in feet above sea level. In countries where the metric system is used, elevations are measured in meters. Surveyors measure elevations when they gather the information to create a new map.

When you move your finger along a contour line on a topographic map, the elevation is the same at every point on the line. Your path would be flat if you walked along the course the contour represents in the real world. You would not go uphill or downhill. Contour lines are always connected at both ends. If you follow a contour line on a topographic map, you will always return to the place where you began. Sometimes the ends of a contour line run off the map page. But eventually they connect if you enlarge the map or follow them onto an adjacent map.

A hill on a topographic map is represented by rings of contour lines. The rings become smaller and smaller as they approach the top of the hill. If you move from one contour line to another, you move either up or down in elevation. In real life, if you walk across contour lines represented on the map, you will go either uphill or downhill.

Elevation changes rapidly if contour lines are close together. A steep hill is represented by closely spaced contour lines. If the contour lines are farther apart, they represent a more gradual slope. Some contour lines are thicker than others and have elevations printed on them. These are called **index contours**. The numbers tell the elevations of the index contours. Index contours help determine whether the elevation is rising or falling.

Topographic maps contain other important information. A scale is printed on the bottom of the map in the margin. In the United States, the standard scale of many topographic maps is 1:24,000 (1 inch equals 24,000 inches or 2,000 feet). The scale is shown as a ratio, graphic scale, or both. On some maps, the scale is given in meters. The text in the margin also states the **contour interval**. This is the change in elevation between any two contour lines. A contour interval of 3 meters (m) means that the elevation of each contour line is 3 m higher or lower than the one next to it.

## Colors Used on Most USGS Topographic Maps

**Green** Major vegetation: forest, brush, and orchards
**Blue** Water: lakes, streams, rivers, springs, marshes, the ocean, and glaciers
**Red** Highways or boundaries
**Black** Human-made structures and place names
**White** Absence of vegetation: prairies, meadows, tundra, and deserts
**Brown** Land features, lava flows, sand areas, and contour lines

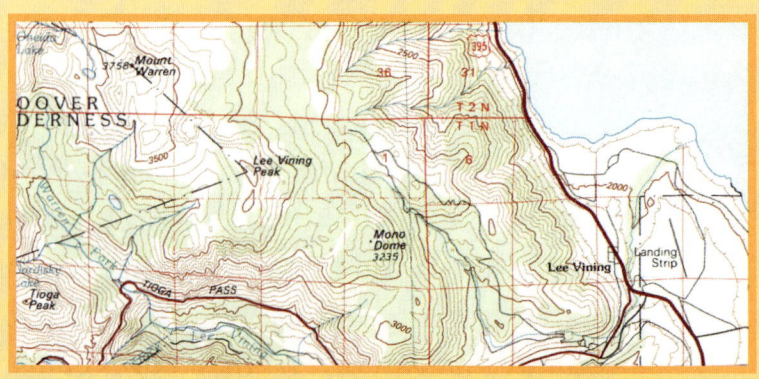

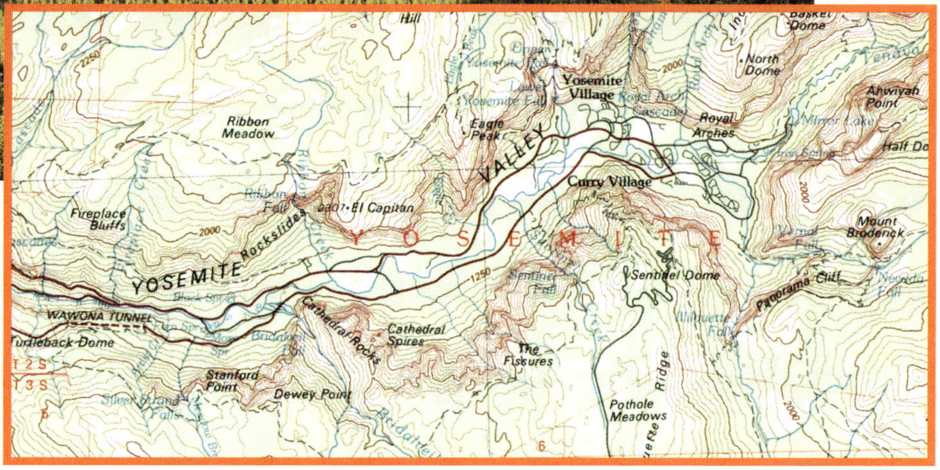

**A topographic map of Yosemite Valley**

Topographic maps contain much more information than changes in elevation. Symbols and colors represent natural **landforms**, vegetation, and structures made by people. USGS topographic maps use a standard set of colors and symbols to represent objects.

## The United States Geological Survey (USGS)

Topographic maps are made by the United States Geological Survey (USGS). This federal agency was established in 1879. Its task is to map, study, and interpret the geology, hydrology, and topography of the country. USGS surveyors use the latest scientific instruments to create accurate maps. They have created topographic maps of the entire country. In addition, the USGS investigates natural hazards such as volcanoes, earthquakes, and landslides.

# The Story of Mount Shasta

*The following is adapted from an account of a night in a snowstorm on Mount Shasta. The story is based on an article by John Muir. The article was published in the September 1877 issue of* Harper's New Monthly Magazine. *Muir (1838–1914) was a naturalist and explorer. He traveled extensively throughout California and wrote about his adventures.*

The climb to the top of Mount Shasta is usually undertaken in summer, during favorable weather. Then the deep snows have melted from the lower slopes. At that time, storms are much less likely to occur. But whatever the season, Shasta's peak is covered in a layer of snow and ice. I agreed to attempt the climb in spring in order to take barometric observations from the summit.

My companion, Jerome Fay, and I began our climb on April 30, 1875. We took packhorses to carry supplies. We made our way toward a camp about 16 kilometers (km) up the mountain trail. We planned to camp overnight and then get an early start the next morning.

**A profile view of Mount Shasta**

A sketch of Mount Shasta drawn by John Muir

We had not expected to encounter snow 1.5 meters (m) deep on the trail. We pushed on throughout the day, but made slow progress. As the Sun began to set, we realized we would not make our destination by nightfall. Determined to go on, we left the horses. We carried a day's provisions and our blankets up the slope to the timberline. There we set up camp, sheltered by a block of red lava. We slept only 2 hours. At 2:00 a.m., we arose to a fine, starry sky. After cooking our breakfast of venison on the coals, we set off for the summit.

Our pulses raced as we were surrounded by the beauty of the morning. We plunged ahead, hardly stopping for breath. Our boots clomped over the red lava apron that leads up the west side of the mountain. We made our way toward the smaller of the two cone-shaped summits. We crossed the gorge that separates the two peaks and swung around the Whitney Glacier.

The hot fumaroles, vents through which volcanic gases and steam escape, hissed and belched as we hiked upward. By 7:30 a.m., we were at the summit.

Fay and I marveled at the landscapes that surrounded us. I took the required barometric measurements and looked to my companion. At first, I did not understand his frown as he stared southward. As I looked into the Shasta Valley, I knew why he was dismayed. The valley was filled with gray and purple cumulus clouds. My first thought was how beautiful the storm clouds were on the mountain. Then I realized our danger.

Fay and I immediately began our descent. We moved slowly down the mountain. By 1:00 p.m. the storm reached the summit and began pounding us with hailstones. As we stood beside a hissing fumarole, I observed that the hailstones were of an unusual shape, with six straight sides and a domelike crown. Fay was interested less in the shape of the hailstones and more in the condition of the storm. All at once, the violence of the storm hit us with its might.

Had I been alone, I might have attempted the descent. However, Fay convinced me that the only sane course was to ride out the storm near the hissing hot springs. The temperature quickly dropped more than 11 degrees Celsius (°C). The wind became violent. Lightning flashed. We had only one chance. We removed as much clothing as possible and lay in the fuming mud on the edge of the hot springs. Thus we spent the night, freezing on one side and boiling on the other.

As we lay in this state, both threatened and protected by the mountain, my mind wandered to the origins of Shasta. The giant cone of Mount Shasta stands in constant snow. It can be seen from anywhere within a 80 to 160-kilometer km radius around the mountain. This majestic mountain of volcanic ashes and lava rises 4,317 m above sea level. It towers more than 3,000 m above the plain on which it sits. Shasta originated from repeated eruptions that built it upward and outward like the trunk of a tree. The mountain is more than 250,000 years old. Its two peaks are the results of multiple eruptions.

The remains of Shasta's violent history can still be found on the sides of the mountain. Gases, mud, steam, and boiling water spew up through cracks from the magma, or molten rock, below. The fumarole in which we were lying was one such outlet.

As quickly as it came upon us, the storm ended. The sky became clear and filled with stars. The temperature was still too cold to attempt our descent of the mountain, so we remained in our cooker until morning. Then we trudged down the mountain in our frozen, stiff clothes.

Luckily we were met at our camp by a friend with horses. As we descended, we could feel the Sun's warmth on our backs. I looked over my shoulder at the great white cone of Mount Shasta. The ordeal of the previous night seemed like a faraway dream.

**A sketch by John Muir**

## A Cascades Volcano

Mount Shasta is located 65 km south of the California-Oregon border. At 4,317 m, it is the second-highest mountain in the Cascade Range. Mount Shasta is an example of a stratovolcano. Stratovolcanoes are volcanoes composed of lava flows, ash, and other material blown out by explosive activity. Shastina, the prominent cone on the west flank of Shasta, was active about 9,200 years ago. The Hotlum cone at Shasta's peak was active only a few centuries ago.

# It Happened So Fast!

Some landforms are so old, you might think they've always been that way. The Sierra Nevada has been uplifting for more than 2 million years, and it continues today. The Colorado River continues to carve the Grand Canyon, as it has for more than 5 million years. Rock in the Appalachian Mountains began folding more than 480 million years ago. Most changes to Earth's surface are so slow, we can't see them happen.

But sometimes changes happen rapidly. Rapid changes affect people and landforms. Here are some examples of fast changes to Earth's surface.

## Yosemite Floods of 1997

Floods caused a lot of damage in northern California in 1997. Three factors created the floods. There was deep snow in the mountains, warm temperatures, and heavy rain.

Yosemite National Park was hit hard. The Merced River, which flows through Yosemite Valley, rose higher than ever before. Water spread out and covered much of the valley.

**Flood water in Yosemite**

A sign showing the water level during the flood

A Yosemite hiking trail after the flood

In some places, the flood water was 3 meters (m) deep. Campsites were washed away. Housing for the people who worked in Yosemite was destroyed. When the water slowed, sand and other sediment were deposited all over the valley floor. The course of the river was different. Flood water has the power to change the land rapidly.

Water flowing out of Canyon Lake over the spillway at the height of the flood

## Canyon Lake Flood of 2002

In the 1960s, a dam was built on the Guadalupe River to prevent flash flooding and to provide a water supply for central Texas. The Canyon Dam created a reservoir called Canyon Lake. The lake became a popular recreation area in the Texas Hill Country between San Antonio and Austin. This area of Texas is known worldwide for its potential for flash floods. In fact, it is part of an area called Flash Flood Alley.

In early July 2002, it began to rain heavily in the upper part of the Guadalupe River watershed. About 1 m of rain fell during 1 week, and it continued to rain. The runoff flowed into the river and down to Canyon Lake. The lake was already full because of the rain falling on it. The water began to flow over the spillway of the dam. A wall of water over 2 m high and 380 m wide went over the dam. For the next 6 weeks, an amount of water equal to one and a half times the amount of water in the lake flowed over the spillway and into a narrow valley behind Canyon Dam. This torrent of water cut into the valley floor. It washed away the oak trees, mesquite, and topsoil and carried tons of sediment downstream.

When the water stopped flowing, the valley became a gorge. The gorge is 1.6 kilometers (km) long, hundreds of meters wide, and up to 15 m or more deep. The new walls of the gorge exposed limestone rocks dating back 100 million years. Those rocks contain fossils of worms and crustaceans, and tracks of ancient insects and dinosaurs. Teams of scientists are carefully observing the area and recording the evidence they find. The limestone is very brittle and breaks away from the canyon walls.

The other feature that was exposed by the flood was an **earthquake** fault. The **fault** was known to be there before the flood, and now 800 m of the Hidden Valley Fault is visible. The gorge has become a fresh, new laboratory for geologists to study faults found in limestone.

The Gorge Preservation Society (GPS) is a local citizen's group that works with the Guadalupe–Blanco River Authority (GBRA) and the U.S. Army Corps of Engineers to protect and study the gorge. They lead public hikes to some parts of the gorge.

The Canyon Lake flood formed this gorge.

## Big Thompson Canyon Flood of 1976

    The state of Colorado was celebrating its centennial on July 31, 1976. People were enjoying their summer vacations camping along the Big Thompson Canyon. The canyon is northwest of Denver. The town of Estes Park is at the western end of the canyon.

Thunderstorms often occur in the Rocky Mountains, especially in the afternoon. On this day, a thunderstorm formed over the western end of Big Thompson Canyon and didn't move. It dumped over 30 centimeters (cm) of rain in less than 4 hours. The canyon is steep and narrow, and there is little soil to retain the water. By 9:00 p.m. that evening, a wall of water more than 6 m high roared down the canyon. It was a flash flood! It sped down the canyon at about 6 m per second. Huge boulders were swept down the canyon by the wall of water.

People in the lower parts of the canyon had no warning. Because the flood happened so fast, the only way for people to escape was to climb to higher ground in the canyon. Many people didn't have time to get out of the way of the water. There were 145 deaths. A lot of things were destroyed, including 400 cars, 418 houses, and 52 businesses. Most of the main highway along the canyon was washed out. More than 800 people were evacuated by helicopter the next morning. The Big Thompson Canyon Flood was one of the deadliest flash floods ever reported in the United States.

Since this event in 1976, early-warning systems have been put in place. This advance notice about possible flash floods helps people move to safety.

**Many houses were destroyed in the Big Thompson Canyon Flood.**

## Mount St. Helens Eruption of 1980

Mount St. Helens is a volcano in the state of Washington. It is part of a chain of volcanoes called the Cascade Range. On March 20, 1980, an earthquake happened. The north side of the mountain started to bulge.

Two months later, with little warning, another earthquake happened. On May 18, at 8:32 a.m., a magnitude 5.1 earthquake shook Mount St. Helens.

The bulge disappeared as a large avalanche of rocky debris slid down the side of the volcano. **Pumice** and ash erupted.

The debris filled the valley below Mount St. Helens. Trees toppled over like toothpicks. Over 600 square km were flattened. Volcanic mudflows called lahars spilled into the rivers. There were 57 people killed. An estimated 12 million fish at a hatchery, and 7,000 deer, elk, and bears were also killed. The eruption destroyed or damaged over 200 homes, 27 bridges, 298 km of highway, and 24 km of railways.

**Mount St. Helens after the 1980 eruption**

The May 18 eruption lasted more than 9 hours. The plume of ash reached to over 20 km above sea level. It moved eastward at an average speed of 100 km per hour. Ash traveled as far as Idaho by noon the next day. It was also found on tops of cars and roofs in Edmonton, Alberta, Canada, the next morning.

Since 1980, Mount St. Helens has had several smaller eruptions. Scientists continue to carefully monitor the mountain to learn more about volcanoes and to warn people if they think another eruption is about to happen.

**A view of the ash in Connell, Washington, after the eruption. Ash fell over 57,000 square km.**

**Two scientists standing by fallen trees in Smith Creek valley**

**Homes and highways damaged in the Northridge Earthquake**

## Northridge Earthquake of 1994

At 4:30 a.m., on January 17, 1994, people living in the Los Angeles, California, area got a jolt. It was an earthquake deep under the city of Northridge, California. The earth shook for 15 seconds. The magnitude of the earthquake was 6.7.

Earth's **crust** has a lot of cracks. The cracks are called faults. Earthquakes happen when huge sections of Earth's crust slide past each other on a fault.

The Northridge Earthquake happened on a fault geologists didn't know about. It was a blind thrust fault. Blind thrust faults don't reach all the way up to Earth's surface. They are hidden faults.

Damage was widespread. Sections of major highways fell. Parking structures and office buildings fell apart. Many apartment buildings were beyond repair. Houses in the towns of San Fernando and Santa Monica were also damaged. About 22,000 people lost their homes.

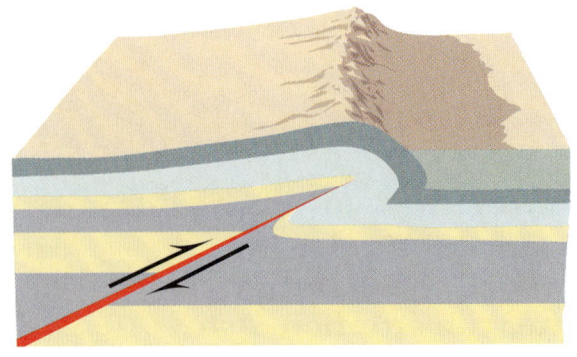

**A diagram of a blind thrust fault**

172

San Francisco soon after the 1906 earthquake, with smoke rising in the background

## San Francisco Earthquake of 1906

Wednesday, April 18, 1906, was the day a big earthquake struck San Francisco, California. People felt the first little shakes at 5:12 a.m. Soon after, the major shaking started. It lasted 47 seconds. People as far away as southern California, Oregon, and central Nevada felt it. The magnitude of the earthquake was about 7.9.

Movement on the San Andreas Fault caused the 1906 earthquake. The fault broke at Earth's surface for a distance of 470 km. Cracks opened and cliffs formed where sections of land fell. Land near the San Francisco Bay settled as a result of the shaking. The settling and shaking caused buildings to fall. Great fires broke out because gas pipes broke. And the fires burned because there was no water to put them out due to water pipe damage.

Earthquakes usually last only a few seconds. Scientists can't predict earthquakes yet, but **engineers** can help people build stronger structures to minimize the damage.

**The town of La Conchita at the base of an unstable hill**

## La Conchita Landslides of 1995 and 2005

Landslides occur when rocks and soil quickly slide downhill. Some areas are more likely to have landslides. The hillside above La Conchita, California, is one of those areas. This small town has had two large landslides. The slides killed people and damaged buildings and cars.

The landslide shown here happened on March 4, 1995. Many people were evacuated because of the slide. Houses nearest the landslide were completely destroyed. No one was killed or injured.

People continued to live in the area below the hillside. Another landslide happened on January 10, 2005. It destroyed or damaged 36 houses and killed 10 people. This kind of land movement happens so quickly, it is often impossible to get out of the way.

This landslide is another example of erosion and deposition. You can see where the sand and mud eroded from the top of the hill. You can also see where the sediment was deposited on the edge of town.

# Yosemite Rockfall of 1996

On July 10, 1996, Ernie Milan was jogging on a trail in Yosemite National Park. Ernie was a trail worker for the National Park Service, so he knew the area well. He heard a loud boom. Dust started swirling around him. Day turned into night. What happened?

A giant mass of **granite**, weighing nearly 70,000 tons, broke loose from a cliff. It fell 600 m to the valley floor. Hundreds of trees were knocked over. One person was killed, and several others were injured. Ernie was not hurt.

Scientists estimated that the rock hit the floor at 400 km per hour. There is no way to stop rockfalls or predict when they will happen again.

Rockfalls happen where loose or cracked rocks are on steep slopes. Rockfalls may happen along road cuts and other excavations. Rockfalls start when rocks are dislodged by freezing or thawing of water or by heavy rainfall. Rockfalls can also be triggered by ground shaking from earthquakes. They generally occur without warning.

Rockfalls happen all over the world. They are a natural kind of weathering and erosion. Most rockfalls are not observed by people. But scientists try to learn what they can from these rockfalls. Some day scientists might be able to predict when a mass of rock is ready to break away.

A 70,000-ton mass of granite fell to the floor of Yosemite Valley.

# Monumental Rocks

Humans build monuments to honor important people and events. Monuments are built to last a long time. They are usually large structures. If you were going to build a monument, what would you make it out of? Rock would be a good choice.

From ancient times to the present, people have made monuments out of rock. Why? Because rock is found everywhere. Rock can be cut and shaped. And most of all, rock lasts a long time. Some rocks are nearly as old as Earth itself. Some structures made of rock have been standing for thousands of years.

**The Great Pyramid and Sphinx**

# The Great Pyramid

Did you know that the Great Pyramid in Egypt is almost completely solid? The only spaces inside are a few hallways and rooms. The pyramid is made out of about 2,300,000 blocks of limestone and granite! The average block weighs about as much as two cars. The largest blocks weigh as much as six cars.

As big as it is, the Great Pyramid was made to honor just one person. It was built around 2700 BCE to hold the body of the pharaoh Khufu. He was a ruler of ancient Egypt.

Each building block in the pyramid was pulled to the site on a wooden sled. Workers used copper axes, chisels, and saws to cut and fit the stones. Today, people wonder how such a building was made without iron tools.

Limestone for the pyramid's center was cut from nearby cliffs. That way, the stone did not have to be moved very far. Granite for the walls and doorways came from almost 1,000 kilometers (km) up the Nile River. Nicer-looking limestone for the outside of the pyramid came from a few kilometers away. By using barges, they floated the limestone down the river to the building site. Today, the polished limestone shell is gone. The stone was "recycled" in the 1300s to rebuild a city damaged by earthquakes.

## What Is Limestone?

Limestone is a sedimentary rock that forms from calcium carbonate. Limestone forms under water. Tiny bits of calcium carbonate, some from shells of organisms, drift to the bottom of the ocean or bays. These pieces of calcium carbonate pile up for millions of years. The layer of calcium carbonate gets thicker and thicker. After a very long time, the bits of calcium carbonate turn into limestone.

# The Taj Mahal

The Taj Mahal in Agra, India, is one of the wonders of the world. Many agree that it is the most beautiful building of all time. The Taj Mahal's designer was Shah Jahan (1592–1666). He built the monument to honor his wife, Mumtaz Mahal (1593–1631).

The Taj Mahal, which means "Crown Palace," is made entirely of white marble. Builders from all over the Middle East worked 22 years to make it. Inside the Taj Mahal, colorful marble was cut and pieced together like a puzzle. Forty-three different kinds of gemstones were used for decoration.

## What Is Marble?

Marble is a metamorphic rock. Metamorphic rocks form when one kind of rock changes into another kind of rock. This usually happens when heat and pressure act on a rock for a long time.

Marble starts out as limestone. When limestone gets buried deep inside Earth, the pressure builds. The temperature goes up. After millions of years, the limestone changes into marble.

# The Vietnam Veterans Memorial

The Taj Mahal and the Great Pyramid each honor a single person. The Vietnam Veterans Memorial was built to honor all the Americans who died in the Vietnam War (1955–1975). It was the idea of Vietnam veteran Jan Scruggs.

A competition was held to design the memorial. Maya Lin's (1959– ) plan was chosen. At the time, Lin was 21 years old. She was a student at Yale University. Lin designed the monument as a black granite wall. The wall forms a V. She wanted the rock to rise out of the ground like two arms to embrace people. One arm points to the Washington Monument. The other arm points to the Lincoln Memorial.

The wall was finished in 1982. The names of more than 58,000 military men and women are written on the wall. Many people didn't like Lin's design at the time. But the memorial she designed is one of the most visited sites in Washington, DC.

Each year millions of people visit the Vietnam Veterans Memorial, designed by Maya Lin (right).

## What Is Granite?

Granite is an igneous rock. That means it started as melted rock deep under Earth's surface. As the melted rock moved toward the surface, it cooled and crystallized. When you look closely at granite, you can see the crystals of the different minerals.

There are only a few places in the world where black granite is found. The beautiful black granite in the Vietnam Veterans Memorial comes from India.

# The Washington Monument

George Washington died in 1799 at his home in Virginia. That year, Congress voted to move his body to the capital city. They wanted to bury it under a marble monument. But Washington's body was never moved, and 85 years passed before a monument was completed. During that time, politicians fought. There were problems raising money for the monument. Sometimes there weren't enough railway cars to deliver the marble. For 2 decades, work stopped completely.

After the Civil War (1861–1865), interest in the monument rose again. People were worried about it. They said the base was not strong enough to support the finished building. Some of the marble blocks were splitting. The original plans had been lost. Many thought the monument was ugly. Some wanted to knock it down and start over. Others wanted a new design. Finally work went on after the foundation was made stronger. The upper two-thirds of the structure was built.

The outside of the monument was constructed from marble taken from quarries in Maryland. At first, the two sections looked the same. But over time wind and rain have caused the marble sections to weather differently. Can you see a color difference between the original marble from one quarry and the later marble from a different quarry?

The great stone monument was finally completed in 1884. It is 169.3 meters (m) tall, which makes it the tallest structure in Washington, DC. It is also the tallest stone structure in the world!

# Geoscientists at Work

Where do **geoscientists** go to do their work? The answer is, just about everywhere. That's because the prefix *geo–* means Earth. Geoscientists observe, investigate, and test landforms all over Earth. Their job is to discover, manage, and protect Earth's natural systems. Earth's rocks, minerals, soils, water, air, plants, animals, and fossil fuels together are called **natural resources**. Geoscientists study the history, distribution, use, and conservation of Earth's limited, valuable, nonliving natural resources.

Most geoscientists spend a lot of time doing fieldwork. That means they are outside in direct contact with Earth. Most geoscientists have a specialty. They focus on one part of the Earth system. And they use instruments designed by and with engineers to collect data about the Earth system they study.

## Marine Geologists

Marine geologists study the ocean floor. They also study the boundary between the ocean floor and the continents, including continental shelves, estuaries, and bays.

Of course, landforms on Earth exist on land, but they can also be found under the water. Mountains, valleys, volcanoes, islands, plains, and canyons all exist in the ocean. In fact, Earth's highest peaks, deepest valleys, and largest flat plains are all in the ocean.

Marine geologists work with acoustic engineers to develop sonar instruments that allow them to "see" underwater structures by bouncing sound waves off rock formations. Sonar can show the size and location of volcanoes and canyons in deep water. Marine geologists use these data to map the bottom of the ocean, one of the most geologically active regions on Earth.

# Atmospheric Scientists

Atmospheric scientists study the composition and activities of Earth's air. They may study weather and the effects of solar radiation on the atmosphere. They may also study atmospheric chemistry, including air pollution, global climate dynamics, and climate change.

Atmospheric scientists depend on a whole family of engineers to develop the instrumentation (weather balloons, gas samplers, aircraft, spacecraft, and satellites) to help them gather the data they need to learn about atmospheric phenomena.

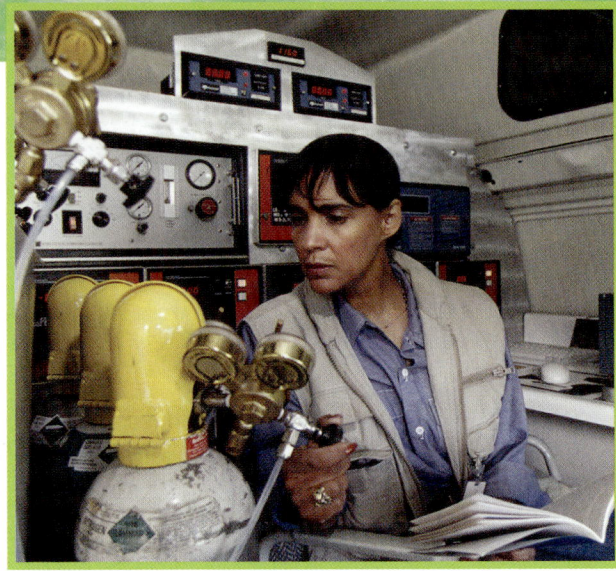

# Seismologists

Seismologists are the earth scientists who study earthquakes. They use seismographs and computer programs to find and monitor fault lines. They place motion-sensing instruments along known faults to collect data. These data help them develop systems to alert people when large, destructive earthquakes are about to happen.

# Structural Geologists

Structural geologists record the shape of Earth's surface. They also study the massive forces that produce earthquakes and create mountains. They use maps and computer programs to analyze changes to Earth's surface.

## Hydrologists

Hydrologists inventory and monitor Earth's fresh water. They measure the quantity and quality of drinking water in lakes, rivers, and wells. They monitor the amount and speed of water flowing in rivers and streams to anticipate the risk of flooding and soil erosion. Hydrologists use tools such as flow meters, depth meters, pH meters, and chemical tests.

## Petroleum Geologists

Petroleum geologists explore Earth for deposits of oil and natural gas. They attempt to find the particular rock formations deep underground that contain these resources to produce petroleum. To do so, they send powerful sound waves into Earth and analyze the reflected sound waves using computer programs. When promising rock formations are detected, engineers then drill down to see if there is actually oil and natural gas. If they find deposits, the resources can be extracted and used as an energy source.

## Volcanologists

Volcanologists study volcanoes and possible volcanic regions. They use tiltmeters, seismometers, and computers to determine when and where volcanoes might erupt. Volcanologists also study areas where volcanic activity is occurring. They determine if geothermal engineers might tap this heat source to generate electricity.

## Soil Scientists

Soil scientists study the composition and quality of soils. They look for ways to keep farm soils stable and fertile for growing food crops. Soil engineers design field layout and maintenance plans to prevent soil erosion.

**Corn and alfalfa crops are planted in alternating rows to protect them from soil erosion.**

**A cotton field with grass planted in rows to prevent wind erosion of the soil**

**A soil scientist field mapping soils using GPS technology**

## Soil Science at Home

Many home gardeners improve their garden soil with compost. Composting is a way to produce humus. With a little simple home engineering, you can make a compost bin. Toss in vegetable waste from the kitchen, lawn and plant clippings, dead leaves, and other plant material. As bacteria and fungi decompose the organic material, it slowly changes into pure dark brown humus. The humus can be worked into soil to enrich its fertility.

Kitchen waste and leaves are collected and broken down in a compost bin.

After several months, the compost has turned into humus and is added to garden soil.

A home gardener uses compost in garden beds to enrich the soil with humus.

Garden plants growing in soil with humus are large and healthy.

Sand, gravel, and pebbles are the aggregates used in concrete.

# Making Concrete

Concrete is a rocklike construction material that is made by people. You have probably seen a lot of places where **concrete** is used. Many highways are made of concrete. Bridges and overpasses are often made of concrete. Dams and stadiums are made of concrete. What is concrete? You might see cement trucks at construction sites. They should be called concrete trucks because the material they carry in the big, round container is actually concrete. Most modern concrete is a mixture of **Portland cement** and aggregates. Aggregates are pieces of rock of different sizes. Small aggregates include sand and gravel. Larger aggregates include pebbles of several sizes.

Portland cement is a fine gray powder made from limestone. Limestone is dug out of a quarry. Then it is heated to a high temperature in a furnace and ground into a fine powder. When Portland cement is mixed with water, it makes a sticky, mudlike mixture. Over time, the cement mixture cures (hardens). The mixture changes into a solid, hard lump. Cured cement is as hard as rock.

In order to take full advantage of this **property** of cement, aggregates are added to the sticky mixture. The cement bonds to the pieces of rock and sand, cementing them together into one strong mass. The mixture of cement, water, and aggregates is a thick fluid that can be poured into forms. The big container on the back of the cement truck is always turning around and around. The motion keeps the concrete moving around so it won't harden inside the truck.

Cement trucks usually don't travel very far from the plant where they load up with ingredients. Many contractors require that the concrete be poured within 90 minutes after loading. If the concrete hardens in the truck, it might be necessary to use jackhammers to break up the concrete. Foundations for buildings are made by pouring concrete into forms. When the concrete foundation is cured, the building is constructed on top of the foundation.

**Cement trucks deliver concrete to construction sites.**

**Concrete is poured into forms to make foundations for buildings.**

**The Roman Colosseum**

The use of concrete for roads, buildings, bridges, and wharfs is not new. Concrete was invented and used widely by Romans more than 2,000 years ago. The Roman Colosseum, built in the year 70 BCE, is the largest colosseum in the world and is still standing. Concrete harbors built about the same time in the Bay of Pozzuoli near Naples are still strong. They have withstood battering from ocean waves and tides. They have endured countless earthquakes for 2,000 years. Modern concrete harbors constructed using Portland cement concrete last as few as 50 years. Why the big difference?

The difference is how the concrete is made. A team of scientists and engineers led by professors of civil and environmental engineering at the University of California, Berkeley, studied the concrete in these old structures. In 2013, the team leaders, Marie Jackson and Paulo Monteiro, announced the results of their analysis of the Roman concrete.

They knew from historical records that Roman-engineered concrete contained slightly different materials than modern Portland cement concrete. Roman concrete used baked limestone (like Portland cement). But it also used locally available volcanic ash, called pozzolan. The pozzolan seems to be the secret ingredient that makes the Roman concrete so strong and durable.

**The wharf area in the Bay of Pozzuoli**

The researchers also discovered that the Romans converted the limestone into lime by heating it to a much lower temperature than the 1,450 degrees Celsius (°C) needed to produce Portland cement. The cooking part of the cement-making process is important. It is important because it takes more fuel to generate the heat to convert limestone into Portland cement. The greater the amount of fuel burned, the greater the amount of greenhouse gas ($CO_2$) produced as a waste product. Using the Roman formula for converting limestone to lime requires less fuel, resulting in less $CO_2$ released into the atmosphere.

The potential engineering advantages presented by these discoveries are huge. The new way for making concrete can produce a stronger building material. Structural engineers can use it to design safer, stronger buildings, bridges, wharfs, and roads. Concrete manufacturers will be able to use much less energy to convert limestone into concrete-grade lime. The Roman concrete recipe will save energy and reduce the amount of $CO_2$ going into the atmosphere. And large deposits of pozzolan are available around the world.

Concrete foundations are different in different regions. For example, concrete in North Carolina is different from concrete in Texas, Wisconsin, or Oregon. That's because the aggregates mixed with the cement are always from the local region. It is too expensive to transport sand, gravel, and pebbles over long distances to make concrete, so the aggregates are local. Where did the aggregates come from to make the concrete foundation used to build your school?

**Concrete can be used as stepping stones in a garden.**

**This school has concrete steps and walls.**

Cutting the clay with a wire

Rolling the clay flat with a rolling pin

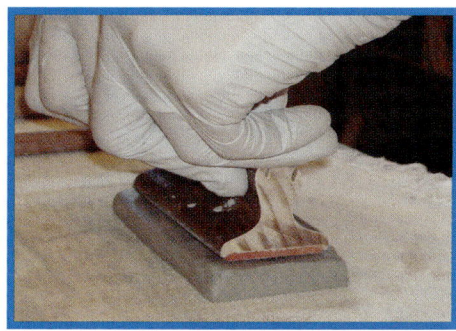

Using a stamp to press a shape into the clay

# Earth Materials in Art

Rose Craig (1943–) is an artist. Rose makes beautiful watercolor paintings, and she is a skilled graphic artist and illustrator. For many years, Rose worked for the FOSS science program, drawing illustrations for articles in the *Science Resources* books. Rose has one other artistic interest, too. Rose makes ceramic tiles. Ceramic tiles are made of clay. As you know, clay is an earth material, so Rose is an earth material artist.

This is how she makes her beautiful tiles. First, she places a big pile of clay on her worktable. She uses a big rolling pin to flatten the clay into one big, thin sheet. The rolling process is very similar to rolling pie dough for a pie crust. When the clay is rolled out just right, Rose uses a straightedge and a knife to cut the slab of clay into rectangular pieces. Rose then uses rubber stamps to press a shape into the surface of the soft clay. She might use a fish shape, a flower shape, or a dragonfly shape, and then trim around the shape. Now Rose has to wait for the clay to dry.

A fish shape stamped in the clay

A kiln is a very hot oven that changes the clay into ceramic tiles.

Finished tiles

After 3 or 4 days, the tiles are dry and ready to be decorated with special paints called glazes. First, Rose paints a background color on the tiles. When that is dry, she presses the design into the clay again and enhances it with bright contrasting colors.

When the tiles are painted just the way Rose likes them, she puts them in a kiln. A kiln is an oven that gets really hot, much hotter than a pizza oven. The intense heat changes the clay into rock-hard ceramic tiles. The colored glaze becomes intensely shiny and hard as glass. The finished product is beautiful and useful. Because ceramic tiles are waterproof, they are good surfaces for sinks and counters that get wet. They are also useful outside in the garden or on a deck because sunshine, rain, or snow will not damage them.

# Where Do Rocks Come From?

**W**here do rocks come from? This question keeps geologists busy. Even though they don't have all the answers, they know a lot about where rocks come from.

Earth is about 4.6 billion years old. The oldest dated rock found on Earth is about 4 billion years old. That's almost as old as Earth. Scientists have also found crystals of a mineral called zircon that were formed 4.4 billion years ago.

There are three big groups of rocks: **igneous**, sedimentary, and **metamorphic**. All the rocks in a group have similar origins, often inside Earth.

Earth is like an egg. An egg has a hard outer layer called the shell. Earth has a hard outer layer called the crust. Earth's crust is made of solid rock.

Under an egg's shell is the fluid egg white. Under Earth's solid crust is the **mantle**, partly melted rock that flows like really thick toothpaste. It is hot inside Earth. It is so hot that rocks and minerals melt.

An egg has a yolk in the center. Earth has a metal **core** in its center. Earth's core is made of iron and nickel.

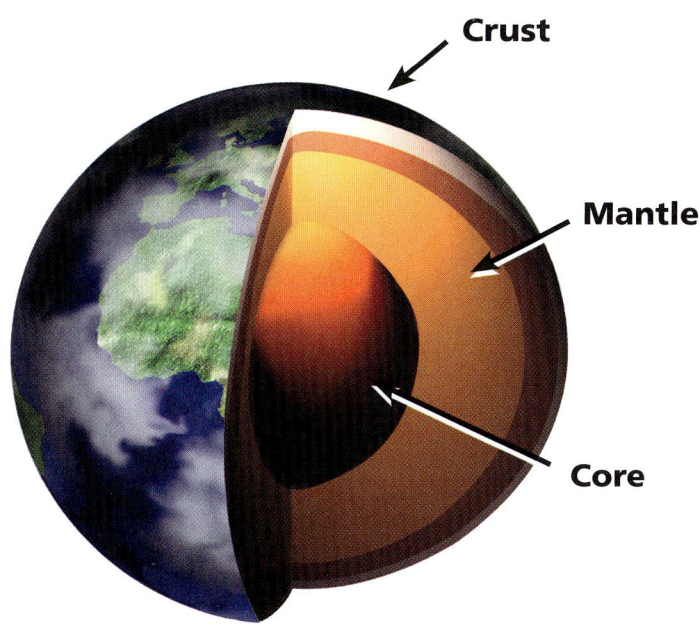

**A cross section of Earth**

## Igneous Rocks

Igneous rocks start out as melted rock deep in Earth's crust. Sometimes the melted rock, called **magma**, comes to the surface in volcanoes. The magma pours out as lava. When lava cools and hardens, it forms new rocks. The basalt you tested for calcite is volcanic igneous rock. Much of the rock in the Cascade Mountains of the Pacific Northwest is basalt.

Other times, magma cools slowly and hardens below the surface. Earthquakes and other changes in Earth's crust might bring these igneous rocks to the surface years later. The granite you studied cooled below Earth's surface. The Sierra Nevada in central California and the Rocky Mountains in Colorado, Wyoming, and Montana are mostly granite mountains.

**Basalt**

**Granite**

Sandstone

## Sedimentary Rocks

Sedimentary rocks form from bits and pieces of recycled rocks and minerals. **Sandstone** is an example of a sedimentary rock. Sandstone starts as big rocks in the mountains. Over time, the rocks crack and break into smaller pieces. This process is called weathering.

Water can cause weathering. Water freezes in cracks in rocks. It expands when it freezes and breaks the rocks apart. Tree roots also cause weathering. Roots grow into cracks in rocks and break big pieces of rock loose.

Loose rocks tumble downhill and break into smaller pieces. Pieces might end up in streams and rivers. The pieces get banged around and broken into smaller and smaller pieces. Eventually the rocks from the mountain are reduced to tiny pieces of sand.

Sand often gets deposited in the ocean and bays. Layers of sand build up. The layers of sand are called sediment. As millions of years pass, the sand gets buried under more layers of sediment. Sand particles are pressed and stuck together. The sand turns into the sedimentary rock sandstone.

Sedimentary rocks often have bits of sand and gravel you can see. Sometimes sedimentary rocks contain fossils of shells, animals, or plants. Sedimentary rocks form in layers. If the rocks are still in their natural site, you can often see the layers.

**Sandstone layers**

**A trilobite fossil**

**A fern fossil**

**A shell fossil**

# Metamorphic Rocks

*Meta-* means change. *Morph* means shape or form. Metamorphic rocks change from one kind of rock into another kind of rock. The starting rocks can be igneous, sedimentary, or even other metamorphic rocks. The rocks change because of heat and pressure. If a rock gets buried deep in Earth's crust or touches hot lava, it will change into metamorphic rock.

Heat and pressure can turn sandstone into quartzite. Limestone can become marble. Shale can change into slate. Heat and pressure can turn granite into gneiss (pronounced "nice").

**Changing into Metamorphic Rocks**

Sandstone changes into quartzite.

Limestone changes into marble.

Shale changes into slate.

Granite changes into gneiss.

# The Rock Cycle

Metamorphic rocks aren't the only rocks that can change. Over time, any kind of rock can change into any other kind of rock. The changes from igneous to sedimentary to metamorphic and back to igneous are the **rock cycle**.

For example, a piece of igneous granite might weather into sediments. The sediments can end up in a layer with other sediments. After a long time, the sediments might change into sedimentary sandstone.

The sandstone could get heated by a lava flow or buried under other sediments. The heat and pressure might change the sandstone into metamorphic quartzite. And finally, the quartzite might be carried down into Earth's mantle where it will melt. After millions of years, the rock material might come back in a new piece of igneous granite.

Rocks don't all follow this path through the rock cycle. The important thing to remember is that all rocks change. Any rock can change into any other kind of rock. Study the rock cycle illustration to see how.

It is even possible for a rock to re-form as the same kind of rock. For example, sandstone might weather into sand. The sand could pile up in a bay. After millions of years, the sand might become new sandstone.

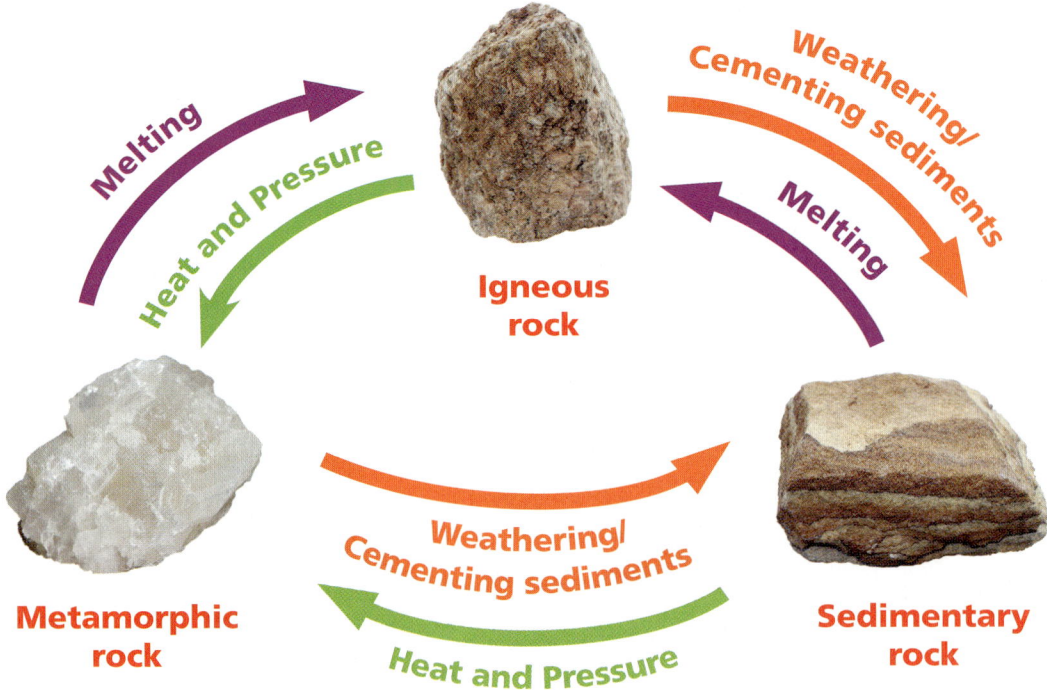

**Any kind of rock can change into any other kind of rock. This is the rock cycle.**

# Rock Samples

This table shows several examples of sedimentary, metamorphic, and igneous rocks. How many of them have you held in your hand?

| Sedimentary | Metamorphic | Igneous |
|---|---|---|
| Limestone | Marble | Basalt |
| Sandstone | Quartzite | Obsidian |
| Shale | Slate | Tuff |
| Conglomerate | Gneiss | Pumice |
| Breccia | Schist | Granite |

Life Science

**FOSS Science Resources**

# Environments

# Table of Contents

**Investigation 1: Environmental Factors**

Two Terrestrial Environments . . . . . . . . . . . . . . . . . . . . . 205
Setting Up a Terrarium . . . . . . . . . . . . . . . . . . . . . . . . . . 215
Isopods . . . . . . . . . . . . . . . . . . . . . . . . . . . . . . . . . . . . . . . 218
Amazon Rain Forest Journal . . . . . . . . . . . . . . . . . . . . . 220

**Investigation 2: Ecosystems**

Freshwater Environments . . . . . . . . . . . . . . . . . . . . . . . 229
What Is an Ecosystem? . . . . . . . . . . . . . . . . . . . . . . . . . 234
Food Chains and Food Webs . . . . . . . . . . . . . . . . . . . . 237
Human Activities and Aquatic Ecosystems . . . . . . . . . . 244
Comparing Aquatic and Terrestrial Ecosystems . . . . . . 248
Animal Sensory Systems . . . . . . . . . . . . . . . . . . . . . . . 250
Saving Murrelets through Mimicry . . . . . . . . . . . . . . . . 257

**Investigation 3: Brine Shrimp Hatching**

Brine Shrimp . . . . . . . . . . . . . . . . . . . . . . . . . . . . . . . . . 260
The Mono Lake Story . . . . . . . . . . . . . . . . . . . . . . . . . . 261
What Happens When Ecosystems Change? . . . . . . . . . 268
The Shrimp Club . . . . . . . . . . . . . . . . . . . . . . . . . . . . . . 273
Variation and Selection . . . . . . . . . . . . . . . . . . . . . . . . 281

**Investigation 4: Range of Tolerance**

Environmental Scientists . . . . . . . . . . . . . . . . . . . . . . . 288
Range of Tolerance . . . . . . . . . . . . . . . . . . . . . . . . . . . . 293
How Organisms Depend on One Another . . . . . . . . . . 295
Animals from the Past . . . . . . . . . . . . . . . . . . . . . . . . . 298
Darkling Beetles . . . . . . . . . . . . . . . . . . . . . . . . . . . . . . 304

# Two Terrestrial Environments

Environmental scientists know a lot about Earth's **environments**. There are **aquatic** environments and **terrestrial** environments. *Terrestrial* refers to Earth's land. There are six major terrestrial environments in the world. They are tropical rain forest, desert, temperate deciduous forest, grassland, taiga, and tundra.

Each environment can be described in terms of **environmental factors**. Environmental factors are **living** and **nonliving** parts of the environment. The living parts of an environment are all the plants and animals that live and **thrive** in that place. The main nonliving components that define the six environments are **temperature**, rainfall, and soil type.

The tropical rain forest environment is different from the desert environment. The tropical rain forest is hot and wet, and the soil is poor because it lacks **nutrients**. The desert environment is dry and sandy. Most deserts are hot, but some are cold. Let's take a closer look at these two terrestrial environments and compare the living and nonliving environmental factors.

**A tropical rain forest environment and a desert environment**

205

# Living Factors in Tropical Rain Forests

Tropical rain forests are home to more kinds of life than any other terrestrial environment. At least half of all the different kinds of plants and animals in the world live in tropical rain forests. Tropical rain forests are also the winter homes for many birds that live in other places the rest of the year.

Life in the rain forest can be divided into layers. Each layer has different plants and animals. Most of the tropical rain forest plants are trees. They grow to heights of 20 to 30 meters (m). Because the trees grow very close to one another, their tops grow together. This forms a broad **canopy**, or roof, above the rain forest.

**A tropical rain forest canopy**

The highest layer in the rain forest is the canopy. There is a lot of sunlight in the canopy layer. This is where most of the rain forest animals live. Monkeys, sloths, and bats spend most of their time here. Tree frogs and snakes live in the treetops along with toucans, hummingbirds, ants, and beetles. These are just a few of the millions of different kinds of animals that live in the canopy. Orchids, ferns, and other "air plants" grow on the branches of the canopy trees. Air plants use the trees for support and get water from the falling rain.

The layer below the canopy is the **understory**. Very little sunlight makes it through the canopy to the understory. It is a dark place full of tree trunks, young thin trees, and broad-leafed plants that thrive in shady conditions. A number of these plants are popular house plants in the United States. The animals living in this layer include jaguars, leopards, frogs, snakes, parakeets, and many kinds of **insects**.

The bottom layer is the forest floor. The forest floor is often covered with moss and wet leaves. Almost no sunlight makes it to the floor. This is where centipedes and scorpions live. Many insects, such as termites, ants, cockroaches, and beetles, also live here. Earthworms and **fungi** use the dead leaves as **food**. Larger animals, such as tapirs, dig up roots in the forest floor.

Can you identify the tapir, frog, and sloth?

207

## Living Factors in Deserts

Some people think of deserts as hot, dry wastelands. That can be true, sometimes. In areas of shifting sand where it never rains and strong winds blow, such as parts of the Sahara Desert in Africa, plants and animals are rare. But deserts have areas that get some water, and those areas are full of life.

Fewer kinds of plants and animals live in deserts than in wetter environments. Desert plants and animals have **structures** and **behaviors** that help them survive in a dry environment. You can see plants and animals with these adaptations in parts of the deserts found in the southwestern United States.

**Sand dunes in the Sahara Desert in northern Africa**

**The Mojave Desert in the American southwest**

In deserts, some plants grow far apart. Their root systems spread over a large area. This distance lets them get water and nutrients without competition from other plants. Some desert plants, such as the mesquite tree, send their roots deep into the desert soil. Mesquite tree roots might go down 81 m to reach water.

Cacti store water in their broad, fleshy blades or columns, which are actually stems. They use the stored water during long dry periods. Cacti don't have leaves but they do have spines. The seeds of some desert plants can lie in the soil for years until it rains enough for them to sprout.

**A saguaro cactus**

A desert tortoise

A desert iguana

A desert bighorn sheep

Animals survive well in the southwest deserts. Insects, spiders, reptiles, birds, and mammals, such as bighorn sheep, live in deserts. Many desert animals are **nocturnal**. Nocturnal animals avoid the heat by coming out only at night.

Desert tortoises are comfortable in the desert. They dig deep **burrows**. When it is too hot or too cold, they have a safe place to stay. Tortoises eat many kinds of plants, especially flowers and fruits. Sometimes they will even eat the moist pads of cactus plants. Tortoises drink a lot of water when they can and store it in their bladders.

A spadefoot toad

Spadefoot toads are **amphibians**. That means they have to **reproduce** in water. Is the desert a good place for them to live? Yes, because they have a behavior to help them survive. When the weather is hot and dry, the toads burrow about a meter underground. They can stay there for up to 9 months. They become **dormant** and live on the fat stored in their bodies. When it rains, spadefoot toads leave their burrows and find mates. The females lay eggs in rain puddles. The eggs soon hatch into tadpoles. The tadpoles grow into young toads. The young toads have to become adults before the puddles dry up or they will die. In a couple of months, the adult toads burrow down into the ground and wait for next year's rain.

Every desert plant and animal has structures and behaviors that allow it to survive and thrive in the hot, dry desert.

The stem of a barrel cactus is round with ribs that are covered with spines.

## Nonliving Factors in Rain Forests

Look at the map to see where tropical rain forests are on Earth. Can you find the ones in Australia? In Asia? In Africa? In Central America? In South America? Where else are there tropical rain forests? Find the line that shows the equator.

**Tropical rain forests are found near the equator.**

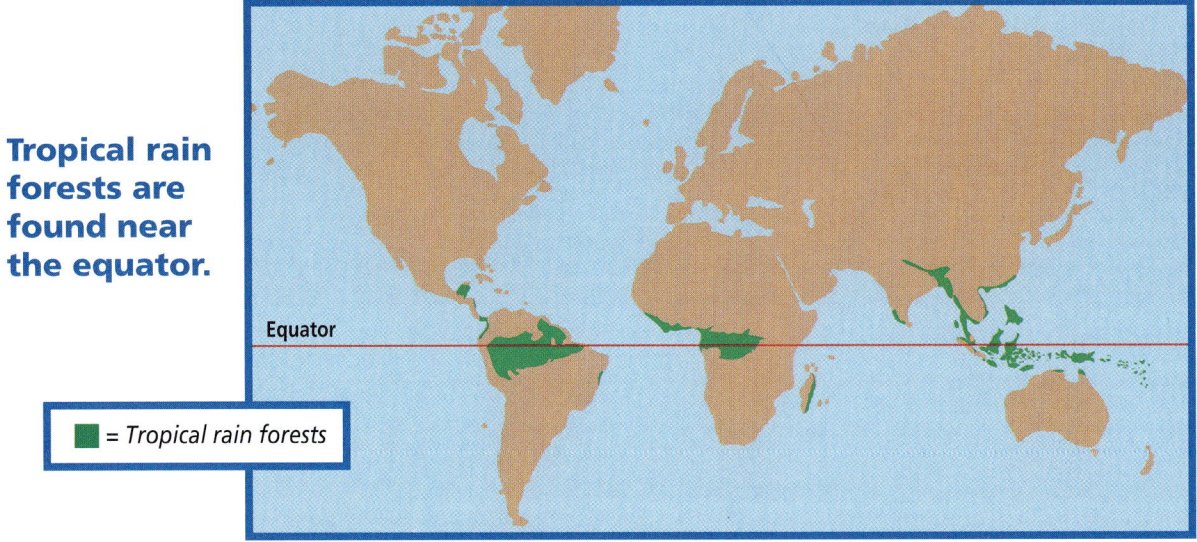

= Tropical rain forests

Tropical rain forests are wet and hot all year. The rainfall in rain forests is about 200 to 450 centimeters (cm) per year. How does that compare to where you live? Here are average rainfalls for five cities in the United States.

- Houston, Texas = 122 cm
- Charlotte, North Carolina = 110 cm
- Chicago, Illinois = 92 cm
- Anchorage, Alaska = 40.5 cm
- Phoenix, Arizona = 21.5 cm

The rain forest soil is shallow and not very **fertile**. Most of the nutrients that plants need to survive are in the trees. If the trees are cut down and taken away, the nutrients are lost to the rain forest environment. This is why it takes a long time for tropical rain forests to grow back once they are destroyed.

**El Yunque National Forest**

## Nonliving Factors in Deserts

Scientists define a desert environment as any place on Earth that receives less than 25 cm of rain per year. Soils are rocky or sandy in deserts. Water runs off the land quickly or sinks into the sand. Water **evaporates**, or dries up, quickly in the desert. Most of the small amount of water that does fall on the desert is lost before plants and animals can get to it. Look at the map to see where deserts are on Earth.

**Deserts are found north and south of the equator.**

Deserts are the hottest places on Earth during the summer. But during the winter, the temperatures can drop below freezing. Snow is seen regularly in parts of the deserts in southern California, China, and South America.

About 20 percent of Earth's land surface is desert. The small amount of rain, high temperatures, and large temperature changes from season to season make life challenging in the desert.

**Snow on Joshua trees in the Mojave Desert**

**A tropical rain forest environment**

**A desert environment**

## Thinking about Environmental Factors

1. What are the environmental factors that define a tropical rain forest environment?
2. What are the environmental factors that define a desert environment?
3. What are some of the structures and behaviors that help organisms survive in the desert?

# Setting Up a Terrarium

People enjoy having plants around. Some people grow plants in gardens. Others grow plants in pots in their homes. Some people grow plants in **terrariums**. A terrarium is a container with plants growing inside. A terrarium can also be a **habitat** for small animals found in a garden.

Terrariums can be any size and shape. Any clear container can be made into a terrarium. It should have a deep layer of soil and a lid to keep moisture inside. It also needs to be large enough to hold the plants and animals you want to keep inside it. A well-planned terrarium provides a good environment for living things.

So what makes a good terrarium environment? All **organisms** have needs. Plants need air, water, nutrients, light, space, and the proper temperature. Animals need air, water, food, space, shelter, and the proper temperature. Plants can be a very good source of food or shelter for some animals.

Not every kind of plant needs the same environment. Some plants need a lot of water. Others require only a small amount. Some plants need bright light, while others thrive in shade. Some plants grow best in cool temperatures, and others thrive in heat. Plan your terrarium to suit the organisms that will live in it.

**Terrariums are many sizes and shapes.**

215

**Plants need light and space to grow.**

An organism's environment is *everything* that surrounds and affects it. Each part or component of an organism's environment is an environmental factor. An environmental factor can be nonliving, such as water, light, and air temperature. Environmental factors also can be living, like all the plants and animals surrounding an organism.

So, when making a terrarium, you need to think about the environmental factors for the plants and animals that will live in it. What kind of soil will you use? Will you have one kind of plant or several kinds? How much water will you provide for the organisms and how often? How will air flow through the container? Where should the terrarium be placed in the room for light and temperature?

A terrarium can be created to represent a desert, grassland, woodland, or rain forest environment. You can add small animals that live in these natural habitats to the terrarium and observe them over time. Reptiles, amphibians, insects, **crustaceans**, worms, and spiders are good animals to place in a terrarium.

**Water is a nonliving environmental factor.**

## Homemade Terrarium

You can make your own terrarium at home using a **recycled** 2-liter (L) clear plastic bottle. Here's how.

### What You Need

- 1 2 L plastic bottle (colorless, clear)
- Soil
- Gravel or small pebbles
- Seeds or small plants
- Scissors
- Water
- Small garden animals
- Piece of carrot

### What You Do

1. Remove the label from the plastic bottle. With help from an adult, cut the bottle about 10 centimeters (cm) from the bottom. Leave the cap on the bottle.

2. Cut four 2 cm slits along the bottom edge of the top part of the bottle.

3. Put a layer of gravel or small pebbles in the base. Add a layer of soil. If you are planting seeds in the terrarium, fill the base with soil almost to the top. Then plant your seeds. If you are planting a small rooted plant, dig a hole in the soil. Place the roots of the plant in the hole. Fill soil in around the roots. Water the soil.

4. Add small garden animals, such as earthworms or isopods. Put a piece of carrot in the terrarium for food.

5. Place the top section of your bottle on the base, fitting the slits over the base. Place the terrarium in an area with some light. Observe how your organisms grow in their environment.

## Thinking about Words

The word *terra* means "earth" or "land." The suffix *-arium* means a place. What do you think *aquarium* means?

# Isopods

**P**ill bugs! Sow bugs! These are two common names people give to **isopods**. Some people confuse isopods with insects. Isopods are not insects because isopods have seven pairs of legs. All insects have only *three* pairs of legs.

All seven pairs of an isopod's legs have the same **function**. Their scientific name indicates this: *iso* means "similar" or "equal," and *pod* means "foot." Isopods use all seven pairs of legs for walking, and nothing else. Insect legs are used for many functions. These include feeding, grasping, jumping, swimming, and carrying. This is another way that isopods are different from insects.

**Isopods**

**Pill bugs**

There are many kinds of isopods, but all are crustaceans. Crustaceans are animals with shells, jaws, and two pairs of antennae. Crustaceans include crabs, shrimp, and lobsters. Most crustaceans live in water and breathe with gills. Isopods are a little different. They can live on land. But they have to be in a moist environment most of the time. As long as they keep their gill-like breathing structures wet, they can breathe. If these structures become dry, the isopod cannot survive. The gills are located behind the last pair of walking legs on the isopod's underside.

Did you observe two different kinds of isopods in class? One kind is dome-shaped and has short antennae. When this isopod senses danger, it can roll up into a ball. That's why it is called a pill bug.

The other isopod is flatter and has longer antennae. It is called a sow bug. A sow bug cannot roll up to protect itself from a hungry spider or insect. But it can run faster than a pill bug.

Sow bugs and pill bugs feed on dead leaves and decaying fruit and seeds. They play an important role in recycling dead plant material in many environments. Where have you found isopods?

**A sow bug**

# Amazon Rain Forest Journal

My name is Lee. My mother is an **entomologist**. That's a biologist who studies insects. She has traveled to the Amazon River in Brazil many times. Her stories about the rain forest always sounded so exciting. I begged Mom for a long time to take me on one of her trips to the rain forest. Finally, she surprised me with a special birthday trip. I wrote a journal about my trip to share my experiences with everyone at school.

## Monday, July 21

It's early morning, and I am sitting in the Manaus airport in Brazil. I can't believe that I'm so far from home in Austin, Texas. Home is 5,472 kilometers (km) away!

We are waiting for a small plane to take us down the Amazon River to the city of Santarém. That's where the ecology research station is. Mom is one of more than 100 scientists who works there.

It's early afternoon now. The flight was great. The rain forest below looked like a green carpet as far as I could see. Mom's friend Kopenawa met us at the airport. She has known Kopenawa for a long time. He has guided her safely through the rain forest many times. He is ready to take us for a short hike in the rain forest. Mom says he knows more about the rain forest environment than almost anyone else.

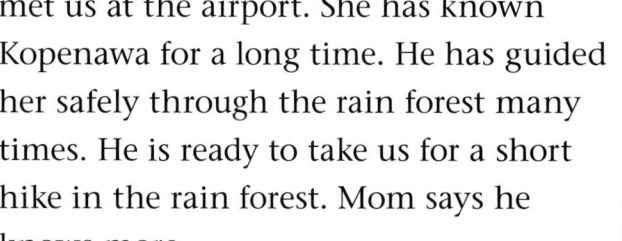

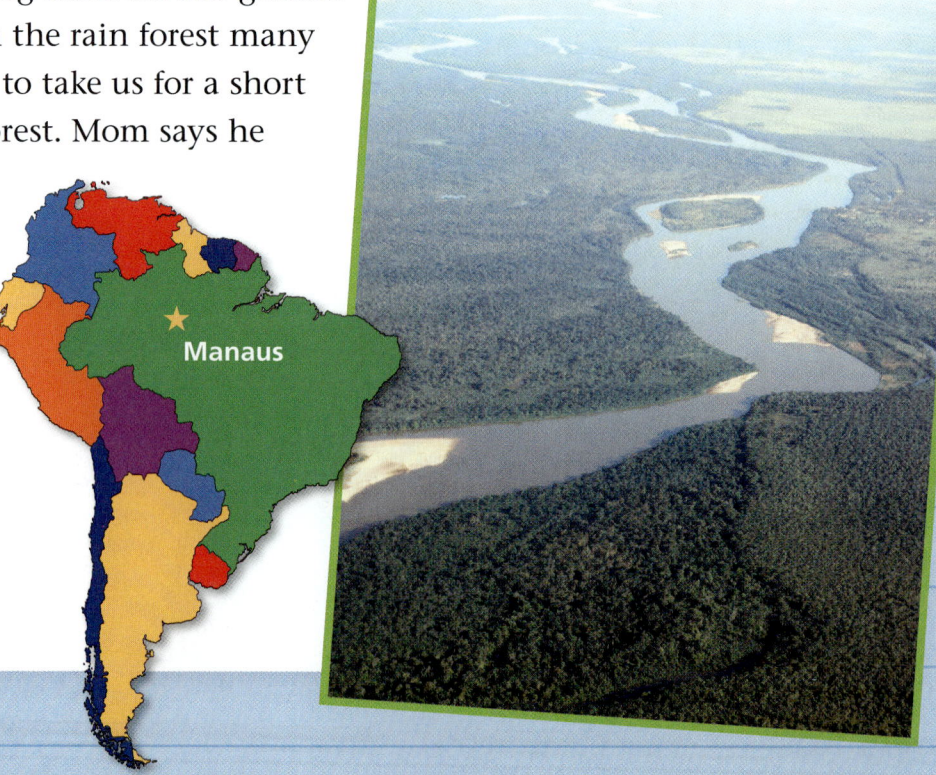

**A green lizard can blend in with plants.**

We're going down the biggest river in the world. Once the boat moves away from the city, I know I am in a new environment. The air is really hot and humid. I can feel sweat soaking my clothes. Everything I see is huge! The trees are the tallest I've ever seen, and there are interesting plants with gigantic leaves everywhere I look.

After traveling a short distance, Kopenawa guided the boat over to the riverbank. We're going into the rain forest!

We are back in Kopenawa's boat after a short hike in the rain forest. From the riverbank, the rain forest looked really dense. I didn't think we would be able to walk through it. But it was much easier to walk when we got away from the river and into the trees. Mom said this is because the tops of the trees form a canopy, or cover. Only a little light can make it through the canopy, so few plants actually grow on the forest floor.

I saw my first rain forest animal. It was a big green lizard! I nearly stepped on it because it blended in so well with the plants. Kopenawa said the lizard's camouflage makes it very hard for **predators** to see. It was hard for me to see, too.

**Leaf-cutter ants**

### Tuesday, July 22

After our short hike in the rain forest yesterday, Kopenawa took us to the research station. We have a little room in a cabin with just screens on the windows. The sounds of the birds and monkeys woke me up early. I ate breakfast in a room full of long tables. Scientists were talking about rainfall, soil, temperature, seed sprouting, parrots, beetles, and a lot more. I was ready to find out more for myself.

Near the cabin I saw a line of thousands of very large ants. They were marching through the rain forest on a trail they made. When I got closer, I could see that many of the ants held pieces of green leaves over their heads. They looked like they were carrying tiny umbrellas. They really looked funny. I asked Kopenawa if they were protecting themselves from the rain. He laughed and told me that they were leaf-cutter ants. They cut pieces out of leaves and carry them back to their underground nests. Their nests are made of hundreds of small rooms, called chambers, under the earth.

The leaf-cutter ants don't eat the leaves. In fact, some of the leaves are poisonous. The ants use the leaves to grow a type of fungus. They chew the leaves. This makes a bed of leaf pulp where the fungus grows. The fungus is what the ants eat.

I asked Kopenawa if the ants ever get lost in the rain forest. The ground is covered with roots, rocks, and plants. I thought they must have trouble finding their way home. Kopenawa explained that the ants put down drops of a chemical, called a pheromone. The pheromones mark the trail for other ants to follow.

**These ants use leaves to grow their own food.**

**Red army ants**

Leaf-cutter ants reproduce with **complete metamorphosis**, like all ants. The queen ant lays eggs that hatch into **larvae**. The adult ants feed fungus to the larvae until the larvae pupate. Soon after, the adults come out. The new ants are called workers. They get right to work cutting leaves and growing fungus.

We kept walking. In half an hour, Kopenawa stopped and pointed to a spot near the trail. More ants! But this time, a battle was going on. A group of red army ants was attacking a group of wasps. Army ants do not eat leaves or fungus. They eat other insects such as wasps, moths, and grasshoppers. Wasps and ants are called social insects because they live together in groups. We watched the ants swarm over the wasps' nest. There were so many army ants that the wasps could not defend themselves. The wasps could only fly away and leave their larvae and eggs behind. The ants carried the wasp eggs and larvae back to their own nest. The eggs and larvae would be food for the rest of the army ants.

A short distance away, we saw a ball of army ants the size of a basketball. Kopenawa said the ants were making a temporary nest. This is the only kind of nest they ever make. The ants hook themselves together in chains. The chains form chambers for the queen and growing larvae. It was like something out of a science fiction movie, a living fort.

Mom told me that the army ants have to keep moving. They eat all the insects and other small animals in their path. They need to keep finding new places to get food.

A coral snake

### Wednesday, July 23

Today we got up very early and went for a hike right after breakfast. Suddenly, Kopenawa put out his hand and stopped me in my tracks. A coral snake was slithering through the leaves on the ground. The snake had bright bands of yellow, red, and black. Some rain forest animals are brightly colored. Often the brightly colored animals are poisonous. The bright colors warn predators to stay away. I kept my distance. Then the snake disappeared into the rain forest.

### Thursday, July 24

Today I went with my mom to her study area. She studies plants and the insects that eat them. I was surprised to hear that most of the trees we were walking under were poisonous. Mom said that's how trees defend themselves against the millions of hungry insects in the rain forest. If the plants didn't have defensive chemicals, all their leaves would be eaten and they would die.

Mom studies why some insects are not affected by the poisonous leaves. Every kind of tree seems to be eaten by one or two kinds of insects. Why can those insects eat leaves that are poisonous to every other kind of insect? That's what Mom tries to figure out.

Mom pointed out a small tree and warned me not to touch it. I thought it might be poisonous, but Mom said no, it was the ants that lived on it. Because this small tree grows in the rain forest understory, it doesn't get much light. It needs every leaf to survive. The ants attack any leaf-eating animals that come close to the tree. The ants make it possible for the tree to survive.

**Ants live inside these large, hollow thorns.**

The small tree has hollow thorns that provide shelter for the ants. The tree also feeds a number of sap-sucking insects called aphids. The aphid herds produce a sweet substance called honeydew. The ants feed on the honeydew. The tree makes it possible for the ants to survive.

Seeing the ant tree reminded Mom of a tree called the swollen-thorn acacia. She observed it on a study trip to the rain forest in Costa Rica in Central America. The leaves of this acacia tree are not poisonous, but the tree is not eaten by insects. It has another way to survive.

The acacia tree produces sugar syrup and little fruitlike bulbs. The bulbs are rich in vitamins and proteins. But only one kind of insect, an ant, eats the abundant food. Why?

Again, the ants protect the tree! When a hungry insect lands on the acacia tree, the ants attack it. If a vine touches the tree, the ants chew through the vine and cut it from the tree. As the acacia tree grows, the ants cut away the ends of the branches on the neighboring trees. The large, swollen acacia thorns are hollow. The ants live safely inside the thorns.

It's amazing. The acacia tree provides food and protection for the ants, and the ants protect the tree. The tree and the ants depend on each other for survival.

**Ants sipping sugar syrup**

### Friday, July 25

This was the best day of all. I had been looking forward to it all week. I actually went into the top of the rain forest today, up into the canopy. The research station has a set of walkways in the canopy. The trip to the canopy started with an elevator ride. Mom called it a "lift." The lift carried us up 30 meters (m). When the lift stopped, we stepped onto a maze of walkways that stretched through the treetops. Each tree trunk had a strong wooden platform around it. The platforms were big enough for a few people to stand on them. As I looked around, I felt like I was on top of the world. We were in the rain forest canopy.

It would be hard to describe all the animals I saw. I observed many kinds of birds. I saw colorful macaws and toucans. Many of the trees were covered with small berries. The branches were full of howler monkeys, dwarf squirrels, and tree frogs. I was amazed that the top of the rain forest was so full of life. It was very different from the forest floor.

**A toco toucan**

**A red-eyed tree frog**

**A scarlet macaw**

**A howler monkey**

### Saturday, July 26

This was my last day in the rain forest. I spent so much time hiking around that I am too tired to write very much. Even though the weather was hot and humid and it rained every day of the trip, I didn't mind. There were so many new things to see and hear!

I'll miss Kopenawa. It was hard to say goodbye to him today. And I'll never forget all the animals, the toucans, howler monkeys, snakes, and the rest. It was amazing to see so many different kinds of plants and animals living together. Everything seems to fit together and work together. It's like fitting all the pieces of a puzzle together to make a beautiful picture. I'll keep this picture in my mind all the way back to Austin.

**The rain forest canopy**

**The canopy walkway**

### Studying the Rain Forest

Lee's mother is an entomologist. She studies insects in the rain forest. These organisms, like many plants, animals, and fungi, can survive only in the rain forest. The cutting of trees is destroying the rain forest and causing the **extinction** of many plants and animals. Little is known about many of the organisms in the rain forest. Studying them is important because of the potential benefits this knowledge may bring to the world.

## Thinking about Rain Forests

1. What did Lee learn about ants on the rain forest adventure?
2. How do ants communicate with each other about navigating through the rain forest?
3. In what ways do animals depend on plants in the rain forest environment? How do the plants depend on the animals in the rain forest environment?
4. What environmental factor changes as you go from the rain forest canopy to the rain forest floor?

Lake 12,460 in Sequoia National Park, California

# Freshwater Environments

Let's begin our tour of aquatic environments on Earth. There are two kinds of freshwater environments, standing-water environments and flowing-water environments. Lakes are the most common standing-water environments. Other standing-water environments are ponds and **vernal pools**. Rivers, streams, and creeks are flowing-water environments.

## Lakes

Lakes are bodies of water surrounded by land. They are all over the world. Some lakes are low in valleys, like the Finger Lakes in New York State. Others are high in mountains, like Lake 12,460 in Sequoia National Park. It's high in the Sierra Nevada range in California.

Less than 1 percent of Earth's water is in freshwater lakes. Although lakes are called standing-water environments, the water in lakes is always moving. Water moves from one part of the lake to another. Streams flowing into the lake move the water. When the weather gets cold, water near the surface gets cold and sinks toward the bottom. Moving water carries oxygen and nutrients to other parts of the lake.

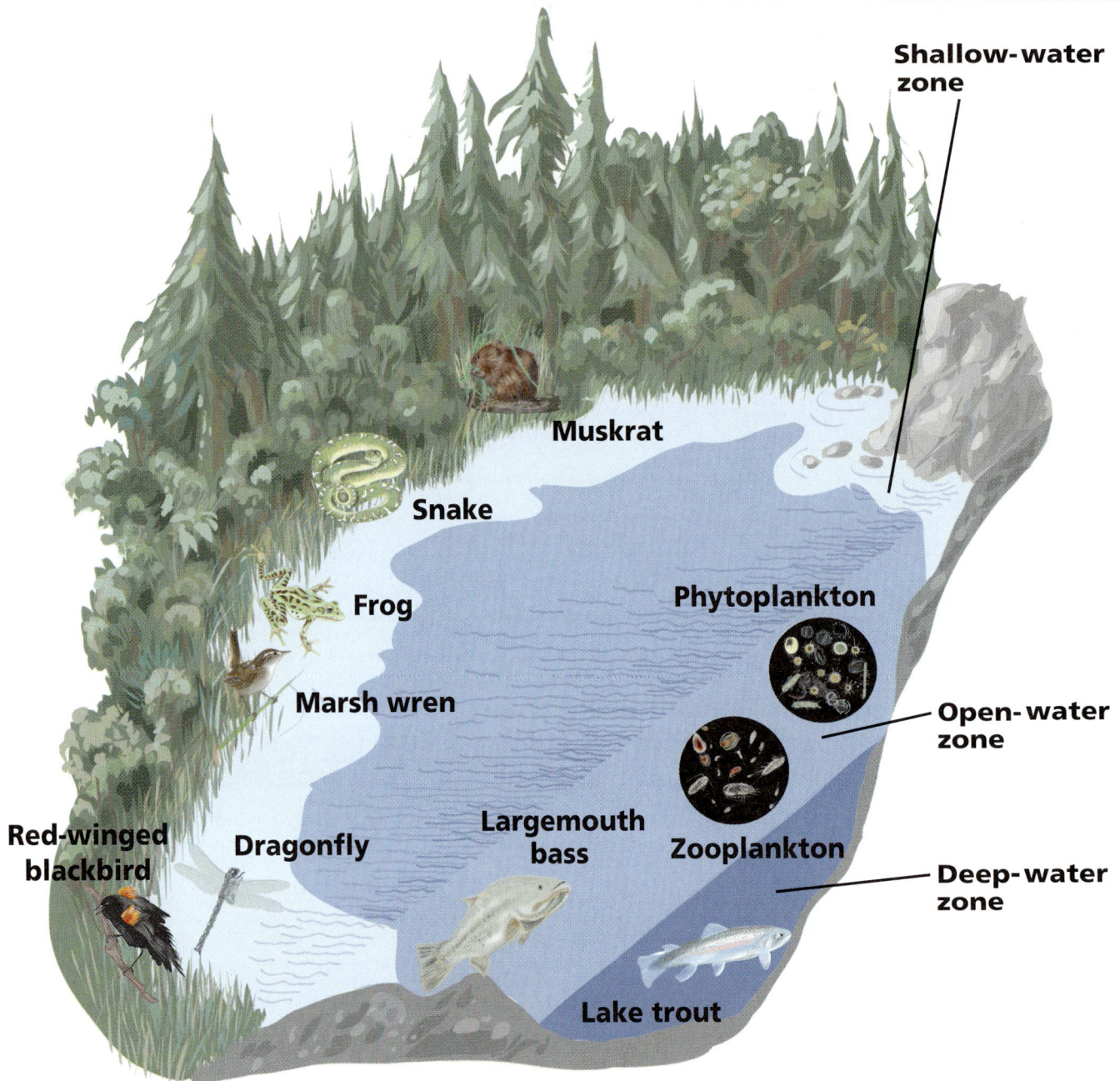

Large lakes often have three different zones. These are the shallow-water zone, the open-water zone, and the deep-water zone. Each zone provides a different environment.

The shallow-water zone is near the shore. The water is shallow enough for sunlight to reach the lake bottom. The shallow-water zone often has rooted plants, such as water lilies, growing in the muddy bottom. Floating plants and **algae** may cover the surface of the water. Insect larvae swim around the plants and burrow into the mud. Insect larvae are food for larger animals, such as fish and frogs. Ducks, other birds, and small mammals live in the shallow-water zone.

The open-water zone is farther out in the lake. The water is deeper. There are no rooted plants. Sunlight is bright near the surface of the open-water zone. The light is dim in the deeper water.

Two important kinds of microscopic organisms live in this open-water zone. **Phytoplankton** are tiny plantlike organisms. They are the "grass" of the lake environment. They are eaten by **zooplankton**.

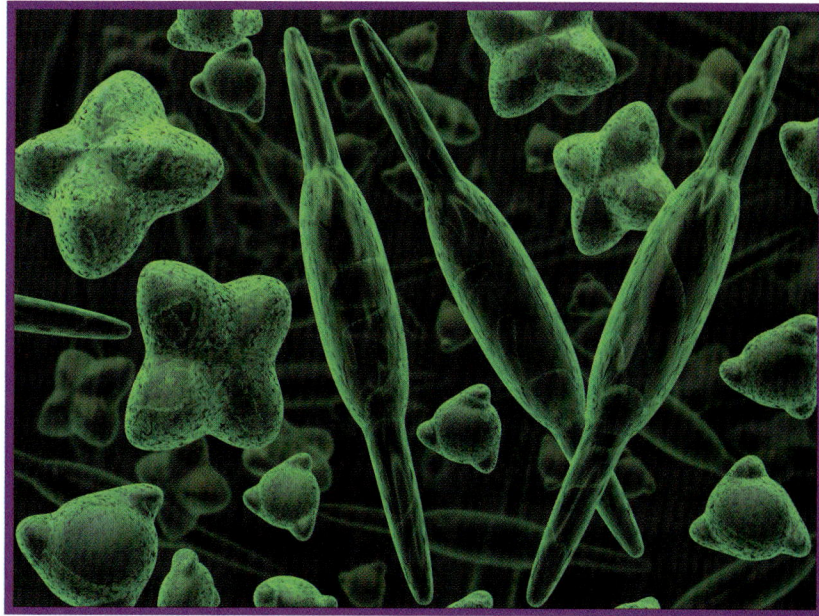

**Phytoplankton are tiny plantlike organisms.**

Zooplankton are microscopic animals in the lake environment. The zooplankton are food for insects and baby fish in the lake. Larger fish, such as trout and largemouth bass, live in the open- and deep-water zones. Birds, such as ducks, gulls, and grebes, also live in the open-water zone.

In big lakes, there is a deep-water zone. This zone is dark, and the water is cold all the time. Water from higher levels in the lake doesn't mix with the deep water, so there is less oxygen in the deep-water zone. Only animals that need little oxygen and light live at the bottom of the lake. These animals include some insects and lake trout.

### The World's Five Largest Freshwater Lakes
(based on surface area)

| Lake | Location | Area in square kilometers |
|---|---|---|
| Lake Superior | North America | 82,103 |
| Lake Victoria | Africa | 69,484 |
| Lake Huron | North America | 59,596 |
| Lake Michigan | North America | 57,757 |
| Lake Tanganyika | Africa | 32,893 |

## Ponds

A pond is a small, shallow body of water. Sunlight reaches the bottom of the pond. Plants and algae may cover the entire surface of the pond. Plants may be rooted or floating. Ponds also have large numbers of phytoplankton and zooplankton. Some animals that live in ponds are fish, birds, crayfish, frogs, snails, scuds, insects, turtles, and worms.

**Plants and algae can grow over the surface of a pond.**

### Lake Baikal

Lake Baikal in Russia is the world's deepest freshwater lake. It is also the largest freshwater lake by volume. Twenty percent of the fresh water on Earth is in this one lake. It is 1,637 meters (m) deep and has a surface area of 31,468 square kilometers (km). The lake formed about 25 million years ago and is the oldest lake in the world. There are over 1,0 kinds of animals that live only in the Lake Baikal region.

Pollution from a nearby paper-making factory almost destroyed many of these animals in the 1950s and 1960s. Efforts to clean up the pollution have brought back much of the wildlife. However, Lake Baikal remains threatened by pollution.

## Vernal Pools

A vernal pool is a shallow, temporary pond. *Vernal* means "spring." Vernal pools form when water collects in low places in the land. This happens during the rainy season or when snow melts in the spring. Vernal pools dry up during the dry season or the summer. When it is filled with water, the vernal pool is full of life. When it is dry, it looks like a mud flat. Vernal-pool plants and animals remain dormant during dry periods. When the pools fill with water again, the organisms reproduce and thrive. Salamanders, frogs, and many insects reproduce in vernal pools.

## Rivers

Rivers are large bodies of moving fresh water. They usually flow into other rivers or into the ocean. Rivers often flow faster near their **source** in the mountains where the land is steep. Animals that live in the upper part of a river survive by being good swimmers or by holding tightly to rocks and twigs. Trout are strong swimmers. Insect larvae have hooks for holding on. As rivers flow toward the ocean, their currents may slow. Plants and animals in the lower parts of rivers are more like those that live in lakes. Smaller moving-water environments include creeks, brooks, and streams.

### The World's Five Longest Rivers

| River | Location | Length in kilometers |
|---|---|---|
| Nile | Africa | 6,825 |
| Amazon | South America | 6,437 |
| Yangtze | Asia | 6,300 |
| Mississippi/Missouri | North America | 5,970 |
| Yenisey | Asia | 5,540 |

## Thinking about Freshwater Environments

1. What living and nonliving factors define a lake's shallow-water zone?
2. What role do phytoplankton play in a freshwater environment?
3. How are lake and river organisms different?

233

# What Is an Ecosystem?

An **ecosystem** is a **community** of organisms **interacting** with its nonliving environment. A terrarium is an ecosystem. When you put plants and a few small animals in a closed or semi-closed environment, the plants and animals are the living community. The soil, air, and water are the main nonliving factors in a terrarium environment.

An aquarium is also an ecosystem. Aquariums have a community of fish, snails, and water plants. Water is the main nonliving factor in an aquarium environment.

Terrariums and aquariums are two kinds of ecosystems. There are many more. When you go to the forest, you are visiting a natural ecosystem. Trees, grass, squirrels, birds, and insects are some of the organisms interacting with the nonliving environment in the forest ecosystem.

**Ecologists** are scientists who study ecosystems. They find out what kinds of plants, animals, and other organisms are living in an area. They also observe properties and measure the nonliving environmental factors in the area (the air temperature, soil, water, and light). Then they study how the community of organisms and the nonliving environmental factors interact.

**A terrarium**

**An aquarium**

## Matter and Energy in an Ecosystem

Living organisms need food to survive. Food provides **matter** and **energy**. Matter is stuff. Everything that takes up space is matter. Air, water, rock, wood, metal, machines, buildings, and organisms are all matter.

Energy makes things happen. Energy makes it possible for organisms to grow and move. Organisms use energy to sense their environment and to reproduce.

Organisms get both matter and energy from food. But the way plants get the food they need for life is very different from the way animals get their food.

Plants *make* the food they need for life. Plants get the matter and energy they need to make food from air, water, and light in the environment.

Animals *cannot* make their own food as plants do. Animals get the food they need for life from other organisms. The way animals get food from other organisms is to eat them.

**A forest ecosystem**

Energy for most ecosystems comes from the Sun. Energy from the Sun is captured by plants' green leaves. Plants use water ($H_2O$), carbon dioxide ($CO_2$), and sunlight from the nonliving environment to make sugar. This process is called **photosynthesis**. Plants then use the sugar as food.

When animals eat plants, the energy of the sugar transfers to the animal. But even though animals get the energy from plants, it is really energy that came from the Sun. All the energy that makes living organisms move, grow, and reproduce in most ecosystems comes from the Sun.

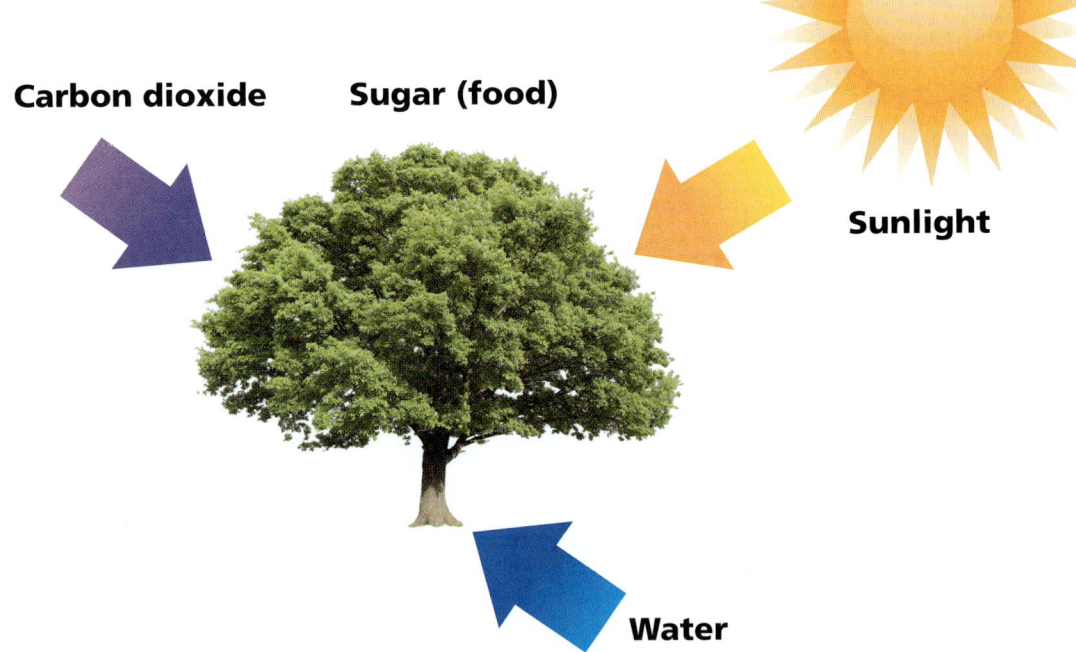

Plants use water, carbon dioxide, and sunlight to make their own food.

# Thinking about Ecosystems

1. How do plants and animals get the food they need to survive?
2. Explain how energy from the Sun helps animals survive.
3. What is an ecosystem?

# Food Chains and Food Webs

In any ecosystem, a lot of eating is going on. Do you remember why? Eating is the way animals get the food they need to survive. What is it about food that makes life possible? Food is a source of matter and energy. The matter in food provides the raw materials an organism needs to grow and reproduce. Energy is like fuel that makes things happen.

One way to think about ecosystems is who eats whom. When you know how an organism gets its food, you can put it into a group. Let's look at the groups.

## Producers

Some organisms don't eat anything. They don't have to because they make their own food. Organisms that make their own food are called **producers**. In terrestrial ecosystems, the most important producers are plants. Grasses, trees, and bushes are producers. In freshwater and ocean ecosystems, algae are the most important producers.

Algae are organisms that play an important role in aquatic ecosystems. Many algae are microscopic. Algae produce most of the food in freshwater and ocean ecosystems. They use water ($H_2O$), carbon dioxide ($CO_2$), and sunlight to make their own food, just like plants. Algae are the food source for many kinds of crustaceans, insects, fish, and worms. In your goldfish aquarium, you might have seen algae growing. Did the water turn green? Did a green layer form on the sides of the aquarium? If so, then you saw algae.

**A type of freshwater algae called *Oedogonium***

But wait! If algae are **microorganisms**, how can you see them? When a few algae are in your aquarium, you won't see them because they are so small. But they start to reproduce. And after a week or two, the population of algae will be in the billions! That's what you see. Any one of those microorganisms by itself is much too small to see. You need a microscope to see just one. But huge numbers of them can affect the color and clarity of the water, making it look green and cloudy.

What happens to the algae? In a freshwater lake, insects and fish eat the algae. In the ocean, algae are food for baby clams, barnacles, corals, and thousands of young fish, crabs, and snails.

Producers use the food they make as a source of matter and energy. They don't eat other organisms for matter and energy. Any organism that makes its own food is a producer.

**Algae on a pond**

A ground squirrel

Caterpillars

A vulture

A snake

## Consumers

Organisms that eat other organisms are **consumers**. Consumers can't make their own food. Consumers have to eat other organisms to get their matter and energy.

Some consumers eat plants and plant parts. Deer eat grass and leaves. Gophers eat roots. Squirrels eat grass, nuts, and berries. Caterpillars eat leaves. Animals that eat only plants to get their food are called **herbivores**.

Some animals don't eat plants. Snakes don't eat nuts and berries. Hawks don't eat grass. Spiders don't eat leaves. So how do they get their matter and energy? They eat other animals. Snakes and hawks eat gophers and squirrels. Spiders eat insects. Animals that eat other animals are called **carnivores**.

Some consumers, like humans, bears, raccoons, robins, and crayfish, eat both plants and animals. They are called **omnivores**.

**Scavengers** are consumers that eat dead organisms. Some scavengers, like vultures, eat only dead animals. Others, like isopods and termites, eat dead leaves and wood. Coyotes, rats, ants, and earthworms will eat just about anything that is dead.

## Decomposers

There is a hidden world in every ecosystem. Millions of insects and invisible microorganisms use the last bits of dead plants and animals for food. They can be thought of as the cleanup crew. These organisms are called **decomposers**.

*Decompose* means "to break into parts." Insects, such as ants and termites, break down dead plants and animals into tiny pieces. Then the decomposers, the **bacteria** and fungi, take over. Bacteria and fungi break down dead plant and animal matter into simple chemicals (nutrients). The simple chemicals are returned to the environment. When decomposers are done with a dead organism, there is no energy to transfer, and there is no longer any food value. The simple chemicals are the raw materials used by producers to make more food. Decomposers are the ecosystem's recyclers of matter.

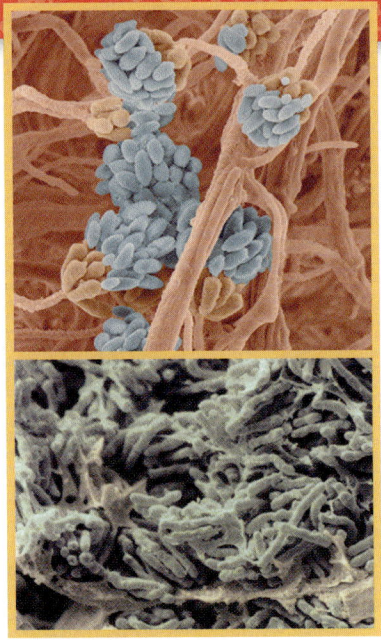

**Soil bacteria**

Bacteria are the smallest organisms in the world. They are found in all environments. Bacteria play a very important role in every ecosystem. Bacteria decompose dead matter and waste. After bacteria finish their work, there is no energy to transfer from the matter, and the raw materials are returned to the environment. Some bacteria can cause disease, but most bacteria have important roles in ecosystems.

Fungi are important decomposers, too. They come in different shapes, sizes, and types. We know them as molds, mildew, and mushrooms. Like bacteria, fungi can live everywhere. They can live in both terrestrial and aquatic ecosystems. They are in the soil, in your home, on plants and animals, and even on you. A spoonful of soil might contain 120,000 fungi. Some are harmful to living plants and animals. But most fungi are important in recycling dead matter for raw materials in the environment.

**Mushrooms are fungi.**

# Food Chains

When a spider eats a fly, the matter and energy in the fly go to the spider. This feeding relationship can be shown with an arrow. The arrow always points in the direction that the matter and energy flow.

fly → spider

If a praying mantis eats a spider, the matter and energy in the spider go to the praying mantis.

fly → spider → praying mantis

It's possible in a woodland ecosystem for a blue jay to eat the praying mantis, a weasel to eat the blue jay, and a hawk to eat the weasel. Matter and energy pass from one organism to the next when they are eaten. This is called a **food chain**. And at the beginning of the food chain is a producer. Energy for producers comes from the Sun.

In this case, the producer is a fruit from a tree, a plum. You can draw arrows from one organism to the next to describe a food chain. The arrows show the direction of energy flow. They point from the organism that is eaten to the organism that eats it.

plum → fly → spider → praying mantis → blue jay → weasel → hawk

Another example of a food chain might have grass as the producer. A chipmunk eats the grass seed. A hawk eats the chipmunk. Bacteria decompose any dead organisms or uneaten parts. You can always draw arrows from dead organisms to the decomposers.

### A simple food chain

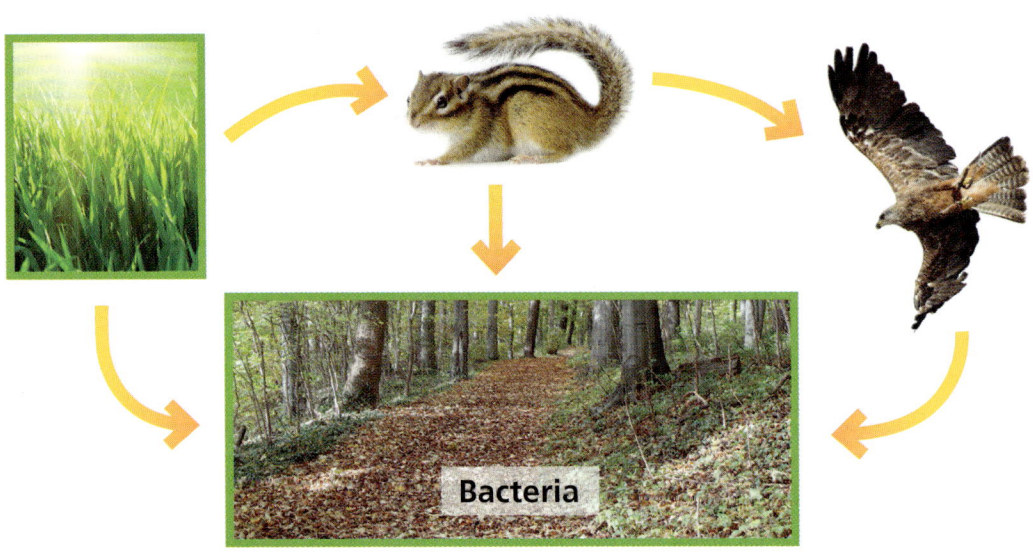

# Food Webs

There are many feeding relationships in an ecosystem. If you draw *all* the arrows that show who eats whom, you have a **food web**, not a food chain. The food web for a freshwater river might look like this.

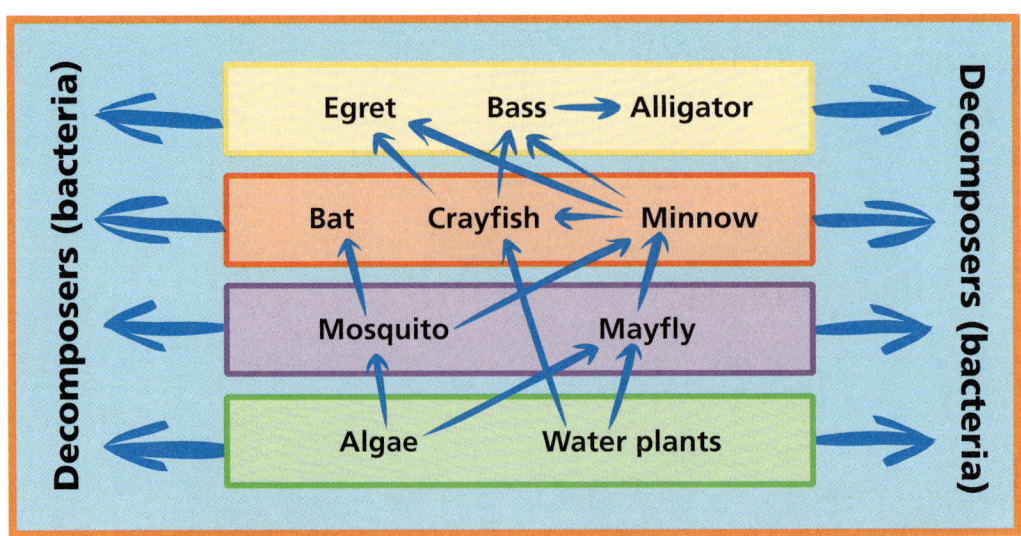

**This is an example of a food web for a freshwater river. Bacteria decompose all the organisms when they die.**

Locate the crayfish in the example of a food web. Crayfish are food for both egrets and bass. If the river has a lot of crayfish, egrets and bass will both have plenty to eat. But if there are few crayfish, the egrets and bass will have to **compete** with each other for food.

The animal that can get more food is the one that is more likely to survive. In this river ecosystem, egrets and bass compete for crayfish. Are there other competitions for food in the ecosystem?

Organisms in ecosystems depend on one another for the food they need to survive. Herbivores depend on producers to make food. Carnivores depend on consumers for food. Omnivores depend on both producers and consumers for food. Decomposers depend on dead organisms and waste for food. And producers depend on decomposers for raw materials to make food. In a healthy ecosystem, some organisms will be eaten so that other organisms will survive.

**Egrets eat crayfish.**

# Thinking about Food Chains and Food Webs

1. What is food? Why is it important?

2. Do plants need food? Why or why not?

3. What is the role of producers in an ecosystem?

4. Look at the food web for a freshwater river. Give three examples of animals that compete for a food source.

5. What is the role of decomposers in an ecosystem?

6. How might a forest fire affect the food web in a forest?

# Human Activities and Aquatic Ecosystems

## The Lake Erie Story

Lake Erie is one of the five Great Lakes on the border between the United States and Canada. The other four lakes are Lake Superior, Lake Michigan, Lake Huron, and Lake Ontario. Together they form the largest freshwater body in the world. In fact, 95 percent of our nation's fresh water is in the Great Lakes.

Humans caused an ecological problem in Lake Erie. For years, sewage, farm runoff, and industrial waste were dumped and washed into Lake Erie. By the 1960s, the lake had become very **polluted**. The environment had changed. Too much algae grew in the water. The amount of oxygen in the lake dropped. This made it difficult for fish to survive. There were large areas of the lake bottom where life did not exist. The lake's aquatic organisms were dying. The ecosystem was in serious trouble.

A coal power plant at Lake Erie, New York

In the 1970s, people started to save Lake Erie. The United States and Canada cleaned it up. Together, the two countries spent millions of dollars to develop a plan to save Lake Erie. Here is part of the plan.

- Build new and better sewage treatment plants.
- Reduce the use of detergents containing phosphates. Phosphates act as **fertilizer** for algae.
- Manage the use of fertilizers and **pesticides** on farms.
- Stop industries from dumping waste into the lake.

The efforts of both governments and the people living and working around Lake Erie paid off. The lake began to recover. After many years, the lake is much safer and healthier. The lake environment now supports many fish and other animals.

Lake Erie still has problems. More than 300 human-made chemicals are in Lake Erie. Some are poisonous. The United States and Canada continue to study ways to improve the water quality. Much has been done to help this important aquatic ecosystem. But the fight to save Lake Erie is not over.

The Lake Erie story is an important one in US history, but there are similar stories to be told everywhere. There are lakes, rivers, streams, and creeks all over the country that are suffering from human pollution. Let's dig deeper into the sources of this pollution.

**A nuclear power plant on Lake Erie**

245

## Sources of Water Pollution

- **Farming** Pesticides are poisons used to kill pests on crops. Fertilizers are used to make crops grow faster and larger. When farmers use too much pesticide and fertilizer, the extra can wash into rivers and lakes. Pesticides kill plants and animals in the water. Fertilizers cause too much growth of aquatic plants and algae. This upsets the balance in aquatic ecosystems.

- **Sewage** Human sewage and waste from farm animals can also get into aquatic systems. These act like fertilizers, causing aquatic plants and algae to grow. Sewage can also carry microorganisms that cause diseases in humans.

- **Sediment** Runoff is water that flows over the land and then into large bodies of water. Runoff can carry soil and chemicals from mines, fields, forests, and cities. These materials settle to the bottom of lakes as sediments. Sediments can bury aquatic plants and animals. This burial can damage the environment and the organisms that live there.

- **Acid** Industrial gases from smokestacks enter the air. The gases form acid in clouds. Acid rain falls from these clouds and changes the acid levels in aquatic ecosystems. Many aquatic plants and animals are sensitive to acid. When the acid level changes, some organisms continue to survive, some survive poorly, and some cannot survive at all.

- **Petroleum** Oil spills and runoff from city streets can put oil and other **petroleum** products into lakes. Oil is harmful to animals that live on the lake surface, like waterbirds. It also harms organisms that live on the lakeshore, like snails, insects, and crayfish.

## World Lakes Getting Warmer

In addition to water pollution, there is another concern for the health of freshwater environments. In 2010, NASA scientists published a study comparing surface temperatures of 167 lakes around the world. The scientists used satellite data to determine the water's surface temperature. The data were collected over a 25-year period, starting in 1985. The scientists used only summertime measurements to avoid winter weather and clouds that would block the satellite's view. They used only nighttime measurements to avoid effects of reflected sunlight. They selected lakes that were large, at least 500 square kilometers (km). All the lakes were inland, far from coastal shores. The measurements were taken in the middle of the lakes to avoid interference from the land.

What did they find out? The temperatures rose significantly in these lakes over the 25 years. The average increase in surface temperature was 0.05 degrees Celsius (°C) for every 10 years. In some lakes, the increase was as high as 0.10°C. That might not seem like a lot, but a small temperature change can have a big effect on a lake ecosystem.

Think about a lake freezing during the winter. If the lake freezes later each year and warms up earlier each year, that can have a big impact on the organisms that live in the lake. For example, nonnative **species**, either a plant or a fish, could become established in the warmer lake. A nonnative species might use the food resources in the lake and make it more difficult for native species to compete for food.

**Human activities impact Earth's aquatic systems.**

This is one of the important studies looking at **climate** change worldwide and its impact on freshwater lakes. Other studies have documented that the temperature of Earth's land and water surfaces are increasing in large part because of human activities.

## Thinking about Aquatic Systems

1. What organism causes most of the pollution in Lake Erie? Give examples of why you think so.
2. What is the effect of climate change on large freshwater lakes?

247

**A terrestrial ecosystem**

# Comparing Aquatic and Terrestrial Ecosystems

Aquatic and terrestrial ecosystems are very different. But they are the same in some ways. Let's compare.

The nonliving factors of the two environments are different. Aquatic ecosystems are in water. Terrestrial ecosystems are on land. The temperature in an aquatic ecosystem changes slowly. The temperature in a terrestrial ecosystem can change rapidly over a short period of time. The amount of water in an aquatic ecosystem is predictable. Water in a terrestrial ecosystem can vary widely.

The organisms are different in the two ecosystems. Most aquatic organisms can live only in water. If they were moved to a terrestrial ecosystem, they would die. The same is true for terrestrial organisms moved into aquatic ecosystems.

**An aquatic ecosystem**

**A heron is a consumer of crayfish in an aquatic ecosystem.**

**A fox is a consumer of mice in a terrestrial ecosystem.**

Both ecosystems, however, are organized in similar ways. The organisms in aquatic and terrestrial ecosystems all need matter and energy to stay alive.

- Both ecosystems obtain energy from the Sun and matter from the environment.
- Both have food chains and food webs.
- Both have consumers that depend on producers to make food.
- Both have decomposers that break down dead organisms and recycle the raw materials (nutrients).
- Herbivores, carnivores, omnivores, and scavengers live in both ecosystems.

In both ecosystems, organisms compete for the resources they need to survive. Plants compete for light. Animals compete for food. Organisms need space and shelter from predators and changes in the nonliving environment. The organism that outcompetes the others is the organism that will survive.

# Animal Sensory Systems

How do you get the information you need to survive in your environment? You get information through your five **senses**. You use your sense of hearing, touch or feel, sight, smell, and taste.

Your senses make you aware of suitable food through smell and taste. They make you aware of things far away through sight and hearing. And they help you sense things that are close, through smell and touch or feel. The sense of touch or feel has many dimensions. Through touch, you can detect many kinds of input to your skin. Human touch can detect pressure, heat, cold, pain, tickle, itch, and textures such as smooth, rough, slippery, and sharp.

**Sensory receptors** on your body get information from the environment. Some of this information travels to your brain, which processes it. Then it sends information to your body to take action.

Animals use these same senses, or **variations** of these senses, to get the information they need to survive in their environments. Some animals use senses that are beyond the reach of humans.

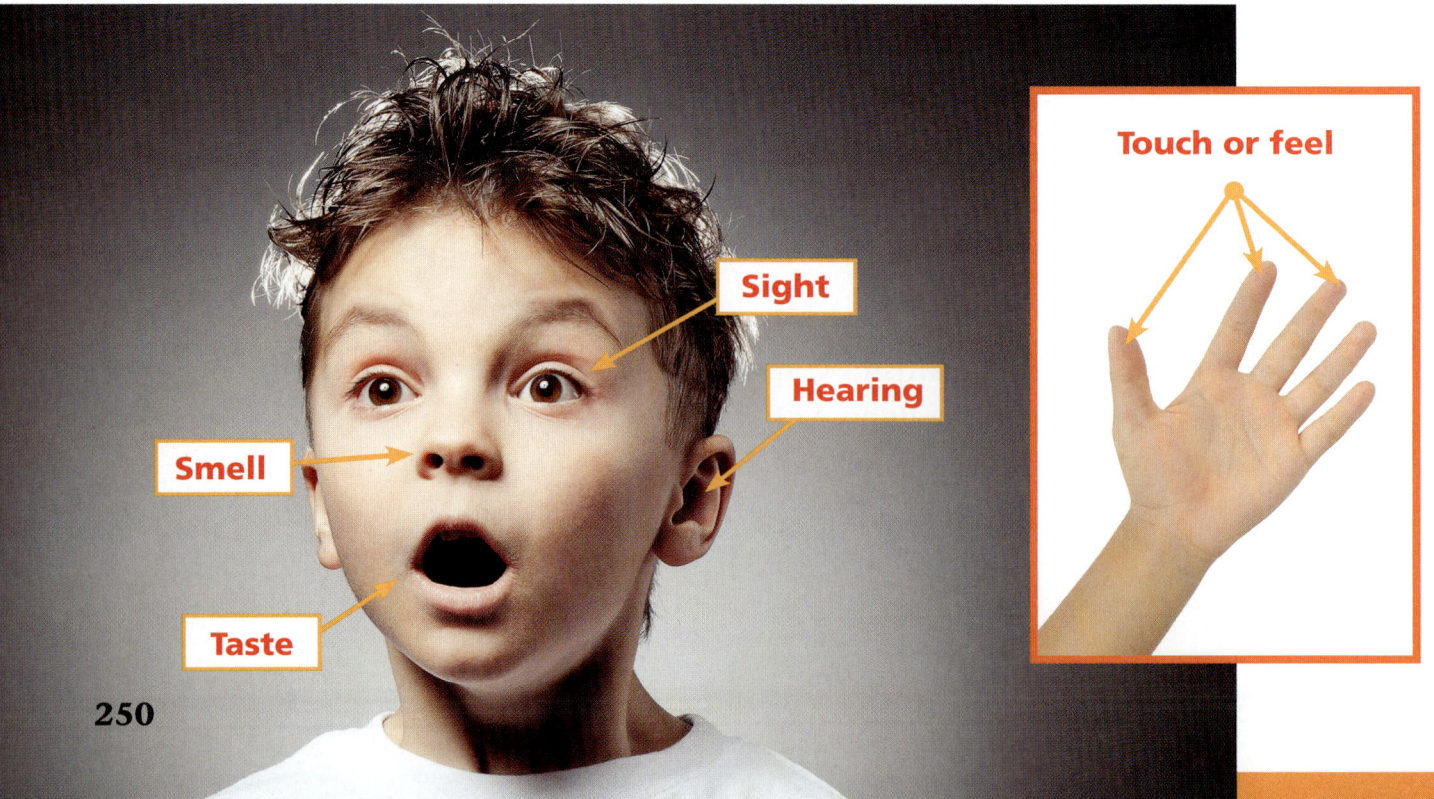

Rattlesnakes are members of a family of snakes called pitvipers. Pitvipers have a sensory receptor on their face that detects heat. With this structure, rattlesnakes locate **prey** such as mice and rats. These small animals give off body heat. The snakes can sense the heat. Put a blindfold on a rattlesnake, and it can still sense and capture prey. A rattlesnake can find a meal even in complete darkness.

American pitvipers include 16 kinds of rattlesnake, the copperhead, and the cottonmouth. Other kinds of pitvipers live in Central and South America.

**A western diamondback rattlesnake**

**Close-up of a rattlesnake's head showing heat-sensing pit**

pit

Honeybees must find flowers with sweet nectar and pollen to survive. Their eyes are part of a sensory system that provides important information about flowers. The light that we see reflected by flowers provides information for bees. But honeybee eyes also detect ultraviolet light. The light reflected from a flower looks quite different to a bee than it does to us. Many flowers appear to have a bull's-eye design. That design helps the bee locate nectar quickly. A white circle with a red center tells the bee to go to that flower and get the nectar and pollen.

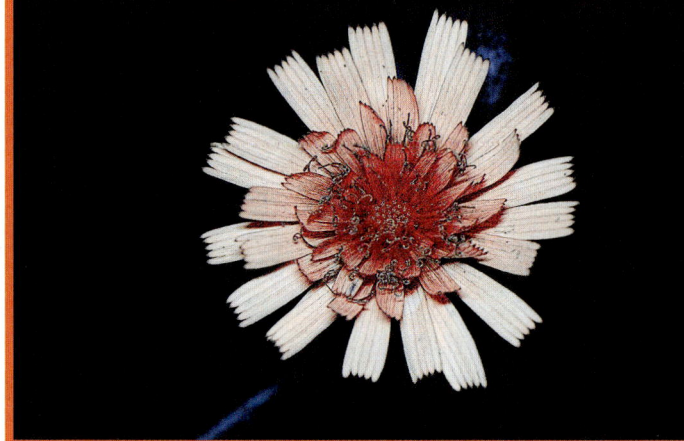

**This flower appears uniformly bright yellow to a human eye, but white with a vivid red center to a honeybee.**

**This flower also looks yellow to the human eye. But it appears white with a bright red center to a honeybee.**

These small fish are swimming in a group called a school. Schooling fish can swim close to one another and change direction all together. They do this without colliding because they have a sensory system called a lateral line. The lateral line looks like a line of little dots running from the head to the tail.

**Lateral line**

The lateral line detects changes in water pressure along the fish's side. Sensing changes in pressure allows thousands of fish to swim together safely in a single school.

Pressure information can be helpful to large predator fish and small prey fish. Changes in pressure can alert predator fish to potential prey swimming nearby. This same information can signal prey fish that a predator is nearby.

The lateral-line sense is most like hearing in humans. However, humans cannot detect pressure changes in the same way.

Humans have no sensory system to detect magnetism. But evidence shows that some animals on Earth can sense and use magnetic information.

Some fish and birds can sense Earth's magnetic field. These animals might use this information to find their way when traveling long distances.

People carry homing pigeons in dark boxes to unfamiliar locations far from their home. When the pigeons are released, they fly up into the air. They circle a little while and then start flying directly toward home. Scientists have discovered that the pigeons have a space in their beaks that contains iron particles. The space and iron particles act like a compass.

**Homing pigeons**

Salmon may also have a magnetic sensory system. Scientists think that salmons' magnetic sensory system helps guide the fish back to the river where they were born. Salmon live as adults in the ocean for several years. Then, they swim up river to their birthplace to mate and reproduce. Their sense of smell also helps them find their birthplace.

**Salmon**

Scientists also suspect that sea turtles use magnetic information to guide them back to the beach where they were born. Adult sea turtles return to their birthplace after several years of life in the ocean.

**A green sea turtle**

**Bats use hypersound to navigate and find insects to eat.**

Bats are excellent navigators in the dark. They can fly through caves and catch insects during the darkest nights. Is this because their eyes are different than ours? No, bats do not use eyesight to navigate in the dark. They use **hypersound**.

Hypersound has very high frequencies that are too high for human ears to detect. But bat ears can hear hypersound. Bats produce hypersounds that bounce off objects such as insects and the walls of caves. Their large ears then detect the reflected sounds. This high-frequency hearing lets a bat know the exact locations of objects in its environment.

Other animals, like the cricket, also use hypersound to communicate. The familiar chirping of crickets is called **stridulation**. The cricket's stridulations are made of different sounds. They are something like the many sounds of an orchestra. Some sounds in a stridulation are within human hearing range. But much of a stridulation is so high that it can be detected only by another cricket.

Crickets can produce several kinds of stridulation by rubbing their wings together. Male crickets make a loud, harsh stridulation to claim a territory. This sound tells other males to stay away. They use a softer, sweeter, stridulation to attract a female. This sound allows cricket pairs to find each other.

**A cricket**

Very large animals, like elephants and whales, can produce and hear **ultrasound**. These ultrasounds are so low that most sensory receptors cannot detect them. If you were standing near an elephant producing ultrasound, you might feel a rumbling. It might feel like the shaking of the ground when a large truck drives by. But your ears would not hear the elephant sound. Low ultrasounds can travel long distances through air or water. These sounds allow elephants and whales to communicate at a distance with others of their kind.

Sharks have an awesome set of sensory systems. They have good eyesight at close distances. Like cats, sharks have excellent night vision. Like all fish, sharks have a lateral line to detect changes in water movement and pressure.

The shark's sense of smell is also exceptional. With two large nostrils on the sides of its head, a shark can sense a smell and tell its direction. Sharks can follow the smell of a tiny amount of blood in the water to locate and eat an injured fish.

In addition, the shark has a structure called the ampulla of Lorenzini. This structure allows the shark to detect electric signals in its environment. Injured fish produce electric signals. The electricity is not like the electric shock you could get from an electric circuit. The electricity produced by an injured fish is very weak. Sharks use the electricity sensors in their snout to find the injured fish.

Awareness of the environment and quick responses are essential for survival. Animals have different kinds of sensors that pick up clues from the environment, both far and near. Each animal has different systems for interpreting the information and responding. A human's brain processes sensory input and decides what action to take.

**Tiny dots on the shark's snout (red circle) hold the electricity-sensing ampullae of Lorenzini.**

A marbled murrelet

# Saving Murrelets through Mimicry

The marbled murrelet is a robin-sized seabird. It spends most of its life in the open ocean from Alaska south to central California. Marbled murrelets eat fish and other small ocean animals. They have streamlined bodies for diving, and strong, sharp beaks for capturing food. The murrelets' structures and behavior suit them for life on the open ocean.

Like all birds, murrelets must leave the water when it is time to breed and to raise their young. Most seabirds build nests on cliff ledges. But marbled murrelets raise their young in trees in coastal forests. Once a year, a breeding pair of murrelets will fly to the top of a tall redwood or other large tree. They nest in the same tree each year. There, the female lays a single egg on a moss-covered limb. The parents take turns sitting on the speckled blue-green egg. For 2 months, the parents fly back and forth from the nesting tree to the ocean to get food. Each trip might be 50 kilometers (km).

Murrelet females lay only one egg a year. The loss of an egg means that a murrelet pair will not produce any offspring that year.

257

**Stellar's jays are major predators of murrelet eggs.**

Wildlife biologists are concerned about the survival of marbled murrelets. Their survival mainly depends on two factors. The murrelets need large mature trees near the ocean for nesting. And they need safety for their eggs and chicks. Predators often eat unguarded murrelet egg. One frequent egg predator is the Steller's jay. When a jay spots an unguarded murrelet egg, it swoops into the nest. The jay uses its sharp beak to break the egg and eat it.

Biologists are testing ways to change the jay's behavior so they won't destroy the murrelet eggs. One experiment involves painting small chicken eggs to look like murrelet eggs. The biologist injects a drug into the murrelet-egg mimic. The drug makes the jays vomit, but doesn't do any lasting harm to them. The biologist then puts the mimic eggs in the trees near where the murrelets nest. The mimic eggs are low in the trees, and the real eggs are high in the trees. When a jay eats a mimic egg, it immediately vomits.

In the experiment, jays that ate mimic eggs learned to avoid all speckled blue-green eggs. These smart birds might even be able to warn other jays not to eat those eggs.

Jays are corvids, a particularly intelligent family of birds. The corvid family includes jays, crows, and ravens. There is research that suggests that corvids are able to communicate what they learn to others of their kind. A jay that has tried the mimic egg and gotten sick, may communicate the message to others that says, "Don't eat those blue eggs with the brown marks; you'll get sick!"

Biologists are trying to decrease the number of jays living near murrelet nests. The population of jays has increased because human visitors to the forest are feeding them. Humans feed the jays for fun or accidentally by leaving picnic crumbs behind. More jays stay in the area because they can easily find food. Biologists are teaching people to not feed the jays. Jays will be less likely to stay in the area and less likely to find and eat the murrelet eggs.

In a 2010 study, biologists have estimated that up to 80 percent of the murrelet eggs along the central California coast were lost to predators each year. They predicted that this murrelet population could disappear within 100 years. But this might not happen now. By placing the mimic eggs in the murrelet habitat, keeping picnic areas clean, and preserving the largest forest trees, people are helping murrelet eggs survive. This is good news for the chances of the continuation of the central California population of marbled murrelets.

**These coast redwoods in which murrelets nest are the tallest trees in the world.**

# Brine Shrimp

Brine shrimp (*Artemia*) are small crustaceans. They live only in salty aquatic environments, such as salt lakes and brine ponds. Unlike their relatives, crabs and lobsters, brine shrimp cannot live in the open ocean. But brine shrimp can live in environments where most other organisms cannot.

An adult brine shrimp is about 1 centimeter (cm) long. Its partly transparent (clear) body is divided into segments. Between 11 and 19 of the brine shrimp's segments have legs. The legs are used for swimming and feeding. As it swims, it pulls nearby microscopic bits of food into its mouth.

Salt is an important nonliving factor in the environment of brine shrimp. Brine shrimp can live in a **range** of salt **concentrations**. The brine shrimp living in Mono Lake thrive when the salt concentration in the environment is 80 parts salt per 1,000 parts water. If the salt concentration drops below 60 parts salt, the brine shrimp will survive, but not as well. If the salt concentration falls below 20 parts per 1,000, or goes over 100 parts per 1,000, the brine shrimp will not survive.

Brine shrimp eggs can survive during long periods of dryness. They can stay dormant for up to 3 years before hatching. Live adult brine shrimp are sold as food for larger fish. Brine shrimp are sometimes sold as pets called sea monkeys.

**Magnified view of a brine shrimp**

**Actual size**

A view of Mono Lake

# The Mono Lake Story

Mono Lake lies at the edge of the Great Basin in northeastern California. It is at least 760,000 years old. That makes it the oldest lake in America. Because it lies between the Sierra Nevada and the desert, Mono Lake is blistering hot in the summer and freezing cold in the winter. Mono Lake's water is salty, even saltier than the ocean.

At first glance, Mono Lake looks lifeless. But it isn't. What looks like a lifeless lake is a rare and important ecosystem.

The story of the Mono Lake ecosystem starts with the lake water itself. Because it is so salty, no plants or common lake animals can live there. There are no fish, frogs, or mosquitoes in the water. But two kinds of algae thrive in the salty water. They are tiny floating algae and bottom algae. Floating algae drift around in the lake, and bottom algae grow on the lake bottom. These algae are the only producers in the Mono Lake ecosystem.

**Pink clouds of brine shrimp in Mono Lake**

**A close-up of a brine shrimp**

**Tufa towers made of calcium carbonate form in Mono Lake.**

## Brine Shrimp

The most important animal in Mono Lake is the brine shrimp. Over the winter, the bottom of the lake is covered with billions of brine shrimp eggs. In late spring, the water starts to warm. The eggs start to hatch. The tiny brine shrimp are no larger than the period at the end of this sentence. The shrimp eat the floating algae and grow. In a few weeks, they are full-sized adults. They start to reproduce. By early summer, there are trillions of brine shrimp in the lake. Mobs of several million shrimp form pink clouds all over the lake.

Many birds **migrate** from winter feeding grounds to spring nesting grounds. Mono Lake plays an important role in the survival of several kinds of birds. About 50,000 California gulls migrate from the ocean to Mono Lake to breed. The gulls make nests on the two islands in Mono Lake and feed on the brine shrimp. When their eggs hatch, the gull parents catch brine shrimp to feed their chicks. By the middle of the summer, the chicks can fly. They follow their parents over the mountains to the ocean.

There is still more happening at Mono Lake. Small shorebirds called phalaropes and waterbirds called eared grebes also stop at Mono Lake to eat and rest. They reproduce in Canada and then fly farther south for the winter. Without Mono Lake as a place to rest and feed, they would not be able to finish their migration.

An amazing 150,000 phalaropes and between 1 and 2 million grebes come to Mono Lake during the summer. By midsummer, there is not much algae remaining in the lake. The brine shrimp have eaten most of the algae. There are trillions of brine shrimp in the lake. The phalaropes and grebes eat and eat and eat. By the time the birds are ready to continue their migration, only a few billion brine shrimp are left in the lake.

As the water cools in the fall, the last brine shrimp females lay eggs. These eggs don't hatch. They settle to the bottom of the lake. With the brine shrimp gone for the time being, the floating algae reproduce in huge numbers. The brine shrimp eggs lay dormant until the next spring. When the water warms up again, the eggs hatch. The new shrimp begin eating the algae, and the whole cycle happens again.

**A Wilson's phalarope**

**An eared grebe**

**California gulls at Mono Lake**

Brine flies along the water's edge

Close-up of brine flies

California gulls feed on brine flies.

## Brine Flies

While the brine shrimp are eating the floating algae, the larvae of the brine fly are eating the bottom algae. When the larvae are full grown, they come to the lake's surface and pupate. In a few days, the **pupae** open and the adult flies come out. There are billions of them on the shore of Mono Lake.

The brine flies are another food source for the phalaropes, gulls, and grebes. In the past, brine flies were food for the native people living in the Mono basin. The word *mono* might be a Native American word that means "fly eater." The Native American people who lived in the basin would gather millions of the pupae, dry them in the sunshine, and store them for winter food. The pupae have a lot of protein and fat, and they were easy to harvest.

## Humans and the Mono Lake Ecosystem

For thousands of years, Mono Lake was where the California gulls came to reproduce. In 1941, things began to change.

The Los Angeles Department of Water and Power began taking water from four of the seven streams that flow into Mono Lake. The water was sent 560 kilometers (km) away for the people in Los Angeles. The result was an ecological disaster for Mono Lake. The lake shrank to half its size. The salt concentration in the lake water doubled.

In 1982, the salt concentration in Mono Lake was making it hard for algae and brine flies to survive. The brine shrimp were in trouble, too. These changes affected the California gulls. They didn't have as much food to eat.

The lower water level created a land bridge between shore and one of the California gull nesting islands. Foxes and coyotes could walk to the island and eat the eggs and chicks. Because of the predators and lack of food, the California gulls did not raise any chicks that year.

## Mono Lake Makes a Comeback

In 1978, a young man named David Gaines (1947–1988) became concerned about the poor environmental condition of Mono Lake. He formed an action group called the Mono Lake Committee. Under his leadership, the committee worked with government agencies, environmental groups, and the Los Angeles water department to solve the problem.

In 1994, a decision was finally reached. Less water would go to Los Angeles. This would allow the water level in Mono Lake to slowly rise.

Today the water in the lake has returned to a good level. The salt concentration has gone down. The land bridge to the island is again underwater. The brine shrimp and brine flies are thriving. The California gulls are raising chicks. The Mono Lake story shows that people can take positive action to restore the environment and save important ecosystems.

**David Gaines**

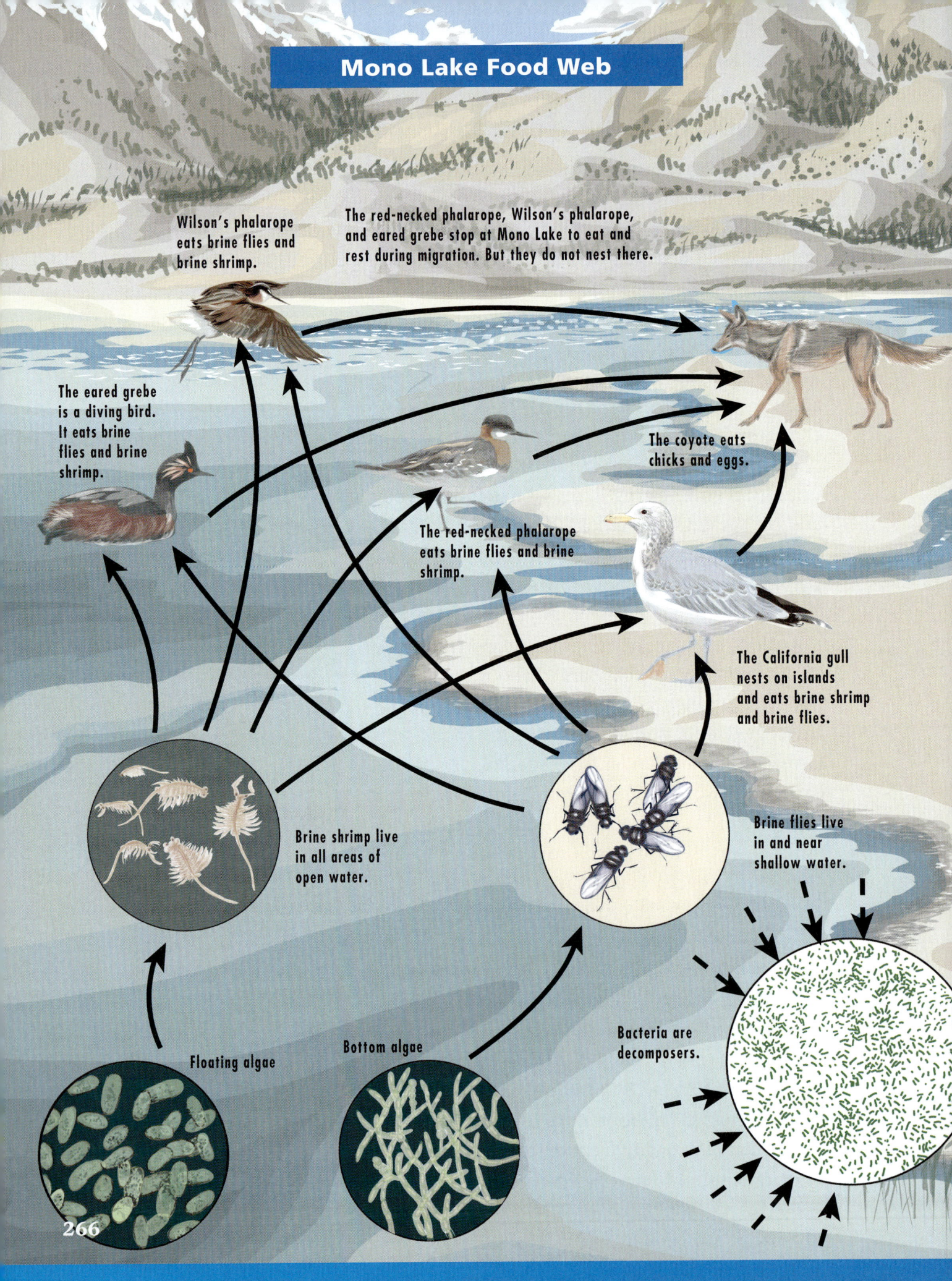

# Reviewing the Mono Lake Ecosystem

Mono Lake is a very salty ecosystem. Most aquatic organisms cannot survive in Mono Lake because of the high salt concentration. But a few kinds of algae thrive in the lake. These algae are the producers that support the Mono Lake ecosystem.

Some algae are small and float around in the lake. One individual alga is too small to see. That makes it a microorganism. But when countless billions of algae fill the lake, you can see them. The water turns green.

Like all ecosystems, Mono Lake has consumers. The two most important consumers are the brine shrimp and the brine flies. Millions of migrating birds stop at Mono Lake every year. The birds eat the brine shrimp and brine flies. The migrating birds rely on this food to survive.

Bacteria are the decomposers in Mono Lake. These microorganisms break down the dead algae, brine shrimp, brine flies, birds, and waste into simple chemicals. The simple chemicals recycle back into the ecosystem. These chemicals are the raw materials used by algae to make food the next year. Bacteria are an important part of the Mono Lake ecosystem.

One way to diagram the Mono Lake food web is shown on the previous page. Follow the arrows to see how energy moves in the ecosystem. A simple Mono Lake food web might look like this.

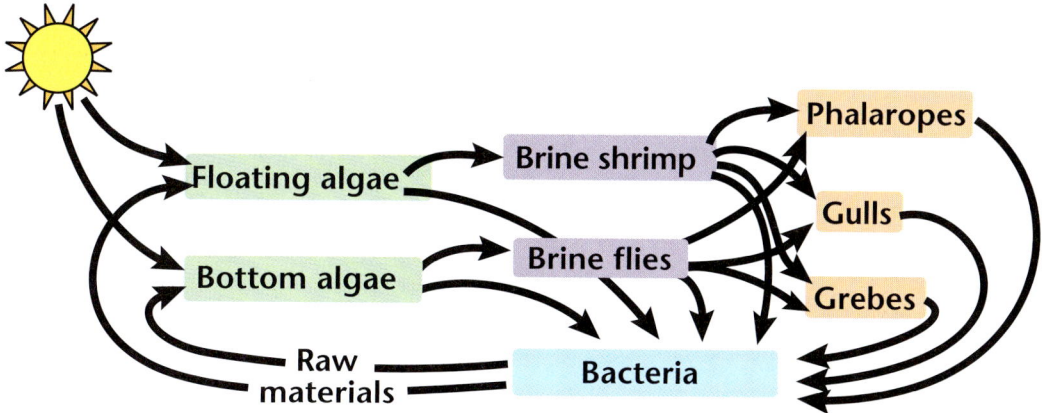

# Thinking about Mono Lake

1. What is the main environmental factor that affects the health of the Mono Lake ecosystem? Explain your answer.
2. Why did the California gull chicks not survive at Mono Lake in 1982?

# What Happens When Ecosystems Change?

Two things define an ecosystem. The first is the organisms. The second is the nonliving environment. The Sonoran Desert ecosystem of the southwest United States is partly defined by its common organisms. Cacti, lizards, and coyotes live in the desert. Spiders, insects, birds, scorpions, and snakes also live in the desert. The environment is hot and dry most of the time. The desert ecosystem thrives with these organisms and environmental conditions.

**A desert ecosystem**

**A tropical marine ecosystem**

The coral reef ecosystem of the Florida Keys National Marine Sanctuary is very different from the Sonoran Desert. The Keys Sanctuary is the only living coral barrier reef in North America. It is the third largest system of coral reefs in the world. The most important organisms in the reef ecosystem are coral and algae. Marine snails and parrot fish feed on the coral, and damselfish eat the algae. Fish of all sizes, shapes, and colors can be found swimming along the reef. Organisms such as spiny lobsters and long-spined black urchins come out from their hiding places and feed at night. Between the barrier reef and the shore are lagoons with calm water. On their sandy bottoms, turtle grass grows. Bottom dwellers, such as the southern stingray and gulf flounder, settle into the sand to feed. The environment is the tropical ocean.

Moving desert organisms to the ocean would be silly. Cacti and snakes from the desert would not survive in a marine environment. The environment is too different. Organisms have needs. Those needs are met only by the environment in which the organisms live. But what happens when the environment changes a little bit? Are organisms affected?

We can look at the Colorado River as an example. Before 1963, the river flowed through Grand Canyon. Each spring the melting snow upstream caused a flood in the river. The flood of cold water roared through the riverbed. It washed away the sandy beaches. It cleared out plants growing on the banks of the river.

During the summer, the river slowed. Sand settled on the edges of the river. The water warmed up. Plants began to grow on the new sandy beaches. The organisms in the river thrived in this environment.

**The Colorado River ecosystem**

**The Glen Canyon Dam changed the Colorado River ecosystem.**

In 1963, the Glen Canyon Dam was completed. The dam stops the flow of flood water each spring. Cold water flows through the bottom of the dam at a steady rate. There are no more floods. The water flowing in the river is cold all year long.

This change in the environment was small. But it affected the balance of organisms in the ecosystem. Trout need cold water to thrive. After the dam was completed, the trout population grew because the water was cold all year. The trout became predators of the young humpback chub living in the river. The humpback chub is a large fish that can live up to 40 years. It lives only in the Colorado River Basin. The humpback chub population got smaller because more trout were in the river.

Trout have a **range of tolerance** for temperature. If the water gets warmer than they can tolerate, or colder than they can tolerate, they will not survive. Before the dam was built, the warmer summer water was within the range of tolerance for trout, so they survived. But it was not the best temperature for the trout. After the dam was built, the colder water was the **optimum** (best) temperature for trout. As a result, the trout thrived, their population grew, and they ate more of the chub.

The willows and other plants that grew on the sandy beaches were no longer washed away in the spring floods. More plants grew in the changed environment. The plants stopped the sand from moving in the riverbed. As a result, the shallow water where the baby chubs and river snails grew disappeared. So the chub and snail populations became smaller.

In March 1967, the humpback chub was placed on the federal list of **endangered** species. The reasons were habitat loss because of changes in water temperature and water flow, and competition from the trout. Recently, the chub populations are starting to increase, but they are still endangered. Here are two possible reasons for the increase.

- People have removed many rainbow trout and brown trout from the river. These two fish prey on young fish and compete with humpback chub for food.
- Starting in 2003, the area experienced a drought. As a result of the drought, water temperature increased in the Colorado River. This warmer water helped native fish, including the chub.

This Colorado River story shows how living and nonliving environmental factors affect organisms. The environment controls which organisms will thrive, survive, and die. Small changes in temperature, water flow, or population size can change the balance of an ecosystem. The change favors some organisms and makes it harder for others.

**A humpback chub**

## Thinking about Populations

How did the change of water temperature after the dam was completed affect the chub population? Why?

# The Shrimp Club

After reading about the endangered humpback chub, our teacher told us about another endangered species, the Attwater's prairie chicken. In the early 1900s, millions of Attwater's prairie chickens lived in the huge grasslands in eastern Texas. Today there might be as few as 100 breeding pairs. What caused such a decline in the number of prairie chickens?

The prairie chicken completely depends on the grassland habitat for its survival. As human populations have grown, the grassland habitat has been lost. Some habitat has been developed for towns and roads. Some habitat has been changed into fields to grow crops. Habitat loss is the main reason that Attwater's prairie chicken is endangered. There is not enough good habitat left to provide grassland for food and space to raise young chicks.

In Texas, wildlife biologists and conservation groups are working together to restore grasslands and prevent existing grasslands from being destroyed. The future survival of Attwater's prairie chicken is looking better.

**A prairie chicken**

Our class was wondering if students could do anything to help an endangered animal. Our teacher told us about an endangered freshwater shrimp living in streams in Northern California. Students in Marin County, California, and their teacher, Laurette Rogers, started the Shrimp Club to see how they could help the endangered shrimp survive. We interviewed Ms. Rogers to find out more about the Shrimp Club.

**Q: Are you still doing the Shrimp Club project?**

**A:** I work doing ecological (habitat) restoration to help endangered Northern California species. My commitment to this work started when I was a teacher at the Brookside School in Marin County, California, in 1992. My fourth-grade class worked together to form the Shrimp Club. The Shrimp Club grew and changed into the Students and Teachers Restoring a Watershed (STRAW) Project, an organization that coordinates many restoration projects.

**Q: What inspired you to do a restoration project to help an endangered species?**

**A:** I didn't plan to do this work. In 1992, my class watched a video on endangered species. John, a student, asked, "What can we do to help?" I knew I couldn't ignore the question. The class felt we had to do something real, and we needed to help. I believe school should be about real life so that students can practice being leaders and then continue to be leaders as adults.

**Laurette Rogers**

1 cm

**The endangered California freshwater shrimp**

**Q: What endangered species did your class decide they wanted to protect, and why?**

**A:** The Adopt a Species organization in California suggested that we choose between three Northern California endangered species that live in our creeks: a trout, a salmon, and a freshwater shrimp. The entire class voted, and the shrimp won. We chose California freshwater shrimp *Syncaris pacifica*.

We found out that
- The shrimp have lived in local creeks since dinosaurs roamed Earth.
- Males are 3 centimeters (cm) long; females are 5 cm long.
- They feed on dead and decaying streamside vegetation.
- They are weak swimmers. They must cling to the roots of willows growing along the banks of the creeks.
- The shrimp live and reproduce in protected, shaded pools.
- Most of the creeks run through ranches where cows eat the streamside vegetation and tramp through the water, destroying the shrimp habitat.

The class was excited to study something obscure and local rather than something cute and fluffy living far away. The shrimp was something no one else was protecting. As we learned about the shrimp, we grew to love them. This was the start of what my students fondly started to refer to as the "Shrimp Club."

**Q: How did your students decide what to do?**

**A:** My 28 students and I brainstormed ideas of what to do. We figured out we had to restore the creeks to their condition prior to the introduction of cows into the watershed. We organized the class into committees that met regularly. Each committee prepared a goal sheet that included what they were working on and the current status of their part of the project.

The T-shirt committee's goal was to raise money. The newsletter committee developed a regular newsletter to share information with the school community. The public relations committee made presentations in front of companies and news media, and encouraged journalists to come to our restoration days to report on our work. One committee met with ranchers to plan where we could restore native vegetation by the streams on their land. The stamp committee made a huge rubber stamp that explained what the Shrimp Club was trying to do. They took home brand-new paper bags from grocery stores, stamped them, and returned them to the store for customers to read. A comic-strip committee formed because a student wanted to draw and write comics about the shrimp project.

> **"** I always thought the teacher made the path and we followed, but in this case the students made the path and the teacher followed. **"**
>
> *Adam (age 10)*

**Young native plants arrive in tubes for planting.**

**Q: What were some of the exciting things the students got to do?**

**A:** In the spring of 1993, we did our first fieldwork on Stemple Creek within the Estero de San Antonio watershed. We planted native plants. We wrote letters to government officials, and students were invited to testify at hearings before local government agencies about the Endangered Species Act. We actually traveled to Washington, DC, to present the Shrimp Club to the National Fish and Wildlife Foundation (NFWF), to the Environmental Protection Agency (EPA), and to our representatives in Congress, Senator Barbara Boxer and Congresswoman Lynn Woolsey. It was a very big deal. We were even on the news. That was exciting!

The less glamorous work was exciting, too. We worked with professional stream-restoration scientists to remove invasive plant species and reintroduce a lot of native willow and oak trees. One day, we watched as a calf was born on a ranch. Students loved being around ranch animals and learning about ranch life. We saw snakes, hawks, and even a badger. Most importantly, we got to do real work to make a difference in our community.

**Q: We heard you won an award. What did you win?**

**A:** In 1993, we won the grand prize in the "A Pledge and a Promise" environmental awards, and the award included a check for $32,000! The whole community went nuts, and some were even dancing in the streets. But we were not doing the work to win awards. We were doing it to restore the habitat for our shrimp.

**Q: It sure seems like everything went really well. Did you have problems?**

**A:** We made a lot of mistakes. A lot of phone calls didn't produce results. Sometimes journalists would hang up on my students. One time the public relations committee arranged for a reporter to show up at a restoration field trip, but the students forgot to confirm it, and the reporter didn't show. We learned a lot from these experiences.

Despite all the challenges and obstacles, it felt like there were people waiting to help us. For example, a banker helped us set up a checking account with a 9-year-old student as a cosigner. The student got to write a check for $25,000. One tiny shrimp opened up the whole world.

**Q: What exactly is a watershed? Why do we need habitat restoration in some areas?**

**A:** When water falls on the land, it flows downhill, usually ending up in a creek or stream. A watershed is the area of land that drains into a particular body of water. The watershed is usually named for the body of water into which the water flows. The watershed starts at the highest point of land, and all the water that flows into a single creek defines a watershed.

We need habitat restoration because the way people have used land in the past has made the land less usable for the native plants and animals that lived there before people moved in. We try to make the land work for the native plants and animals again. We try to work hand in hand with nature and the people who live there now to make the ecosystem work well for the native organisms that live there. At one particular ranch, we observed 8 species of birds before restoration. Now we see 28 species.

**Students plant native trees and shrubs.**

Lots of equipment is needed to restore a watershed.

**Q: What plants are used to restore a watershed?**

**A:** We use native plants, the plants that evolved to live in that spot. Nonnative plants are plants that were brought in by people. Sometimes during restoration work, we're just removing invasive species, making space for the native species to grow and expand.

**Q: Can one class make a difference?**

**A:** Yes, if you have a good plan. If you want to be involved in a creek restoration project, you should have a professional creek restorationist to help you. A wildlife scientist will help make sure you do the right thing and not accidentally do more damage. If you follow a plan and get the cooperation of the community, then yes, absolutely! One class can make a big difference.

**Q: Are you still involved in this work?**

**A:** It is my whole life, and I'm in my 19th year of watershed-restoration work. I still go to most restoration fieldwork days.

Each year, STRAW brings about 100 classes to local creeks that we have identified as needing restoration work. I work with a team of professionals with incredible scientific expertise and other STRAW faculty who go into K–12 classrooms to give pre-field lessons. Students often say, "It was hard work, but it was fun."

**Q: How did the restoration work that students did in 1992 impact their lives?**

**A:** The main thing is the students feel empowered to make a difference in their lives. From my experience, I've seen that students gain self-knowledge about who they are in the world. It's important that students have their hands on the reins of their own learning, that you trust them, and give them the freedom to have creativity and ownership.

**Students can make a difference.**

**Q: How is the California freshwater shrimp doing?**

**A:** I was told it would take 50 years to see if the restoration would work, but the shrimp have already expanded their range because of the work students did. They have moved downstream holding on to the roots of the willows students planted.

STRAW continues as a project of Point Reyes Bird Observatory (PRBO) Conservation Science.

> " I think this project changed everything I thought we could do. I always thought kids meant nothing . . . [But] kids can make a difference. We are not just little dots. "
>
> *Megan (age 10)*

> " I have diary entries from your class. Wanting to be a marine biologist, I remember writing furiously to express how excited I was about all you taught.
>
> Thank you so much for teaching me more than a college degree and 4 years of 'real world' work experience could have taught me. I will carry memories from your class always. I hope that as I enter graduate school, I can experience that same thrill and excitement I had when I was 10. Your class has stuck with me more than any other over the years. "
>
> *Megan (age 28) in a letter to her fourth-grade teacher Laurette Rogers*

# Variation and Selection

If every person in your school brought their pet dog to class, you would see a lot of variation. There might be a tiny Chihuahua or a big Bernese mountain dog. There might be short-legged dachshunds or tall golden retrievers. There might be thin dalmatians or round-looking bulldogs. Where did they all come from? Why do they look so different?

Evidence suggests that pet dogs evolved from the wolf. Scientists think that one kind of wolf might have been comfortable around humans as far back as 135,000 years ago. These wolves were not pets, but they lived near humans. Much later, about 2,500 years ago, humans used some kinds of dogs for hunting, protecting livestock, and carrying loads. Today, there are about 400 different breeds (kinds) of pet dogs. How did 400 breeds of dog come from the wolf?

**Pet dogs evolved from the wolf.**

**Dogs show a lot of variation.**

## Selective Breeding

Suppose you wanted a hunting dog to chase badgers out of their burrows. The dog would need short legs. So you would find a dog with short legs and make sure it produced offspring. You would breed the offspring with another dog with very short legs. And when those pups grew up, you would again breed the short-legged offspring. In a few **generations**, you might have a lot of short-legged dogs. Some of these dogs would be able to go into burrows to catch a badger. This might have been how the short-legged dachshund breed came to be.

**A dachshund has short legs.**

Selective breeding is when humans select individual organisms to breed to produce offspring with certain traits. Humans decide which qualities they want in a dog. They find individual dogs in the population that have these traits. Then they breed them to produce offspring with those same traits.

Selective breeding has produced the 400 different breeds of dogs. It has also produced many breeds of horses, cats, dairy cows, wheat, peppers, tomatoes, and corn. The desirable traits can be very different. You might want a plant that grows fast or produces fruit with no seeds. Humans are good at using selective breeding to meet their needs.

**Peppers and tomatoes have many different breeds.**

There is more competition for food during the winter.

Young moose (offspring) inherit traits from their parents.

## Natural Selection

In nature, the environment (not humans) selects the individual organisms that will produce offspring. Some individuals are selected to reproduce, and some are not.

Life is a struggle. Animals compete for food. They also compete to find a mate. Changes in the environment, such as climate change, can place pressure on organisms. Individuals in populations that are adapted to their environment have ways to respond to these pressures.

In all populations, there is variation from one individual to the next. Some individuals will be better at getting food. Others will be better at avoiding predators. Some will be better at dealing with cold weather. These variations are important when the environment changes.

A change in the environment can add more pressure to a population. The change might be a new predator, a forest fire, or less food to eat. Some individuals in the population will be able to live successfully in this changed environment. These successful individuals will reproduce. They will leave offspring with the traits that allow them to survive in the changing environment. The traits of the survivors are passed to the next generation as **inherited traits**. That's natural selection.

# Darwin's Finches

In 1835, Charles Darwin visited the Galápagos Islands off the shore of Ecuador. He observed and described many kinds of birds with different beaks. Later, other scientists studied these same birds. These birds are known as Darwin's finches, and there are 13 of them. These finches gave scientists a new way of thinking about how changes occur in populations.

We now know that all 13 different finches on the Galápagos Islands evolved from one species of finch. That original species of finch arrived on the islands thousands of years ago. How did one species of finch evolve into 13 different species?

## The Galápagos Islands

**Darwin collected many finches, each with a different beak.**

Scientists speculate that long ago, a big storm blew a small flock of mainland finches out to sea. The flock landed on some small, volcanic islands. The small population of finches was in a very different environment. The islands had food and places to nest, but they were not what the birds were used to.

There were seeds of several sizes from grasses, shrubs, and trees. In the population of mainland finches, there was variation in beak size. Individuals with larger, stronger beaks could crack large seeds. Individuals with smaller beaks could not. Finches with smaller beaks could more easily gather large numbers of small seeds. Individuals with large beaks could not eat the small seeds. Variations in beak size turned out to be helpful.

**Medium male (left) and female (right) ground finches found on the Galápagos Islands**

Finches that fed on large seeds mated and produced offspring with large, strong beaks. Their beaks allowed them to survive when large seeds were plentiful. Over time, the finches lived as separate groups because of the seeds they ate. Over many generations and many years, the large-beaked finches and the small-beaked finches were so different that they could no longer mate with each other to produce offspring. They had evolved into two new species. And the new species were different from the original mainland finches.

This same process of eating different foods based on beak size and shape produced other differences in the populations. Over time, all the differences created 13 different species. Each species was adapted to feed on a different food source.

What would happen to the large-beaked finches if the large seeds became scarce? They would have to find a new food source. It might be seeds of a different size or perhaps insects. Within the population of large-beaked finches would be individuals with smaller beaks. The small beaks would make it easier for those individuals to feed on a smaller food source. They would survive and reproduce. Their offspring would inherit the trait of smaller beaks. Individuals who survived would pass their traits to the next generation. The pressure of finding food would cause the population to shift to finches with smaller beaks. This would take many generations.

## Darwin's Finches Today

Recently, the environment on the Galápagos Islands changed again. Fly larvae are like a **parasite** to baby finches. They burrow into a chick's body and make it sick. The finches now have to deal with this new pressure. It is not clear whether individuals in the finch populations have adaptations to protect themselves from the deadly fly larvae.

The struggle for survival goes on. Because the environment is always changing, the populations that survive and thrive are always changing. Sometimes the change in the environment is so fast or so extreme that no individuals in a population survive. Then the entire population dies or becomes extinct. Extinction is part of the process of natural selection.

**A large female ground finch opening a seed**

**A common female cactus finch**

# Environmental Scientists

The behaviors of humans can change ecosystems throughout the world. Environmental scientists study changes to environments and ecosystems. They also research ways to save native habitats and prevent destruction. These environmental scientists have made a difference in environmental science.

## Rachel Carson

In 1962, Rachel Carson's book *Silent Spring* was published. Many people think it is the most important book ever written about ecology. It changed how Americans think about their place in nature.

Carson (1907–1964) studied marine biology in college. In 1936, the US Bureau of Fisheries hired her. She was the first woman biologist ever hired by the bureau. During the 1940s and 1950s, she studied and wrote about life in the sea. She also started to see some disturbing things happening in the environment. Animals were dying. She figured out that the cause was pesticides.

Pesticides developed in the 1940s were used widely to kill mosquitoes, fruit flies, cabbage worms, and lots of other pests. Carson discovered that the poisons also killed all the other insects in the area where the pesticide was sprayed. The poison killed everything.

When pesticide spray drifted over a friend's bird sanctuary, the birds died. Carson was alarmed. She imagined a spring when no birds returned to the woods near her home. In 1957, she started writing a book. The horrible thought of spring without the music of singing birds became the name for her book, *Silent Spring*.

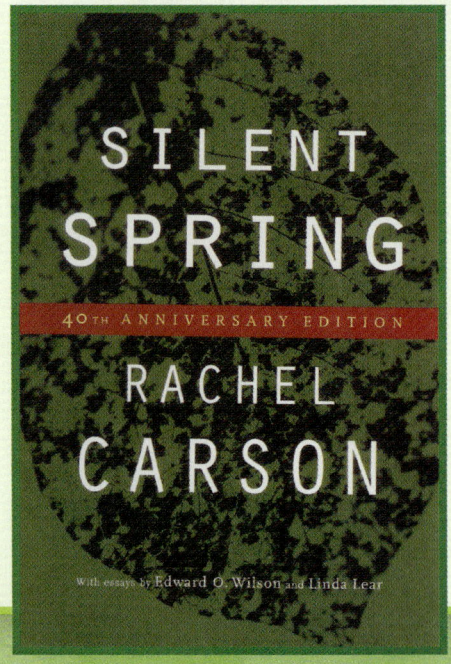

**Carson writing in her study**

The book got a lot of attention. The companies that made the pesticides tried to get the book banned. They attacked Carson and her scientific conclusions. She fought back and continued to present her evidence. Soon people started to listen, including President John F. Kennedy. President Kennedy ordered studies of a pesticide called DDT to see if Carson's ideas were right.

Carson warned us of a danger to Earth's ecosystems. It was up to others, including many environmental groups, to act on her warning. As a result of *Silent Spring,* DDT was banned in 1972. But Carson never saw that day. In 1964, she died of cancer.

Carson is best remembered for making people aware of the dangers of pesticides. People started thinking about what happens to plants and animals when we change the environment either by accident or on purpose.

# Edward O. Wilson

As a child, Edward O. Wilson (1929–) loved nature. He loved exploring in the Alabama woods and nearby streams. When he was 9 years old, he read an article about ants. Their interesting behavior and the way they worked together fascinated him. Those Alabama ants started young Wilson's career as a scientist. When he was only 13 years old, he discovered the first fire ants in the United States.

Wilson had a hard time with math and some trouble reading. This did not stop him from studying science. He studied biology at the University of Alabama and Harvard University. Later, he became a professor at Harvard.

Wilson continued to study ants. In 1971, he wrote a book about the social behavior of ants. He described how ants and other animals communicate using chemicals called pheromones. In the book, he also compared the organization of ant colonies to human societies.

In 1992, Wilson wrote a book called *The Diversity of Life*. He wrote that human activities were destroying organisms worldwide. Wilson predicted that millions of kinds of plants and animals would become extinct by the middle of the 21st century. Since then, Wilson has been trying to find ways that humans can save the world's ecosystems.

In 2007, Wilson gave a speech challenging everyone to learn more about our biosphere. He asked for the development of an online database of what we know about organisms. His speech gave rise to the Encyclopedia of Life project (EOL), which provides global access to knowledge about life on Earth.

## Tyrone B. Hayes

Tyrone B. Hayes (1967–) is a biology professor at the University of California at Berkeley. He studies frogs. The first frogs he saw were in a swamp near his home in South Carolina. Now Hayes studies frogs in Africa and North America.

Hayes found something strange happening to some of the frogs he studied. Frogs living in the wild were going through sex changes. The "male" frogs were making eggs just like the females.

Hayes and his team studied the frogs' environment. They found small amounts of a common **herbicide** in the water. An herbicide is a chemical used to kill plants. Hayes did more tests in the lab. The tests showed that the herbicide was causing the changes in the frogs.

The companies that make the herbicide challenged the research. But Hayes believes his science is correct. He continues to speak out about what he finds.

## Wangari Muta Maathai

Wangari Muta Maathai (1940–2011) was born in Nyeri, a town in Kenya, Africa. Unlike most of the young women in her country, Maathai was able to go to college. She went to college in Kansas, Pennsylvania, and Nairobi. She was the first woman from eastern Africa to receive a doctorate degree.

In 1977, Maathai founded the Green Belt Movement. The group is mostly women. Their main activity is planting trees to replace those cut down for firewood. They have planted more than 30 million trees! But some people didn't understand the value of planting trees. They didn't see the good Maathai was doing for the environment. Even though people tried to stop her, she did what was right for the environment and for the people of Kenya.

Maathai was elected to the Kenyan parliament in 2002. She was named deputy minister of Kenyan natural resources and wildlife in 2003. In 2004, Maathai received the Nobel Peace Prize for her many years of promoting peace and good living conditions in Africa.

# Range of Tolerance

Ecosystems are defined by the nonliving factors of the environment and the organisms living there. Water is a nonliving factor. Every ecosystem must have water. But the amount of water in an ecosystem can be different. Lake and ocean ecosystems thrive underwater. Rain forest ecosystems thrive with a lot of water. Desert ecosystems thrive with very little water.

Chaparral ecosystems are found on the West Coast of the United States. Chaparral is not quite as dry as desert. But plants and animals living there must survive long summers and falls without rain. The plants are tough and brushy with long roots. Many of the animals burrow deep into the rocky soil.

**A chaparral ecosystem**

**Chaparral ecosystems before and after a fire**

Another challenging nonliving factor in chaparral ecosystems is fire. Wildfires leave the land's surface black and lifeless. But before long, life returns. Animals that hide deep in their burrows come back to the surface after the fire passes. The roots of chaparral plants are still alive. As soon as the rains come, new branches and leaves sprout. The ashes from the burned plants provide nutrients for the new plants to grow and thrive. The chaparral ecosystem can survive well even when wildfire burns it to the ground.

The chaparral ecosystem has plants and animals that can thrive even when there are fires. The plants and animals that live there have a high range of tolerance for heat and fire. Plants and animals whose optimum environment is a forest ecosystem might survive in the chaparral ecosystem, but not nearly as well. They do not have as much tolerance for heat and fire. Plants and animals that live in rain forests would die in the chaparral ecosystem. They have no tolerance for heat and fire.

## Thinking about Range of Tolerance

All plants need water. What does *optimum water* mean for a plant? What does *range of tolerance for water* mean for a plant?

# How Organisms Depend on One Another

Animals depend on plants for survival. Trees provide shelter for birds to build nests. High in the branches, eggs and baby birds are safe from snakes, skunks, and coyotes. The owl in the picture below is protected from weather and predators in a tree. Beetles and isopods live under tree bark. Walking sticks hide on trees to protect themselves from predators. Animals also depend on plants for food. Animals eat leaves, flowers, fruits, seeds, bark, stems, sap, and roots of plants. It's easy to find many ways that animals depend on plants for survival.

Plants depend on animals for survival, too. You read about the swollen-thorn acacia tree. The ants help the tree survive. If an insect lands on the tree, the ants will attack it. If another plant touches the tree, the ants cut it away. The acacia tree depends on the ants for protection. And the ants depend on the tree for shelter and food.

**An owl nesting in a tree**

**A walking stick looks like a twig.**

A bee collects pollen and nectar for food.

## Pollination

What other ways do plants depend on animals? Think about honeybees visiting flowers. Bees collect pollen and nectar from flowers. This is food for the bees. The bees depend on plants for food.

The plants also depend on the bees. Pollen must get from one flower to another for plants to make seeds. This is called **pollination**. Plants can't move, so the pollen must be carried from one flower to another. Bees carry pollen as they fly from flower to flower. (Can you see the yellow dust on this bee's body? That's the pollen.) Bees make it possible for plants to produce seeds. The seeds grow to become adult plants, which make flowers with pollen and nectar. Then the cycle starts over again.

Other insects, such as butterflies and moths, also visit flowers for food. Plants depend on insects to bring pollen, and insects depend on plants for food. Without bees and other insects that visit flowers, plants cannot survive. Without flowers on plants, bees and butterflies cannot survive.

## Seed Dispersal

When seeds are ripe, they are ready to grow. Seeds have a better chance of survival if they sprout away from the parent plant. The new plant will be able to get more light, water, and nutrients. **Seed dispersal** is the term used to describe ways that seeds move away from the parent plant.

Sometimes wind disperses, or scatters, seeds. Wind is dispersing the small seeds of this dandelion.

Animals can also disperse seeds. Squirrels, chipmunks, and birds often take seeds and fruits (acorns, sunflower seeds, berries, and cherries) for food. They may drop the seeds or bury them and forget where they put them. Seeds with hooks can also stick to animals to be carried away from the parent plant.

**Dandelion seeds blowing in the wind**

Animals depend on plants for survival. Plants give animals food and shelter. Plants also depend on animals for survival. Animals help pollinate plants and disperse seeds.

**Sometimes birds drop the seeds they are carrying.**

**A chipmunk eating an acorn**

## Thinking about Dependence

1. Describe three examples of how animals depend on plants for survival.
2. Describe three examples of how plants depend on animals for survival.
3. Do you think animals pollinate flowers and disperse seeds on purpose or by accident? Explain why you think so.

# Animals from the Past

Thirty thousand years ago, people did not live in Los Angeles, California. But animals did. Some of these animals were the same ones you might see in the western United States today. Coyotes, mountain lions, and black bears lived back then. But some of the animals that were alive then are gone today. How do we know those animals lived 30,000 years ago?

Not far from downtown Los Angeles is a place called the La Brea Tar Pits. The area has many pools of hard, black tar. In the summer heat, the tar melts.

When animals stepped into the melted tar thousands of years ago, they got stuck. They couldn't get out. Slowly, they sank into the sticky tar and died.

In 1901, scientists discovered that the tar pits were full of **fossil** bones. Some of the bones were unlike any they had seen before. They dug the bones out of the tar. The scientists carefully put them together to make complete skeletons. Some skeletons were from kinds of animals that no longer live on Earth. Groups of animals that once lived on Earth, but have died out are extinct.

**A tar pit at La Brea**

**La Brea Tar Pits Museum**

**What a ground sloth might have looked like**

**A fossil skeleton of a ground sloth**

Ground sloths were common 30,000 years ago in the western United States. Ground sloths are extinct now. Scientists discovered that ground sloths once lived in this region when they found their bones in the tar pits. The ground sloths are similar to tree sloths that still live in the rain forests of South America.

Saber-toothed cats no longer live on Earth. They are similar to the mountain lions that live in the western United States and other places today. Saber-toothed cats had huge canine teeth that look deadly. Scientists aren't sure what purpose the oversized teeth served. The large cats may have followed prey animals into the tar.

**What a saber-toothed cat might have looked like**

**A skull of a saber-toothed cat**

299

The mastodon is one of the largest animals that lived in this region. It looks a lot like the elephants that live in Africa and Asia. Some of the tar pits might have had a layer of water over the tar. Mastodons that stepped into the pool for a drink could have become trapped in the tar.

Why did the ground sloth, saber-toothed cat, and mastodon become extinct? It's not because they all fell into the tar pits. Only a few were trapped in the tar and died. Organisms become extinct when the environment changes.

The climate was warming up after the ice age. When the environment changed, some animals survived, some animals looked for other places to live, and some died. The animals that are known only as fossils from the La Brea Tar Pits could not survive in the changed environment.

**What a mastodon might have looked like**

**A fossil skeleton of a mastodon**

## Recent Discoveries about Ice Age Animals

Ice age fossils have been discovered recently in other parts of North America. In 1978, the fossil remains of Columbian mammoths were discovered near the Bosque River in Waco, Texas. This is the same kind of mammoth that was found in the La Brea Tar Pits. Researchers from Baylor University worked for 20 years to uncover the fossils and preserve them. The researchers found 22 mammoths, a camel, and the tooth of a young saber-toothed cat. The Waco Mammoth Site holds the record for the most skeletons of mammoths that died at the same time. At least 19 of the mammoths were trapped by flood water some 68,000 years ago. Their remains were buried in the sediments.

The Waco Mammoth Site was closed to the public until the end of 2009. That year, a shelter was completed to protect the bones. Now the fossils can be viewed by the public. There are plans to make this site a national monument, like the Dinosaur National Monument in Colorado and Utah.

**A Columbian mammoth**

More ice age fossils turned up in October 2010 near Aspen, Colorado. A construction worker was using a bulldozer to expand the Ziegler Reservoir. He was digging into the ground and removing peat moss when he observed a few large rib bones poking out. He immediately stopped and called the Denver Museum of Nature and Science.

A team of paleontologists went to the site. They used hand tools and began to carefully uncover the well-preserved bones of a Columbian mammoth. The bones had been buried in a lake during the ice age. The lake was gone, but the sediments were still wet and covered with peat moss. The scientists quickly wrapped the bones in plaster so that the bones would stay moist. If the bones dried out too fast, they would break.

This site is one of the richest fossil sites ever discovered in Colorado. The fossils found so far include American mastodons, Columbian mammoths, ice age deer and bison, a ground sloth, and a tiger salamander. Small animals include iridescent beetles and other insects, snails, and microscopic crustaceans. The large quantity of well-preserved plant material includes wood, seeds, cones, leaves of white spruce, sedges, and other plants.

The scientists could only work for a month at the reservoir fossil site because of the winter snow. Scientists continue to return to this site during good weather, uncover more fossils, and learn more about the animals that lived there 40,000 years ago.

**Uncovering the bones of a mammoth**

**Wrapping the fossils in plaster**

This discovery is important because the elevation is almost 2,700 meters (m). Scientists have never found ice age fossils at such a high elevation before. Little is known about the animals living in high-elevation environments during the ice age.

The other important discovery is nearly two dozen mammoth and mastodon tusks. The tusks have growth rings just like tree trunks. Scientists can use the tusk growth rings to tell how old the animal was when it died. They can even tell what season of the year the animal died. The tusks become a record of the animals' lives. They tell if the female had calves, if the males had been fighting, and other interesting things about their lives. These tusks and other fossils are on display at the Denver Museum of Nature and Science.

Scientists are learning a lot about ice age environments from the fossils found at different sites. They are a way to study animals that lived in a colder environment than exists today. The information might help us understand what will happen as Earth gets warmer.

**Removing the bones of a Columbian mammoth from the ground**

**A close-up of the mastodon tusk in the ground**

**The tip of the tusk**

# Thinking about the Past

1. What does *extinct* mean?
2. What are some animals that once lived in the United States, but are now extinct?
3. What are some animals that are similar to animals that are now extinct?
4. What can cause animals to become extinct?

# Darkling Beetles

Darkling beetles are insects. They live in almost every part of the world, from the desert to the rain forest. There are many different kinds. In North America alone, there are 1,400 kinds of darkling beetles! One kind of darkling beetle is *Tenebrio*.

The adult *Tenebrio* beetle is about 1.9 centimeters (cm) long. It is dark brown to black and usually lives in dark, dry places. Like other insects, the darkling beetle has six legs and three body parts. These parts are the head, thorax, and abdomen. Like other beetles, it has two pairs of wings. The front wings cover and protect the back wings and abdomen. Even with wings, darkling beetles cannot fly.

## Life Cycle

The darkling beetle goes through four stages in its life cycle. The stages are egg, larva, pupa, and adult beetle. Female beetles lay 500 to 1,000 eggs at a time. The eggs at 1 millimeter (mm) are almost too small to see. Tiny larvae hatch from the eggs in about a week.

The larvae of *Tenebrio* beetles are a yellow-gold color. They are called mealworms, but they are not worms at all. The larvae eat cereals and grains. They grow to a length of 3 cm. The larvae molt (shed their tough outer skin) several times in order to grow. After about 3 months, the larvae change into pupae.

The pupa is a resting stage. The insect's body begins to change into an adult beetle. The pupa stage lasts about 2 weeks. Then the beetle comes out as an adult. This cycle of changes is called complete metamorphosis.

**A larva (mealworm)**

**A pupa**

**An adult *Tenebrio* beetle**

# Characteristics

Darkling beetles inherit most of their characteristics from their parents. Darkling beetles get their size and color from their parents. They get their head, antennae, thorax, and six legs from their parents.

Some characteristics are caused by the environment. Things can happen to change how a beetle looks. If a beetle gets into a fight, it might lose a piece of wing cover. It could even lose a leg. The beetle looks different.

If the beetle becomes a parent, what will its offspring look like? Will they have broken wing covers and five legs? No. Changes like these are caused by the environment. They are not passed on to offspring.

In the natural environment, *Tenebrio* beetles live in grasslands where there are plenty of seeds. They also make their homes near humans. They get into cupboards, pantries, and chicken farms. For this reason, darkling beetles might be thought of as pests. But they are harmless to humans.

**Darkling beetles inherit most of their characteristics from their parents.**

## Other Beetles

What makes a beetle a beetle? The most important characteristic that all beetles share is their short, hard front wings called elytra. When a beetle folds its wings, the elytra cover its entire abdomen. This shell gives a beetle its armored appearance. When a beetle flies, it lifts its elytra so that its back wings can move.

All beetles go through the same four stages of growth as the darkling beetle. Females lay eggs that hatch into wormlike larvae. The larvae eat, grow, and pupate. Finally, the pupae change into adults. At least 250,000 kinds of beetles have been described by scientists. Beetles can be less than 1 cm to more than 15 cm long.

**Another kind of darkling beetle**

Beetles live in just about every environment on Earth. They live in rain forests, deserts, mountain lakes, rivers, and northern forests. They can live in people's homes and gardens. They can even live in sewers. The only environment they don't live in is the ocean.

**A metallic-green fig beetle**

Beetles eat almost everything. Some eat leaves, fruit, bark, seeds, and grains. Others are parasites and live on or in living animals. Some beetles are scavengers, living on dead animals or dung. Beetles can be helpful to humans. For example, beetles called ladybugs are predators. They eat small insects that destroy gardens and farm plants.

Beetles have antennae for sensing their environment. These antennae are primarily used to smell, but may also be used to feel.

**A ten-lined June beetle**

What group of insects do you think is the most successful on Earth? Flies? Mosquitoes? Ants? It's the beetles. There are more kinds of beetles than all the other kinds of insects added together.

And how many different kinds of insects are there? No one knows for sure. About 1 million of the 1.3 million kinds of organisms that have been described by scientists are insects. The list of insects is growing at the rate of about 7,000 to 10,000 new kinds every year! Based on work done in rain forests, some scientists think there may be 10 to 30 million more kinds of insects to discover. The estimated numbers of kinds of plants, fish, birds, reptiles, and mammals seem quite small compared to the millions of insects.

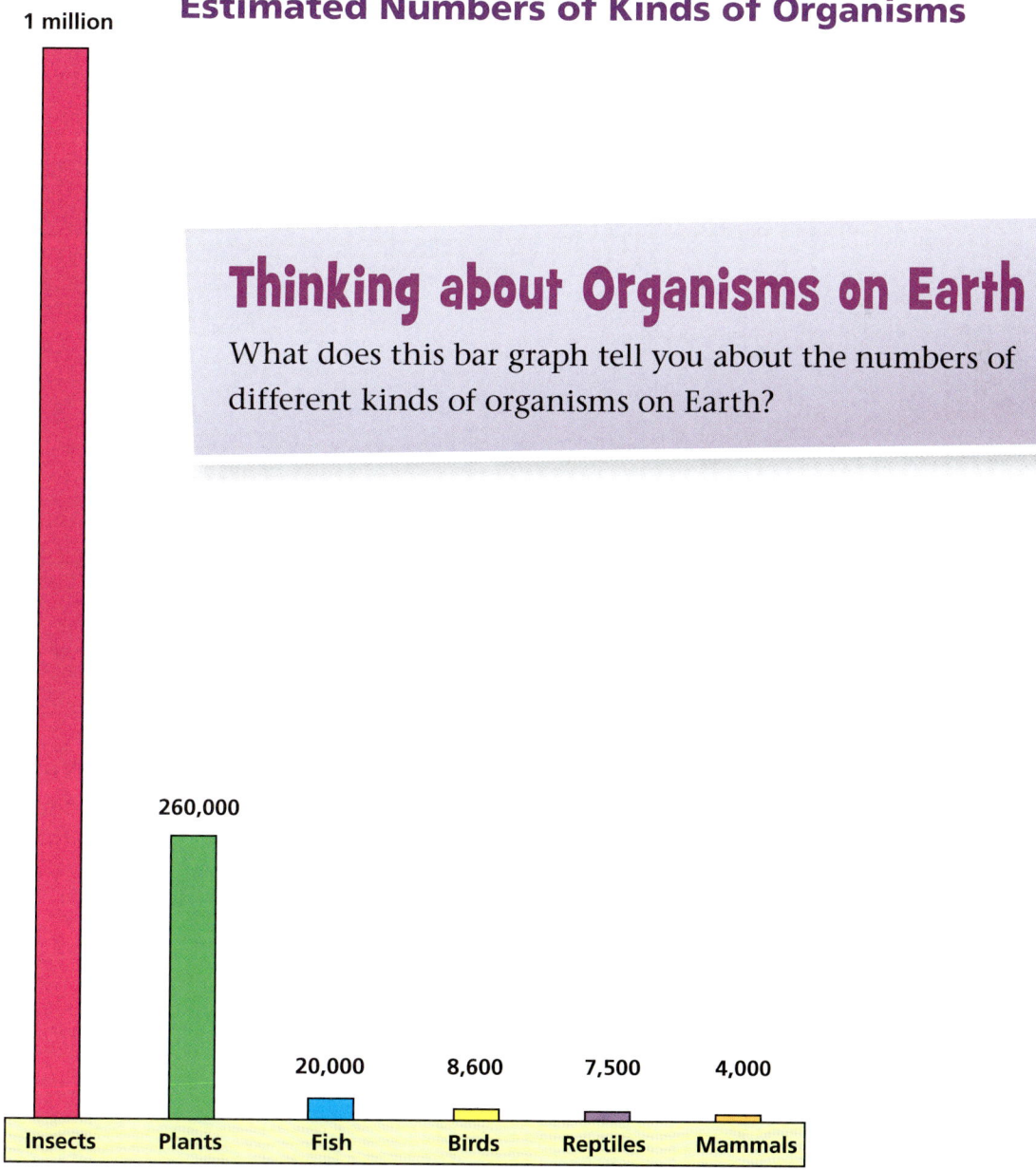

**Estimated Numbers of Kinds of Organisms**

## Thinking about Organisms on Earth

What does this bar graph tell you about the numbers of different kinds of organisms on Earth?

# References

**Table of Contents**

# References

Science Safety Rules . . . . . . . . . . . . . . . . . . . . . . . . . . . **312**
Glossary . . . . . . . . . . . . . . . . . . . . . . . . . . . . . . . . . . . . **313**
Photo Credits . . . . . . . . . . . . . . . . . . . . . . . . . . . . . . . **322**

# Science Safety Rules

1. Listen carefully to your teacher's instructions. Follow all directions. Ask questions if you don't know what to do.
2. Tell your teacher if you have any allergies.
3. Never put any materials in your mouth. Do not taste anything unless your teacher tells you to do so.
4. Never smell any unknown material. If your teacher tells you to smell something, wave your hand over the material to bring the smell toward your nose.
5. Do not touch your face, mouth, ears, eyes, or nose while working with chemicals, plants, or animals.
6. Always protect your eyes. Wear safety goggles when necessary. Tell your teacher if you wear contact lenses.
7. Always wash your hands with soap and warm water after handling chemicals, plants, or animals.
8. Never mix any chemicals unless your teacher tells you to do so.
9. Report all spills, accidents, and injuries to your teacher.
10. Treat animals with respect, caution, and consideration.
11. Clean up your work space after each investigation.
12. Act responsibly during all science activities.

# Glossary

**abrasion** the rubbing, grinding, and bumping of rocks that cause physical weathering **(133)**

**absorb** to take in or soak up **(70)**

**accelerate** to change an object's speed **(81)**

**acid** a substance that geologists use to identify rocks that contain calcite **(134)**

**algae** a large plantlike group of water organisms **(230)**

**amphibian** an animal, such as a frog or spadefoot toad, that reproduces in water **(211)**

**amplitude** the height of the peaks in a wave form **(91)**

**aquatic** referring to water **(205)**

**attract** to pull toward each other **(33)**

**bacteria** microorganisms that act as decomposers **(240)**

**battery** a source of electricity created from stored chemical energy **(11)**

**behavior** the actions of an animal in response to its environment **(208)**

**burrow** a hole or tunnel dug by a small animal **(210)**

**calcite** a common rock-forming mineral in Earth's crust **(134)**

**canopy** the highest layer in a forest, where there is a lot of sunlight **(206)**

**carnivore** an animal that eats only animals **(154, 239)**

**cast** a copy of an organism, like a fossil, that is created by the minerals in a mold **(151)**

**chemical weathering** the process by which the minerals in a rock can change due to chemicals in water and air. Chemical weathering can cause rocks to break apart. **(134)**

**circuit** a pathway for the flow of electric current **(6)**

**climate** the average or typical weather conditions in a region of the world **(247)**

**closed circuit** a complete pathway through which electricity flows **(15)**

**code** a set of signals or symbols that communicate **(62)**

**coil** a series of loops **(9)**

**community** the plants and animals in an ecosystem **(234)**

**compass** an instrument that uses a free-rotating magnetic needle to indicate direction **(42)**

**compete** to rely on or need the same resource as another organism **(243)**

**complete circuit** a circuit with all the conditions necessary to transfer electric energy **(15)**

**complete metamorphosis** the cycle of growth changes for an insect. The stages include egg, larva, pupa, and adult. **(223)**

**component** one item in a circuit **(15)**

**concentration** the amount of a substance, such as salt, in an amount of another substance, such as water **(260)**

**conclusion** a scientific decision based on observations, evidence, and data **(154)**

**concrete** a mixture of gravel, sand, cement, and water **(186)**

**constraint** a restriction or limitation **(24)**

**consumer** an organism that cannot make its own food. Consumers eat other organisms. **(239)**

**contact point** the place on a component where connections are made to allow electricity to flow **(6)**

**contour interval** the change in elevation between any two contour lines **(158)**

**contour lines** the curved lines in a topographic map that represent a specific elevation **(157)**

**core** in an electromagnet, the material around which a coil of insulated wire is wound **(43)**

**core** the center of Earth, made mostly of iron and nickel **(193)**

**crest** the high point of a wave **(89)**

**criteria** a standard for evaluating or testing something **(23)**

**crust** Earth's outer layer of solid rock **(172)**

**crustacean** a class of mostly aquatic animals with hard, flexible shells **(216)**

**decay** when dead plants or animals break down into small pieces **(130)**

**decomposer** an organism that breaks down plant and animal material into simple chemicals **(240)**

**deposition** the settling of sediments **(135)**

**digestive system** the organs and structures that digest food. The digestive system includes the teeth, mouth, esophagus, stomach, small intestine, large intestine, and colon. **(155)**

**dissolve** when a material mixes uniformly into another **(134)**

**dormant** inactive or resting **(211)**

**earth material** any nonliving natural resource that makes up Earth, including soil and water **(129)**

**earthquake** a sudden movement of Earth's crust along a fault **(167)**

**ecologist** a scientist who studies ecosystems **(234)**

**ecosystem** a community of organisms interacting with each other and with the nonliving environment **(234)**

**electric current** the flow of electricity through a conductor **(5)**

**electricity** energy that flows through circuits and can produce heat, light, motion, and sound **(6)**

**electromagnet** a piece of iron that becomes a temporary magnet when electricity flows through coils of insulated wire wrapped around it **(48)**

**electromagnetism** a property of electric and magnetic fields that causes interactions with electric charges and currents **(52)**

**endangered** at risk of becoming extinct **(272)**

**energy source** a place where energy comes from, such as batteries, fuels, the Sun, and objects in motion **(11)**

**energy** the ability to do work; what allows organisms to grow and move **(6, 235)**

**engineer** a scientist who designs ways to accomplish a goal or solve a problem **(8, 173)**

**entomologist** a biologist who studies insects **(220)**

**environment** everything that surrounds and influences an organism. Deserts, forests, and the ocean are environments. **(205)**

**environmental factor** one part of the environment. An environmental factor can be nonliving, such as water, light, and temperature. It can be living, such as plants and animals. **(205)**

**erosion** the carrying away of weathered earth materials by water, wind, or ice **(135)**

**evaporate** to dry up and go into the air **(213)**

**evidence** data used to support claims. Evidence is based on observations and scientific data. **(149)**

**extinction** a species that no longer exists **(228)**

**fault** a break in Earth's crust along which blocks of rock move past each other **(167)**

**fertile** able to support growth and development **(212)**

**fertilizer** any natural or synthetic material used in soil to help plants grow **(245)**

**filament** the material in a lightbulb (usually a thin wire) that makes light when heated by an electric current **(5)**

**flood** a large amount of water flowing over land that is usually dry **(138)**

**food** a form of chemical energy that organisms need to survive **(207)**

**food chain** a description of the feeding relationships between organisms in an environment **(241)**

**food web** all of the connected and interacting food chains in an ecosystem. Arrows show the flow of matter and energy from one organism to another. **(242)**

**force** push or a pull **(36)**

**fossil** any remains, trace, or imprint of animal or plant life preserved in Earth's crust **(150, 298)**

**fossil fuel** the remains of organisms that lived long ago preserved as oil, coal, and natural gas **(73)**

**fossil record** all the fossils on Earth **(152)**

**fracture** the uneven, rounded, or splintered surfaces of some minerals when they break **(148)**

**frequency** the speed at which something oscillates. High-frequency vibrations are rapid vibrations. **(64)**

**function** an action that helps a plant or an animal survive **(218)**

**fungus (plural fungi)** an organism that lacks chlorophyll and gets nutrients from dead or living organisms **(207)**

**generation** a group of organisms born and living at the same time **(282)**

**generator** a device that produces electricity from motion **(11)**

**geologist** a scientist who studies Earth, its materials, and its history **(149)**

**geoscientist** a scientist who studies the use, distribution, and conservation of Earth's natural resources **(181)**

**glacier** a large mass of ice moving slowly over land **(140)**

**granite** an igneous rock that forms inside Earth **(175)**

**gravity** the natural attraction between masses. On Earth, all objects are pulled toward the center of Earth. **(78)**

**habitat** the natural environment of a plant or an animal **(215)**

**heat** observable evidence of thermal energy **(6)**

**herbicide** a chemical used to kill plants **(291)**

**herbivore** an animal that eats only plants or algae **(154, 239)**

**humus (HEW-mus)** bits of dead plant and animal parts in the soil **(130)**

**hypersound** a very high frequency sound that is too high for human ears to detect **(255)**

**igneous rock** a rock that forms when melted rock (magma) hardens **(193)**

**incomplete circuit** a circuit that has a break in it **(16)**

**index contour** the numbers on contour lines that determine whether the elevation is rising or falling **(158)**

**induced magnetism** the influence of a magnetic field on a piece of iron, which makes the iron a temporary magnet **(36)**

**inherited trait** a characteristic that is passed down from generation to generation **(283)**

**insect** an animal that has six legs, a head, a thorax, and an abdomen **(207)**

**interact** to act on and be acted upon by something else **(36, 234)**

**iron** a metal that is attracted to a magnet **(33)**

**isopod** a small crustacean with 14 legs that all function the same **(218)**

**key** a switch that completes a circuit in a telegraph system **(60)**

**kinetic energy** energy of matter in motion **(82)**

**landform** a feature of the land, such as a mountain, canyon, or beach **(159)**

**landslide** the sudden movement of earth materials down a slope **(133)**

**larva (plural larvae)** the wormlike early stage in the life cycle of an insect **(223)**

**lava** melted rock erupting onto Earth's surface, usually from a volcano **(149)**

**light source** anything that radiates light, such as the Sun, a lightbulb, or a flame **(7)**

**light** visible evidence of energy **(5)**

**lightbulb** a filament held by two stiff wires and surrounded by a clear glass globe **(5)**

**limestone** a sedimentary rock made mostly of calcite **(134)**

**living** the condition of being alive **(205)**

**load** a weight or resistance that is moved or overcome when work is done **(76)**

**magma** melted rock below Earth's surface **(194)**

**magnet** an object that attracts to iron or steel at a distance **(32)**

**magnetic field** an area of magnetic influence around a magnet **(36)**

**magnetism** a property of objects or systems that causes them to attract iron or steel **(36)**

**mantle** the solid rock material between Earth's core and crust **(193)**

**marble** a metamorphic rock formed when limestone is subjected to heat and pressure **(134)**

**matter** anything that has mass and takes up space **(235)**

**metamorphic rock** a rock that forms when rocks and minerals are subjected to heat and pressure **(193)**

**microorganism** a microscopic organism, such as bacteria and some algae **(238)**

**migrate** when animals move from place to place with a change in the weather **(262)**

**mineral** an ingredient of a rock **(132)**

**mirror** a shiny surface that reflects light **(63)**

**mold** a space in the sediments that fills with minerals **(150)**

**motion** a change in the position of an object or system **(10)**

**motor** a device that produces motion from electricity **(13)**

**natural resource** living or nonliving materials, such as soil, forests, or water, that come from the natural environment **(181)**

**newton (N)** the standard unit for measuring force in the metric system **(84)**

**nocturnal** active at night **(210)**

**nonliving** referring to something that has never been alive or to things that were once alive and are no longer alive **(205)**

**north pole** the end of a magnet that orients toward Earth's magnetic north pole **(34)**

**nutrient** something that living things need to grow and stay healthy **(130, 205)**

**omnivore** an animal that eats both plants and animals **(239)**

**open circuit** an incomplete circuit through which electricity will not flow **(16)**

**optimum** most favorable to growth, development, and reproduction of an organism **(271)**

**organism** any living thing **(149, 215)**

**orient** to position an object in a certain way **(35)**

**oscillation** a back-and-forth motion **(89)**

**oscilloscope** an instrument that displays electric pulses as a wave form on a screen **(97)**

**paleontologist** a scientist who studies fossils **(149)**

**parallel circuit** a circuit that has two or more pathways for current to flow to multiple components at the same time **(17)**

**parasite** an organism that lives on and gets nutrients from another living organism **(287)**

**particle** a very small piece or part **(129)**

**peak** the high point on a wave form **(90)**

**permanent magnet** an object that sticks to iron **(32)**

**pesticide** a chemical developed to kill animals that are in some way harmful to humans **(245)**

**petrified wood** the fossil remains of trees. The term means "wood turned into stone." **(150)**

**petroleum** an oil that comes from the earth **(246)**

**photosynthesis** a process used by plants and algae to make sugar (food) out of light, carbon dioxide, and water **(236)**

**physical weathering** the process by which rocks are broken down by breaking and banging **(132)**

**phytoplankton** microscopic plantlike organisms in aquatic environments that produce their own food **(231)**

**pitch** how high or low a sound is **(64)**

**pole** the end of a magnet **(34)**

**pollination** the moving of pollen to the female part of a flower **(296)**

**pollute** to make an environment unsuitable for organisms because of substances introduced into air, water, or soil **(244)**

**Portland cement** a kind of cement made from limestone **(186)**

**potential energy** energy that matter has because of its position or condition **(86)**

**predator** an animal that hunts and catches other animals for food **(221)**

**predator** an animal that hunts and catches other animals for food **(154)**

**prey** an animal eaten by another animal **(251)**

**producer** an organism, such as a plant or algae, that makes its own food **(237)**

**property** something that you can observe about an object or a material. Size, color, shape, texture, and smell are properties. **(187)**

**property** something you can observe about an object, material, or system **(99)**

**prototype** the first attempt to build a product **(25)**

**pumice** a type of rock that forms when lava erupts from volcanoes **(170)**

**pupa (plural pupae)** the stage of an animal's life cycle between the larva and the adult stages **(264)**

**range** an amount of variation or difference **(260)**

**range of tolerance** the varying conditions of one environmental factor in which an organism can survive **(271)**

**react** to act or change in response to something **(134)**

**recycle** to use again **(217)**

**reflection** the bouncing of light rays off an object **(103)**

**refraction** the bending of light rays **(107)**

**repel** to push away **(33)**

**reproduce** to have offspring **(211)**

**restoration** putting something back to its original condition, such as building a fossil skeleton **(153)**

**retain** to hold or continue to hold **(130)**

**rock** a solid earth material made of two or more minerals **(129)**

**rock cycle** the processes by which rocks change into different kinds of rocks **(198)**

**sandstone** a sedimentary rock made of sand particles stuck together **(195)**

**scavenger** an animal that eats dead organisms **(239)**

**sediment** pieces of weathered rock such as sand, deposited by wind, water, and ice **(135)**

**sedimentary rock** a rock that forms when layers of sediments get stuck together **(149)**

**seed dispersal** the movement of seeds away from the parent plant **(297)**

**senses** information received from the environment using hearing, touch or feel, sight, smell, and taste **(250)**

**sensory receptor** a specialized cell that gets information from the environment and sends it to the brain **(250)**

**series circuit** a circuit that has only one pathway for current to flow to multiple components **(17)**

**silt** rocks that are smaller than sand, but bigger than clay **(129)**

**sine wave** a repeating s-shaped wave form **(90)**

**soil** a mix of humus, sand, silt, clay, gravel, and/or pebbles **(129)**

**solar cell** an instrument that transfers sunlight directly into electricity **(15)**

**solution** the "answer" to a problem. Engineers solve problems. **(23)**

**sound** observable evidence of energy **(10)**

**sound source** an object or material that vibrates in a way that sends oscillations through a medium **(93)**

**source** the beginning of something, such as where a river starts **(233)**

**south pole** the end of a magnet that orients toward Earth's magnetic south pole **(34)**

**species** a group of organisms that are all the same kind **(247)**

**speed** the rate at which an object changes position **(77)**

**stored energy** energy available for use **(11)**

**stridulation** the chirping sound that crickets make **(255)**

**structure** any identifiable part of an organism **(208)**

**technology** a modification of natural materials or processes done to satisfy human needs or desires **(9)**

**telegraph** a device that uses an electromagnet to send coded messages by closing and opening an electric circuit **(60)**

**temperature** a measure of how hot or cold matter is **(205)**

**temporary magnet** a piece of iron that behaves like a magnet only when it is under the influence of a magnetic field **(36)**

**terrarium** a container with plants growing inside **(215)**

**terrestrial** referring to land **(205)**

**thrive** to grow fast and stay healthy **(205)**

**tool** any device used to perform a specific function **(25)**

**topographic map** a map that uses contour lines to show the shape and elevation of the land **(157)**

**transport** to move or carry from one place to another **(136)**

**trough** the low point on a wave form **(89)**

**ultrasound** a very low frequency sound that is too low for human ears to detect **(256)**

**understory** the layer above the rain forest floor and below the rain forest canopy **(207)**

**variation** difference **(250)**

**vernal pool** a shallow, temporary pond **(229)**

**vibration** a quick back-and-forth movement **(58)**

**volcano** an opening in Earth's crust where lava, cinders, ash, and gases come to the surface **(149)**

**wavelength** the distance from the center of one peak to the center of the next peak on a wave form **(92)**

**weathering** the process by which larger rocks crack and break apart over time to form smaller rocks **(132)**

**wire** a metal or other solid substance through which electric current moves **(6)**

**work** to use force to move an object or achieve another outcome **(10)**

**zooplankton** microscopic animals in aquatic environments **(231)**

**Photo Credits**

Cover and title page: © Matt Gibson; Page 1: © iStockphoto/Cameron Strathdee; Page 5: © akg-images/The Image Works; Page 6: © iStockphoto/henrikroger (lightbulb); © iStockphoto/lishenjun (battery); Page 7: U.S. Dept. of Interior, Nat'l Park Service, Edison Historic Site (top); © Science Source/Photo Researchers, Inc. (bottom); Page 8: U.S. Dept. of Interior, Nat'l Park Service, Edison Historic Site; Page 9: © iStockphoto/mgkaya (top); © iStockphoto/luismmolina (middle); © iStockphoto/AntiMartina (bottom left); © iStockphoto/janda75 (bottom right); Page 10: © Galyna Andrushko/Shutterstock; Page 11: © iStockphoto/davidf (bottom left); © Rodolfo Arpia/Shutterstock (right); Page 12: © iStockphoto/design56 (top); © Mary Kate Denny/PhotoEdit (bottom right); © iStockphoto/andras_csontos (inset); © iStockphoto/Miffycat (bottom right); Page 13: Courtesy, Sacramento Municipal Utilities District; Page 14: © Christian Waadt/Shutterstock (top); © Tatiana Popova/Shutterstock (bottom); Pages 15–17: © Rose Craig/Lawrence Hall of Science; Page 18: © iStockphoto/JLGutierrez; Pages 19–20: © Rose Craig/Lawrence Hall of Science (illustration); © iStockphoto/lishenjun (battery); Page 21: © Darrin Henry/Shutterstock; Page 22: © Valerii Ivashchenko/Shutterstock; Page 23: © Huntstock.com/Shutterstock; Page 24: © Leigh Prather/Shutterstock; Page 25: © iStockphoto/Pamela Moore; Page 26: © demarcomedia (top); © anyaivanova/Shutterstock (left); © suphakit73/Shutterstock (right); Pages 27–28; © Laura Stachel/We Care Solar; Pages 29–30; © Daniel Dekko Goldman; Page 31: © Laura Stachel/We Care Solar; Page 32: © Michael Dalton/Fundamental Photographs, NYC; Page 33: © Rose Craig/Lawrence Hall of Science; Page 34: © Matthew Cole/Shutterstock; Page 35: © Scott MacNeill; Page 36: © iStockphoto/Tommousney; Page 37: © iStockphoto/Melissa Carroll (top); © Rolin Graphics (middle); © Volina/Shutterstock (bottom); Page 38: © Rose Craig/Lawrence Hall of Science; Pages 39–41; © Scott MacNeill; Pages 42–43: © Triff/Shutterstock (background); Page 43: © Rose Craig/Lawrence Hall of Science; Page 44: © Matthew Cole/Shutterstock (left); © worker/Shutterstock (middle); © ARTEKI/Shutterstock (right); Page 45: © Rose Craig/Lawrence Hall of Science; Page 46: © The Museum of National History on Frederiksborg Castle; Page 47: © Scott MacNeill; Page 48: © Rose Craig/Lawrence Hall of Science; Page 49: © Laurie Meyer (top); © Rose Craig/Lawrence Hall of Science (bottom); Page 50: © Rose Craig/Lawrence Hall of Science; Page 51: © John Quick; © Scott MacNeill (top); Pages 52–53: © Scott MacNeill; Page 54: © John Quick (top); © Scott MacNeill (bottom); Page 55: © Scott MacNeill; Page 56: © iStockphoto/eurobanks (top); © iStockphoto/xefstock (bottom left); © Rose Craig/Lawrence Hall of Science (bottom right); Page 57: © Rose Craig/Lawrence Hall of Science; Page 58: © bikeriderlondon/Shutterstock (top); © Jaimie Duplass/Shutterstock (right); Page 59: © Rose Craig/Lawrence Hall of Science (bottom); Page 59: © Rose Craig/David Herrmann (top left); © Lasse Kristensen/Shutterstock (bottom left); © Jaimie Duplass/Shutterstock (right); Page 60: © SSPL/Science Museum/The Image Works (top); © Rose Craig/Lawrence Hall of Science (bottom); Page 61: © Division of Work and Industry National Museum of American History, Smithsonian Institution; © Laurie Meyer (bottom); Page 62: © iStockphoto/Stouffer; Page 64: © The Print Collector/HIP/The Image Works (top); Library of Congress (bottom); Page 65: © SSPL/The Image Works; Page 66: © Juriah Mosin/Shutterstock (top left); © Elnur/Shutterstock (top right); © carroteater/Shutterstock (bottom left); Page 67: © Elena Schweitzer/Shutterstock (top); © www.Foto-Format.com/Shutterstock (bottom left); © Ulga/Shutterstock (bottom right); Page 68: © Adisa/Shutterstock (top); © John C. Hooten/Shutterstock (bottom); Page 69: © Monkey Business Images/Shutterstock (top); © iStockphoto/lightcatcheristockphoto (bottom left); © David Young-Wolff/PhotoEdit (bottom right); Page 70: © Scott MacNeill (top); © Viktor1/Shutterstock (bottom); Page 71: © Michael Newman/PhotoEdit; Page 72: © geraldb/Shutterstock (left); © Dan Kosmayer/Shutterstock (right); Page 73: © iStockphoto/Arpad Benedek; Page 74: © E.G.Pors/Shutterstock (left); © Werner Stoffberg/Shutterstock (middle); © Nikolai Zaburdaev/Shutterstock (inset); Page 75: © Fotofermer/Shutterstock; Page 76: © Andrew Lundquist/Shutterstock (top); © Darryl Ligasan; Pages 76–77: Darryl Ligasan; Page 78: © Lawrence Hall of Science (table); © Artpose Adam Borkowski/Shutterstock (ball); © Guy Shapira/Shutterstock (bottom); Page 79: © Lawrence Hall of Science (table); © Artpose Adam Borkowski/Shutterstock (ball); Page 80: © Fukuoka Irina/Shutterstock (top); © Darryl Ligasan (bottom); Page 81: © iStockphoto/Duncan Walker (top); © Fotofermer/Shutterstock (bottom); Page 82: NASA (top); © Carlos Caetano (bottom); Pages 83–84; © Scott MacNeill; Page 85: © iStockphoto/Sonja Fagnan (left); © iStockphoto/ahmet ercan senkaya (inset); Page 86: © iStockphoto/Rob Friedman; © Tom Wang/Shutterstock (inset); Page 87: © iStockphoto/Reuben Schulz; © colors/Shutterstock (bottom right); © Lucie Lang/Shutterstock (bottom left); Page 88: © Lawrence Hall of Science; © Pavel Vakhrushev/Shutterstock (bottom); Page 89: © Anton Balazh/Shutterstock (top); © Lawrence Hall of Science (bottom); Page 90: © Lawrence Hall of Science (top); © Laurie Meyer (bottom); Page 91: © Scott MacNeill (top); © Lawrence Hall of Science (bottom); Page 92: © Lawrence Hall of Science; Page 93: © Gerald A. DeBoer/Shutterstock; © iStockphoto/GordonHeeley (bottom); Page 94: © Chris Collins/Shutterstock (top); © Blend Images/Shutterstock (bottom); Page 95: © 9george/Shutterstock (left); © Dmitry Skutin/Shutterstock (middle); © wernerimages/Shutterstock (right); Page 96: © Apollofoto/Shutterstock (top); © Vikulin/Shutterstock (middle); © Aitormmfoto/Shutterstock (bottom); Page 97: © Rannev/Shutterstock; Page 98: © Lawrence Hall of Science; Page 99: © Lawrence Hall of Science; © Fotofermer/Shutterstock (bottom); Page 100: © Lawrence Hall of Science; Page 101: © Colette3/Shutterstock (bottom left); © Chros/Shutterstock (bottom right); © Kirsanov Valeriy Vladimirovich/Shutterstock (top) Page 102: © iStockphoto/sewebel; © dwphotos/Shutterstock (inset); Page 103: © Sibrikov Valery/Shutterstock (candle); © imging/Shutterstock (lightbulb); © Luminis/Shutterstock (book); © Yuri Arcurs/Shutterstock (girl); Page 104: © iStockphoto/Studio-Annika (top left); © iStockphoto/MacrocosmPhotography (top right); © Scott MacNeill (bottom); Page 105: © iStockphoto/RTimages (book); © iStockphoto/bmaksym (flashlight); Page 106: © Larry Malone/Lawrence Hall of Science; © iStockphoto/samkee (bottom right); Page 107: © iStockphoto/AngiePhotos; Pages 108–111; © Apryl Stott; Page 112: © iStockphoto/mstay (top); © Viachaslau Kraskouski/Shutterstock (bottom); Page 113: © Tokar Dima/Shutterstock (top); © David Philips/Shutterstock (ball); Page 114: © iStockphoto/bmaksym (flashlight); © iStockphoto/bonnie Jacobs (bottom); Page 115: © Scott MacNeill (top); © Bliznetsov/Shutterstock (bottom); Page 116: © iStockphoto/acilo; Page 117: © iStockphoto/peart (top); © iStockphoto/thebroker (bottom); Page 118: © WDG Photo/Shutterstock; Page 119: © iStockphoto/Lisa-Blue; © iStockphoto/Rhoberazzi (inset); Page 120: © iStockphoto/LydiaGoolia; Page 121: © iStockphoto/rarpia; Pages 122–123: © Compass Light Productions; Page 125: © Daniel Lohmer/Shutterstock; Page 127: © iStockphoto/Ramon Rodriguez; Page 129: © iStockphoto/Donna Coleman (top right); © Victor Newman/Shutterstock (bottom); © Lawrence Hall of Science (bottom right); Page 130: © D. Kucharski K. Kucharska/Shutterstock; Page 131: © Doug Wechsler/Earth Scenes (left); © D. Cavagnaro/Visuals Unlimited, Inc. (right); Page 132: © iofoto/Shutterstock (left); © Sue Jagoda/Lawrence Hall of Science (rights); Page 133: © Sue Jagoda/Lawrence Hall of Science (left); © Fedorov Oleksiy/Shutterstock (top right); © Larry Malone/Lawrence Hall of Science (bottom); Page 134: © Sue Jagoda/Lawrence Hall of Science; © Greg Henry/Shutterstock (bottom right); Page 135: © iStockphoto/Sam Sefton; Page 136: © John Ballard/AGI Image Bank (left); © Larry Malone/Lawrence Hall of Science (right); Page 137: © iStockphoto/Oks_Mit (top); © Sue Jagoda/Lawrence Hall of Science (bottom); Page 138: © Mirek Hejnicki/Shutterstock (top); © Bruce Amos/Shutterstock (bottom left); © Graham Prentice/Shutterstock (bottom right); Page 139: © Kondrachov Vladimirr/Shutterstock (top); © Inc/Shutterstock (middle); © iStockphoto/Eric Foltz (bottom); Page 140: © mountainpix/Shutterstock (top); © iStockphoto/Martina I. Meyer (bottom); Page 141: © iStockphoto/Lew Zimmerman (top); © iStockphoto/jim kruger (top right); © J.Jofriet/Shutterstock (bottom left); © iStockphoto/Amy Kitscher (bottom right); Page 142: © Roman Sigaev/Shutterstock (top right); © iStockphoto/ingmar wesemann (top right); © Sue Jagoda/Lawrence Hall of Science (bottom left); © iStockphoto/Thaddeus Robertson (bottom right); Page 143: © iStockphoto/Dan Barnes (top left); © iStockphoto/Richard Goerg (top right); © iStockphoto/Jose Antonio Santiso Fernández (bottom left); © Sinclair Stammers/Science Photo Library (bottom right); Page 144: © Marli Bryant Miller/Earth Science World Image Bank (top left); © iStockphoto/Valeria Titova (top right); © Suzanne Tucker/Shutterstock (bottom left); © G. R. 'Dick' Roberts/NSIL/Visuals Unlimited, Inc. (middle right); Page 145: © iStockphoto/Stephen Rees (bottom left); © iStockphoto/Phil Augustavo (bottom right); © Roberto Cerruti (right); © Paul A. Souders/CORBIS (top right); Page 146: © iStockphoto/Duncan Walker (top left); © iStockphoto/Robert Bremec (top right); © Vadim Ostrikov/Shutterstock (bottom left); © iStockphoto/Madeleine Openshaw (bottom right); Page 147: © Manamana/Shutterstock (top left); © iStockphoto/Thomas Hopson (top right); © iStockphoto/Alexander Fortelny (middle left); © Hans-Walter Untch (middle right); © W.A.N.T. PHOTOGRAPHY/Animals Animals - Earth Scenes (bottom right); Page 148: © iStockphoto/Bart van den Dikkenberg (top); © Darlene Cutshall (middle); © George Burba/Shutterstock (bottom); © Ken Babione (bottom right); Page 149: © iStockphoto/sumografika™ (left); © iStockphoto/cafafotos (right); Page 150: © APaterson/Shutterstock (top); © markrhiggins/Shutterstock (bottom); Page 151: © Mike Viney, The Virtual Petrified Wood Museum; Page 152: © Condor 36/Shutterstock (top); © holboxx/Shutterstock (bottom); Page 153: © iStockphoto/CowboyRoy (left); © Patti McConville/Getty Images (right); Page 154: Photos courtesy of the Utah Geological Survey; Page 155: © Crestview Studio (left); © Steve Collender/Shutterstock (right); Page 156: © Crestview Studio; Page 157: © Mike Flippo/Shutterstock; Page 158: Courtesy of the United States Geological Survey; Page 159: © Gary C. Tognoni/Shutterstock (top); courtesy of the United States Geological Survey (middle and bottom); Page 160: Francis M. Fritz/Wikimedia Commons (top); © Bryan Brazil/Shutterstock (bottom right); Page 161: Courtesy of the United States Geological Survey; Page 162: © Shutterstock/Vlue; Page 163: Courtesy of the United States Geological Survey; Page 164: © AP Photo/Al Golub; Page 165: © Sue Jagoda/Lawrence Hall of Science; Page 166: © www.cceo.org; Page 167: © Southwest Research Institute®; Technology Today 2007; Pages 168-169: Robert D. Jarret/USGS; Page 170: Austin Post/USGS; Page 171: Lyn Topinka/USGS; Tom Casadevall/USGS (top); Page 172: FEMA News Photo; © Lawrence Hall of Science (bottom right); Page 173: NOAA; Page 174: © AP Photo/Kevork Djansezian; Page 175: © AP Photo/Stockton Record, Beverly Shilling; Page 176: © Maksym Gorpenyuk/Shutterstock; Page 177: © Maksym Gorpenyuk/Shutterstock; Page 178: © iStockphoto/Jean-Yves Benedeyt; Page 179: © Paul Conklin/PhotoEdit (top); © AP Photo/World Wide Photos (bottom); Page 180: © iStockphoto/Jeremy Edwards; Page 181: © NOAA; Page 182: © Dwayne Newton/PhotoEdit (top); © AFP/Getty Images (middle); Mike Lisowski/USGS (bottom); Page 183: © Roberto Schmidt/Getty Images (top); © photo2008/Shutterstock (middle); © iStockphoto/mikeuk (bottom); Page 184: USDA; Page 185: © Chris Price (top left); © iStockphoto/constantgardener (top right); USDA (bottom left and right); Page 186: © iStockphoto/Baris Simsek (left); © iStockphoto/mona plougmann (right); Page 187: © iStockphoto/Chad Truemper (top); © iStockphoto/Charles Schug (bottom); Page 188: © anshar/Shutterstock; Page 189: © onairda/Shutterstock; Page 190: © iStockphoto/kopperhead (left); © iStockphoto/carterdayne (right); Page 191: © Larry Malone/Lawrence Hall of Science; Page 192: © Larry Malone/Lawrence Hall of Science; Page 193: © iStockphoto/inspireme; Page 194: © Laurie Meyer (top and middle); © juliengrondin/Shutterstock (bottom); Page 195: © Jim Lopes/Shutterstock; Page 196: © akva/Shutterstock (top); © Styve Reineck/Shutterstock (middle); © iStockphoto/Michael Marcotte (bottom right); © Tim Burrett/Shutterstock (bottom left); Page 197: © Andrew J. Martinez/Photo Researchers, Inc. (top left); © Kirill Matkov/Shutterstock (top right); © Iain McGillivray/Shutterstock (second from top, left); © Laurie Meyer (second from top, right; second from bottom, left; second from bottom, right); © Bragin Alexey/Shutterstock (bottom left); Page 198: © Bragin Alexey/Shutterstock (bottom left); © Kirill Matkov/Shutterstock (top right); © Andrew J. Martinez/Photo Researchers, Inc. (top left); Page 199: © Lawrence Hall of Science (background); © John Quick (limestone, sandstone, tuff, breccia); © iStockphoto/zoomstudio (marble); © iStockphoto/brytta (basalt); © Joyce Photographics/Photo Researchers (quartize); © steve estvanik/Shutterstock (obsidian); © iStockphoto/Teresa Gueck (shale); © iStockphoto/klemens wolf (slate); © iStockphoto/mikeuk (conglomerate); © Tom Grundy/Shutterstock (gneiss); © iStockphoto/Van Eden (pumice); © iStockphoto/seraficus (schist); © Mars Evis/Shutterstock (granite); Page 201: © Anton Foltin/Shutterstock (top); © Antonio Jorge Nunes/Shutterstock (left); © Anton Foltin/Shutterstock (right); Page 206: © Eky Studio/Shutterstock; Page 207: © Dmitry Savinov/Shutterstock (backdrop); © worldswildlifewonders/Shutterstock (sloth); © Anneka/Shutterstock (frog); © Christian Musat/Shutterstock (tapir); Page 208: © Rechitan Sorin/Shutterstock (top); © James M. House/Shutterstock (bottom); Page 209: © luchschen/Shutterstock (top); © Joao Virissimo/Shutterstock (bottom); Page 210: © Larsek/Shutterstock (left); © iStockphoto/james leonardy (top right); © Casey K. Bishop/Shutterstock (bottom right); Page 211: © Daniel Petrescu/Shutterstock (top); © MBoe/Shutterstock (bottom); Page 212: © Creative Media Applications, Inc. (top); © iStockphoto/Lawrence Sawyer (bottom); Page 213: © Creative Media Applications, Inc. (top); © SoleilC/Shutterstock (bottom); Page 214: © Anton Foltin/Shutterstock (left); © Dhoxax/Shutterstock (right); Page 215: © iStockphoto/MoniqueRodriguez (left); © Dave King/Getty Images (right); Page 216: © S.Borisov/Shutterstock (top left); © ason/Shutterstock (top right); © Elena Elisseeva/Shutterstock (bottom); Page 217: © Scott MacNeill; Page 218: © iStockphoto/Wayne Stadler (left); © iStockphoto/Nancy Nehring (right); Page 219: © Joseph Calev/Shutterstock (top left); © Nicholas Piccillo/Shutterstock (top right); © Steve McWilliam/Shutterstock (bottom); Page 220: © Volina/Shutterstock (left); © Frontpage/Shutterstock (right); Page 221: © Christopher Tan Teck Hean (top); Page 222: © Dr. Morley Read/Shutterstock; Page 223: © Christopher Tan Teck Hean/Shutterstock; Page 224: © Claus Meyer/Getty Images; Page 225: © Paul Opler/Visuals Unlimited (left); © Mark Moffett/Minden Pictures (bottom right); Page 226: © worldswildlifewonders/Shutterstock (bottom left); © iStockphoto/ideeone (bottom middle); © iStockphoto/Richard Sidey (top right); © M Reel/Shutterstock (bottom right); Page 227: © Dr. Morley Read/Shutterstock (top); © Focus_on_Nature (bottom); Page 228: © guentermanaus/Shutterstock (top right); © Larry Malone/Lawrence Hall of Science (bottom right); Page 230: © Rose Craig/Lawrence Hall of Science; Page 231: © Knorre/Shutterstock; Page 232: © Elena Elisseeva/Shutterstock (left); © motorolka/Shutterstock (inset); © iStockphoto/Александр Тараканов (bottom right); Page 233: © Nikolay Mikhalchenko/Shutterstock; Page 234: © Patrick Moynihan/pyronious.com/Getty Images (left); © dragon_fang/Shutterstock (right); Page 235: © Aleksander Bolbot/Shutterstock; Page 236: © kosam/Shutterstock (tree); © hugolacasse/Shutterstock (sun); Page 237: © Lee Prince/Shutterstock (top); © Andrejs Pidjass/Shutterstock (inset); © Catalin Petolea/Shutterstock (bottom); Page 238: © Color-PIC/Animals Animals (top); © J. Michael Eichelberger/Visuals Unlimited (top inset); © Nagel Photography/Shutterstock (bottom); © JOSE ALBERTO TEJO/Shutterstock (bottom right); Page 239: © Christopher Tan Teck Hean/Shutterstock; © Laure Neish (ground squirrel); © JASON STEEL/Shutterstock (snake); © Stefan Fierros/Shutterstock (caterpillars); © iStockphoto/Nancy Nehring (vulture); Page 240: © Dr. Dennis Kunkel Microscopy, Inc./Visuals Unlimited (top); © Simko/Visuals Unlimited (middle); © Pukhov Konstantin/Shutterstock (bottom); Page 241: © Le Do/Shutterstock (fly); © Smit/Shutterstock (spider); © JIANG HONGYAN/Shutterstock (praying mantis); © Mageon/Shutterstock (plum); © Mike Truchon/Shutterstock (blue jay); © IrinaK/Shutterstock (weasel); © iStockphoto/rusm (hawk); Page 242: © Maksym Protsenko/Shutterstock (grass); © Eric Isselée/Shutterstock (chipmunk); © iStockphoto/rusm (hawk); © Michael Schneidmiller/Shutterstock (bacteria); © Rose Craig/Lawrence Hall of Science (bottom); Page 243: © Ivaschenko Roman/Shutterstock (top); © Chris Twine/Shutterstock (bottom); Page 244: © Jeffrey M. Frank/Shutterstock; © Rose Craig/Lawrence Hall of Science (bottom); Page 245: © iStockphoto/Arvid Emtegren (top); © Jerry Sharp/Shutterstock (bottom); Page 246: © Romanenkova/Shutterstock; Page 247: © puwanai/Shutterstock; Page 248: © Caitlin Mirra/Shutterstock (top); © Tim Mainiero/Shutterstock (bottom); Page 249: © FloridaStock/Shutterstock (left); © Kirsanov/Shutterstock (right); Page 250: © VaLiz/Shutterstock; © Butterfly Hunter/Shutterstock (inset); Page 251: © Dennis W. Donohue/Shutterstock (left); © Bildagentur Zoonar GmbH/Shutterstock (right); Page 252: © Bjørn Rørslett/NN; © bjonesphotography/Shutterstock (top right); Page 253: © cbpix/Shutterstock (top); © tantrik71/Shutterstock (bottom); Page 254: © guentermanaus/Shutterstock; Page 255: © bikeriderlondon/Shutterstock (bottom right); © Patryk Kosmider/Shutterstock (bottom left); Page 255: © Sytilin Pavel/Shutterstock (top); © Gucio_55/Shutterstock (inset); © D. Kucharski K. Kucharska/Shutterstock (bottom right); Page 257: © Tim Zurowski/Getty Images (top); © Nick Hatch/Forest Service (right); Page 258: © bshumaker17/Shutterstock (bottom); Page 259: © Krzysztof Wiktor/Shutterstock (bottom left); © Lawrence Hall of Science (top left); Page 260: © OSF/J.A.L. Cooke/Animals Animals; Page 261: © Larry Malone/Lawrence Hall of Science; Page 262: Courtesy of The Mono Lake Committee (top); © patrimonio designs limited/Shutterstock (bottom); Page 263: © Linda De Lucchi/Lawrence Hall of Science (top); © Kenneth Rush/Shutterstock (inset); © Norman Bateman/Shutterstock (right); © SoleilC/Shutterstock (bottom); Page 264: © Doug Wechsler/Animals Animals (top & inset); © Doug James/Shutterstock (bottom); Page 265: Courtesy of The Mono Lake Committee; Pages 266–267: © Rose Craig/Lawrence Hall of Science; Page 268: © Anton Foltin/Shutterstock (top); © Harris Shiffman/Shutterstock (inset); Page 269: © Peter Leahy/Shutterstock; Page 270: © Tom Grundy/Shutterstock; Page 271: © Scott Prokop/Shutterstock; Page 272: © Ken Lucas/Getty Images; Page 273: © iStockphoto/Tom Tietz; Page 274: © Karen Mendelow Nelson/Lawrence Hall of Science; Page 275: © Larry Serpa; Page 276: © Lawrence Hall of Science; Pages 277–280; © Karen Mendelow Nelson/Lawrence Hall of Science; Page 281: © cynoclub/Shutterstock (bottom); © iStockphoto/Holly Kuchera (inset); Page 282: © iStockphoto/Imagesbybarbara; © Jan Hopgood/Shutterstock (bottom left); © marco mayer/Shutterstock (bottom right); Page 283: © Kirsanov/Shutterstock (left); © Volodymyr Burdiak/Shutterstock (right); Page 284: © Mogens Trolle/Shutterstock; Page 285: © Rose Craig/Lawrence Hall of Science; Pages 286–287: © iStockphoto/Michael Stubblefield; Pages 288–289: © Alfred Eisenstaedt/Time Life Pictures/Getty Images; Page 290: AP Worldwide Photos; Page 291: © Durden Images/Shutterstock (left); © Peg Skorpinski (right); Page 292: © John Mcconico/AP Worldwide Photos; Page 293: © iStockphoto/lynn watson (top); © iStockphoto/Alan Tobey (bottom); Page 294: © Ken Lucas/Visuals Unlimited (top left and right); © Tom McHugh/Photo Researchers, Inc. (bottom); Page 295: © Rick Wylie/Shutterstock (top); © mikeledray/Shutterstock (bottom); Page 296: © Rickshu/Shutterstock; Page 297: © Alex_187/Shutterstock (top); © David Koscheck/Shutterstock (right); © iStockphoto/Janet Forjan-Freedman (bottom right); © Bruce MacQueen/Shutterstock (bottom left); Page 298: © Caitlin Mirra/Shutterstock (bottom); Page 299: © Tom McHugh/Photo Researchers, Inc. (top); © A.J. Copley/Visuals Unlimited (top right); © Ralf Juergen Kraft/Shutterstock (bottom left); © Jason Speros/Shutterstock (bottom right); Page 300: © CORBIS/Bettmann (top); © A.J. Copley/Visuals Unlimited (bottom); Pages 301–303: ALL RIGHTS RESERVED, DENVER MUSEUM OF NATURE & SCIENCE; Page 304: © D. Kucharski & K. Kucharska/Shutterstock (left & top right); © Henrik Larsson/Shutterstock (bottom right); Page 305: © John Quick; Page 306: © vblinov/Shutterstock (top); © mrobert67/Shutterstock (middle); © Vishnevskiy Vasily/Shutterstock (bottom); Page 307: © Rose Craig/Lawrence Hall of Science; Page 312: © Delta Education.